Living With the Psalms

Presented to:

Kent Scott

By:

the members of
Halsbury Bapt. Church
May 24, 1981

May God's Richest
Blessings Be Upon You
in Your Future!

LIVING WITH THE PSALMS

LEROY BROWNLOW

BROWNLOW PUBLISHING COMPANY, INC
P. O. Box 3141
Fort Worth, Texas 76105

Brownlow Gift Books

Flowers That Never Fade

Flowers for You

Flowers for Mother

A Father's World

Flowers of Friendship

The University of Hard Knocks

Longfellow Birthday Book

Better Than Medicine

By His Side

Making the Most of Life

Aesop's Fables

A Time to Laugh
—or Grandpa Was A Preacher

With the Good Shepherd

Thoughts of Gold
in Words of Silver

For Love's Sake

The Story of Jesus

The More Years the More Sunshine

Peace Be With You

Daybreak

Windows

Living With the Psalms

Today Is Mine

Foreword

Living With the Psalms is a day-to-day guide containing 365 essays — devotionals — based on Psalms, which is the world's most popular book.

The Psalms continue to live and grip the attention of needy humanity. Fads blossom and wilt, generations come and go, civilizations rise and fall, but the Psalms continue to survive the ages. No other book has been so fondly read and so freely commented on. The inescapable conclusion is — it has something helpful for man in every circumstance of life.

Psalms is a stupendous and marvelous book, enormous in teaching, amazing in faith, astonishing in trust and astounding in relevancy. It is something! It covers the whole scope of living: everything that accompanies the farflung and eventful life of man. Its extensive, up-to-date thoughts testify that man has ever had to face the same problems. How little man changes through the ages! And as we read them, we realize that — with slight variations of circumstances —the author could be speaking of us this very hour.

The Psalms are our common heritage, filling common needs. They contain guidance for the errant, power for the weak, courage for the trembling, rest for the weary, cheer for the despondent, hope for the faint-hearted and comfort for the afflicted. By lifting high the rulership and interposition of God to aid man, they encourage him to live a victorious life, marked with optimism and jubilation. "For all's well that ends well."

In this volume, *Living With the Psalms,* at least one devotional is based in numerical order on everyone of the 150 Psalms — no Psalm is omitted. To have one for each day (365), we took more than one from some of them.

Additional thoughts could have been given, but for the sake of brevity each treatise was limited to one page.

While the essays are to some extent explanatory and analytical of the text, in keeping with the tenor and occasion of each Psalm, this volume was not meant to be a commentary. Rather, it was the aim of the author to give each topic and text, as much as it would permit, a relevant treatment and a suggestive application to assist man in gaining instruction, inspiration and power for a wiser, fuller and nobler life.

This volume is by no means a book to be read at a sitting. Its nourishment and stimulation are too concentrated for such reading. It can be used to greatest profit a little at a time. It is what it was meant to be — a daily meditation. However, in addition to the daily thought, a person can read and think on the particular devotional best adapted to his particular mood and circumstance that calls for help.

Believing in the power of daily meditation, convinced that men's thoughts constitute the army that conquers the world, we present this volume from the voice of yesterday with the hope that it will be a helpful voice today and the herald of tomorrow.

—LEROY BROWNLOW

The Blessed Man

BLESSED is the man that walketh not in the counsel of the ungodly, nor standeth in the way of sinners, nor sitteth in the seat of the scornful. But his delight is in the law of the Lord; and in his law doth he meditate day and night. —1:1, 2

The Book of Psalms appropriately begins with the blessed or happy man. This is a preface to the whole book. Happiness is largely due to our own making; and if we would make it, there are conditions to meet, both negative and positive. This is understandable, for man cannot follow the constructive course without refraining from the destructive one.

Negatively: The man described as blessed refuses to be guided by the counsels of the ungodly. This is vital, for no person can become better than the principles or plans by which he walks.

He does not stand in the way of or closely associate himself with confirmed sinners. Neither does he sit with scorners: jokers of good, mockers of morals and ridiculers of religion.

Positively: His delight, pleasure or happiness is in the Lord's law. His heart, out of tune with the world, is in tune with Divinity.

The Written Word is precious to him. He reads it and meditates on it. It is a part of his life, a pleasant portion; so happiness is his fortune.

> *The blessed man is one who will*
> *Not harbor wrong in his breast,*
> *But op'ns it for God's domicile*
> *That every right may be his guest.*

The Futility of Opposing God

WHY do the heathen rage, and the people imagine a vain thing? The kings of the earth set themselves, and the rulers take counsel together, against the Lord, and against his Anointed, saying, Let us break their bands asunder, and cast away their cords from us. —2:1-3.

The second Psalm deals with conflict: Messianic power and sinners' rebellion.

In the rebels' rebellion they *rage, imagine, set themselves, take counsel against the Lord and say what they shouldn't.* Evil men have always felt that God's rule is too restrictive; so as these sinners chafe and gall in their ill-fated desire for uninhibited living, they say, "Let us break their [God and His Anointed] bands asunder, and cast away their cords from us" (ver. 3). No bands. No cords. No controls. What a terrible picture.

However, their evil imaginations are vain, to no avail. They are left defeated and crushed. The Lord shall laugh at their foolishness. Hold them in derision. "Vex them in his sore displeasure." And "break them with a rod of iron." God is merciful but firm. How silly for man to think he can win in opposing God. God's rule cannot be overthrown. Every attack against Him rebounds against the attacker. Against Him, you face defeat. With Him, you are a sure winner.

> *He always wins who sides with God,*
> *To him no chance is lost;*
> *God's will is sweetest to him when*
> *It triumphs at his cost.*
>
> *—Frederick William Faber*

Peril and Prayer

LORD, how are they increased that trouble me! many
are they that rise up against me. Many there be which
say of my soul, There is no help for him in God. Selah.
But thou, O Lord, art a shield for me; my glory, and
the lifter up of mine head. I cried unto the Lord with
my voice, and he heard me out of his holy hill. —3:1-4

We have here the peril, struggle, prayer and victory
of an Old Testament character. It gives the experience
of the *him* and the *then*—and hope to the *us* and the
now. For we are all brothers in trial, the difference
being only in time and degrees.

David's own son Absalom led a revolt against him.
Trouble in the family. Trouble in the kingdom. When
a man's family does not stand with him, it multiplies
his hardships.

The scoffers got busy. They always do. They said,
"There is no help for him in God." A common joy
of sinners is to taunt the people of God in their trials
with the ridicule that they are God-forsaken.

But the writer never lost faith. In the face of peril,
David turned to prayer: "I cried unto the Lord with
my voice." His enemies used their voice to defy God.
But he used his voice to address God. What a dif-
ference! And enough to always make a difference.
For God heard him. He won. They lost.

Repose came to David. He could sleep (ver. 5).
He was sustained. But more trials are ahead, and
trust must go with him and it does. Thus he says,
"I will not be afraid . . . " (ver. 6).

When in Distress

HEAR me when I call, O God of my righteousness: thou hast enlarged me when I was in distress; have mercy upon me, and hear my prayer. O ye sons of men, how long will ye turn my glory into shame? how long will ye love vanity, and seek after leasing? Selah. But know that the Lord hath set apart him that is godly for himself: the Lord will hear when I call unto him. —4:1-3

"Hear me when I call, O God," was the constant plea of David. "Have mercy," he begged—not justice; for justice would doom him and all of us.

"I was in distress," he acknowledged. Actually, this is the plight of the whole race, and fortunate is he who knows it.

In his anguish, caused by humanity, he found consolation in Divinity, in two assuring thoughts: First, God sets apart for Himself the godly. Second, God answers prayer. How strengthening: hope to lift sinking hearts and faith to energize lagging steps.

Let us, therefore, bravely take the world's blows, for we can bear them. David could. You can. I can. With God's help, no tribulation can overwhelm us. As David concluded, let us stand in awe of God, stick with Him, sin not, be still, sacrifice and trust Him (vers. 4, 5).

When, counting slumber,
The hours I number,
And sad cares cumber
  My weary mind.
This thought shall cheer me:
That thou art near me,
Whose ear to hear me,
  Is still inclined.

Who Will Give Us Good?

THERE be many that say, Who will show us any good?
Lord, lift thou up the light of thy countenance upon
us. Thou has put gladness in my heart, more than in
the time that their corn and their wine increased. I will
both lay me down in peace and sleep: for thou, Lord,
only makest me dwell in safety. —4:6-8

Among David's supporters there were pessimists.
Nothing new. They have always been numerous and
vocal. In this instance, they asked, "Who will show
us any good?" In these hard times who will give us
good? Who will give us satisfaction? Who will give
us peace? They saw only the visible aspects of life.

For a true answer, however, David looked beyond
the gloomy circumstances and prayerfully appealed
to the source of all good: "Lord, lift thou the light of
thy countenance upon us" (ver. 6). Somewhere there
must be an answer to man's cry in the night for light,
peace and rest. David knew that the *somewhere* is with
God, that the answer beams from His countenance.

In contrast with worldly views, the psalmist stated
that the fulfillment of man's greatest needs is not in
materialism—corn and wine (ver. 7)—but rather in
an attachment to the Lord that provides a deep gladness and a broad safety that enables one to lie down
in peace. All other answers are no answers—only
vain echoes in empty hearts.

> *If I him but have,*
> *Glad I fall asleep;*
> *Aye the peace His heart gave*
> *My poor heart I shall keep.*
>
> *—Adapted, George Macdonald*

A Plan for Living

Give ear to my words, O Lord. —5:1

The fifth Psalm contains an excellent plan for living:

Meditation: "Consider my meditation" (ver. 1). One of the grievous errors of this age is our fast pace which leaves no time to think and meditate.

Morning prayer: "In the morning will I direct my prayer unto thee" (ver. 3). A good way to start the day. God's help is needed.

Upward look: "And will look up" (ver. 3). Look up to God. This gives optimism.

Acceptance of mercy: "I will come into thy house in the multitude of thy mercy" (ver. 7). Man is imperfect. Mercy is needed. And if you accept God's mercy which forgives, then forgive yourself and put your mistakes behind you.

Worship: "And in thy fear will I worship" (ver. 7). Approach God with reverential fear. He is God. You are human. Never try to humanize Him. Keep the distinction. Worship Him. The need is as old as man.

Right leadership: "Lead me, O Lord, in thy righteousness" (ver. 8). The wrong leadership has wrecked many a life.

A straight way: "Make thy way straight before my face" (ver. 8)—not smooth, not easy. Just let the way be Thine and show me clearly.

Trust: "But let all those that put their trust in thee rejoice" (ver. 11). Trust lets you see the rainbow in the cloud. Our days should be lived joyfully—not in serving a rigorous sentence.

Self-destruction

DESTROY thou them, O God; let them fall by their own counsels; cast them out in the multitude of their transgressions; for they have rebelled against thee. —5:10

Some people rise, others fall. And a determining factor is counsel. In wise counsel there is success, but in foolish counsel there is failure.

The ill-advised suffer bitter defeat, because they do not "with good advice make war" (Proverbs 20:18). Poor counsel! Multitudes land at the wrong place when misdirected. Legions see their houses collapse, because they listen to the grasshopper philosophy which suggests that it is too strenuous to dig deep enough to build on the rock.

Seething in materialism, glorying in defiance of righteousness, crawling in the mire of their blackguard rebellion, the wicked miss the good life. It is their own doing, or rather their own undoing. They fall for they have no internal strength.

God does not help the rebels in their sins. The transgressors are doomed to perish. It is God's appointment that they be destroyed by their own devices. And on they go to their self-made woes. It is as Isaiah recorded:

WOE to the rebellious children, saith the Lord, that take counsel, but not of me. —Isaiah 30:1

They get lots of advice, but from the wrong ones. It's a case of human destruction, resulting from human misdirection.

O Lord, How Long?

O LORD, rebuke me not in thine anger, neither chasten me in thy hot displeasure. Have mercy upon me, O Lord; for I am weak: O Lord, heal me; for my bones are vexed. My soul is also sore vexed: but thou, O Lord, how long? —6:1-3

Here is a man who was being tested to the limit. He was exhausted. There was a question as to whether he could survive.

He was conscious of some grievous sin in his life; and though he deserved rebuke, he asked that the chastisement be applied in love rather than anger.

Bodily ailment plagued him. "My bones are vexed."

Additionally, his soul was vexed. The mental suffering was more agonizing than the physical. Always is.

In his affliction he had groaned until he was weary. He had cried and cried. "All the night make I my bed to swim; I water my couch with my tears" (ver. 7).

As his enemies continued to torment him, he asked "O Lord, how long?" How long can I endure? How long can I suffer? How long must I wait for relief? In the depths of despair, this has ever been the question on the lips of man—how long?

The writer was conscious of his weakness—"I am weak"—but this was a sign of strength. The weakest are those who are not aware of it and never seek help. Though he was weak, he was strong enough to pray. His supplication was heard and that sufficed (vers. 9, 10). There was strength enough in God, but not in himself alone. This is our lesson, and blessed are we if we learn it.

If I Have Done Wrong

O LORD my God, if I have done this; if there be iniquity in my hands. —7:3

The seventh Psalm apparently was written during the earlier part of David's public life. As is true of all public men, he had persecutors. And King Saul, encouraged by the detractors, sought his life (ver. 2). But David returned good for evil and spared the king (I Samuel 26:1-25).

In referring to the charges against him, David said, "If I have done this." Done what? If I "sought the king's hurt" (I Samuel 24:9). "If there be iniquity in my hands" (ver. 3). "If I have rewarded evil unto him that was at peace with me" (ver. 4).

The charges were false. In his denial, David stated that if he were guilty, he would be willing to pay the penalty: "Let the enemy persecute my soul . . . tread down my life . . . lay mine honor in the dust" (ver. 5).

Now, in his innocence, David lays his burden on God and makes a fivefold petition:

— Save me (ver. 1).
— Arise, O Lord, do something (ver. 6).
— Judge me, vindicate me (ver. 8).
— End their wickedness (ver. 9).
— Establish the just (ver. 9).

If man is guilty, he should not grumble at having to pay sin's penalty; if not, let him take hope in that God is knowledgeable of all false rumors and is capable of defending the defamed.

If One Turns Not From Evil

GOD judgeth the righteous, and God is angry with the wicked every day. If he turn not, he will whet his sword; he hath bent his bow, and made it ready. He hath also prepared for him the instruments of death; he ordaineth his arrows against the persecutors.

—7:11-13

God, in a just judgment, will vindicate the righteous. When they are assailed by their enemies, He will interpose to lift them up.

Concerning the wicked — God is angry with them everyday. His love for righteousness necessitates strong feelings against wickedness (they are antipodal); and consistency requires Him to feel the same way everyday. Being God, His feelings do not vary as the sentiments of fickle, temperamental humans. If sin is wrong today, it is wrong tomorrow; and, accordingly, God's view of it remains constant.

If justice requires God to bless the righteous, it also compels Him to punish the wicked. The whole world recognizes the equity of this principle; and by following it civilization is maintained.

However, God tempers justice with a mercy that civil magistrates do not follow (they cannot look into the heart); and thus Divine execution of punishment is against only him who refuses to repent—"if he turn not." All who turn may escape. Mercy like this is found nowhere else—only in God. But if the sinner doesn't turn, justice prescribes punishment. The decision is his. No person can repent too soon, because he doesn't know how soon it may be too late.

Trapped in One's Own Pit

HE made a pit and digged it, and is fallen into the
ditch which he made. His mischief shall return upon
his own head, and his violent dealing shall come down
upon his own pate. —7:15, 16

Doing mischief to hurt another returns to harm
the mischief-maker. The pit he digs to entrap another becomes his own pitfall (ver. 15).

The writer alludes to a method of hunting wild
beasts in ancient times. A pit would be dug and
covered over with brush and leaves. As unsuspect-
ing animals were driven over it they would fall
through and be trapped.

The lesson is that the person who lays a deceptive
plan for the destruction of others will be ensnared by
his own devices. Such retribution is not uncommon
among the crafty who are caught in the consequences
of their own devilment. They become entangled in
the recoils of their own cunning. They are trapped
in self-dug pits. They are caught in self-made nets.

History is replete with examples. Many a Haman
has been hanged on the gallows he prepared for another (Esther 7:10). Many a Judas has sold himself
with his own kiss (Matthew 26:48).

WITH what measure ye mete, it shall be measured to
you again. —Matthew 7:2

No one can overestimate the danger of a crooked
and mischievous policy. Neither can one overvalue
the worth of an open and straightforward course in
dealing with others — both friends and foes.

What Is Man?

WHAT is man, that thou art mindful of him? and the son of man, that thou visitest him? For thou has made him a little lower than the angels, and hast crowned him with glory and honor. —8:4, 5

The God who created the heavens, the vastness and complexity of the celestial bodies, was mindful of man and visited him with a position and destiny just a little lower than the angels, crowning him with glory and honor.

That such a powerful God would regard man so highly should inspire him to praise and thank his Creator. Though he was made of clay, he was given an image like his Maker.

Endowed with the capacities that distinguish him from all other creatures, man was made to rule. He was given dominion over the works of his Designer's hands. All things were put under his feet. His nature gives him the advantage over the lower creatures who tend no flocks, sow no harvests, plant no forests, build no hospitals and entertain no hope of immortality. Man is really something! Too bad he sometimes drops beneath his greatness.

That God is mindful of man is perhaps the most moving and inspiring thought ever to pass through the mind of man. It won't let him settle for a lower existence. It rouses in him the exclamation, "O Lord our Lord, how excellent is thy name in all the earth!" (ver. 9)

Whole-hearted Praise

I WILL praise thee, O Lord, with my whole heart; I will show forth all thy marvelous works. I will be glad and rejoice in thee: I will sing praise to thy name, O thou Most High. —9:1, 2

David stated that he would praise the Lord with all his heart. This is essential. God will not accept a divided service.

A half a heart never finds him —

AND ye shall seek me, and find me, when ye shall search for me with all your heart. —Jeremiah 29:13

Laudations from a forked tongue is no praise at all—

OUT of the same mouth proceedeth blessing and cursing. My brethren, these things ought not so to be. Doth a fountain send forth at the same place sweet water and bitter? Can the fig tree, my brethren, bear olive berries? either a vine figs? so can no fountain both yield salt water and fresh. —James 3:10-12

A double eye (one for Him and one for the world) never sees Him —

IF therefore thine eye be single, thy whole body shall be full of light. But if thine eye be evil, thy whole body shall be full of darkness. —Matthew 7:22, 23

So with a whole heart, a straight tongue and a single eye, let us lift up our praises to the Most High. For the First and Great Commandment is: "Thou shalt love the Lord thy God with all thy heart, and with all thy soul, and with all thy mind" (Matthew 22:37). Anything less than this is unacceptable.

May Men Know They Are Only Men

PUT them in fear, O Lord: that the nations may know themselves to be but men. —9:20

What a needed lesson! The poet understood this—his humanity and God's Divinity. But the heathen nations didn't — they rejected God. The ninth Psalm makes plain the distinctions:

— Man falls and perishes (ver. 3), but not God.

— Imperfect man often supports the wrong and evil cause, but God maintains only the right (ver. 4).

— The name of the mushroomer flourishes for a while (ver. 5), but the name of God lives eternally.

— Memorials to men perish with them (ver. 6), but the rainbow (a memorial to God) still forms.

— Man lives threescore years and ten, but God never dies (ver. 7).

— Man judges imperfectly, but Jehovah's judgment is in uprightness (ver. 8).

— Man is limited in his ability to help, but Jehovah is always a refuge in time of trouble (ver. 9).

— Because of their fickleness, men are forsakers, but not God: "for thou, Lord, hast not forsaken them that seek thee" (ver. 10).

— The ears of men are more turned to the cries of the rich and the proud, but God "forgetteth not the cry of the humble" (ver. 12).

— Men are taken by their own pits and nets (vers. 15, 16), but God never fails.

— Man can oppose God, but never win (ver. 19).

Thus may men know that they are only men.

Why Doesn't God Do Something?

WHY standest thou afar off, O Lord? why hidest thou thyself in times of trouble? —10:1

One thing about this life — it is filled with trouble. While it comes in degrees, it comes to all.

MAN is born unto trouble. —Job 5:7

But it seems the psalmist had more than his share: envious enemies, callous calumniators and family fightings, plus the ordinary distresses we all experience.

When trouble comes, it is natural for downtrodden man to ask, "Why?" Why me? Why do I have to suffer? Why doesn't God come to my rescue? Why does God permit the wicked to continue in their blackguard ways? Is God going to let them get away with it (ver. 11)? Why doesn't He lift up His hand against them (ver. 12)? Doesn't God require anything of them (ver. 13)? Why doesn't He break their power (ver. 15)? Why? Why? Why?

Such questions indicate that man is too impatient; that his ways are not God's ways. God will take care of the trouble in His own time and in His own way. Vengeance belongs to Him. Fret not. Furthermore, some suffering on the part of His children can be chastening and rewarding.

After asking *Why?* as humans do, David extols his Maker as the God who answers prayer and helps "the oppressed, that the man of the earth may no more oppress" them (ver. 18).

The Ways of the Troublemaker

BREAK thou the arm of the wicked and the evil man: seek out his wickedness till thou find none. —10:15

In the tenth Psalm the writer entreats God for help from his enemies, troublemakers, described as:

Proud and harassing: "In his pride doth persecute" (ver. 2).

Cunning: "The devices they have imagined" (ver. 2).

Boasts of his wealth: "Boasteth of his heart's desire" (ver. 3).

Blesses the evil: "Blesseth the covetous" (ver. 3).

Too proud to seek God: "Through the pride of his countenance, will not seek after God" (ver. 4).

Doesn't think of God: "God is not in all his thoughts" (ver. 4).

Having no morals, his ways produce grief: "His ways are always grievous" (ver. 5).

Thinks he can sweep his enemies away with a breath: "He puffeth at them" (ver. 5).

Never thinks of the future: "For I shall never be in adversity" (ver. 6).

Profane, fraudulent and vain: "His mouth is full of cursing and deceit and fraud" (ver. 7).

Engages in underhandedness and treachery: "He sitteth in the lurking places . . . He lieth in wait secretly as a lion (vers. 8, 9).

Thinks he can hide from God: "He hath said in his heart, God . . . will never see it" (ver. 11).

But he is deceived! grossly deceived!

Advice From the Timid

IN the Lord put I my trust: how say ye to my soul,
Flee as a bird to your mountain? For, lo, the wicked
bend their bow, they make ready their arrow upon the
string, that they may privily shoot at the upright in
heart. If the foundations be destroyed, what can the
righteous do? —11:1-3

When David was suffering from calumnious accusations, his friends advised him to flee to the mountain.
Their reasons were: The enemy is after you; and if
the foundations be destroyed, there is no hope left
for the righteous. There are always reasons for running, but ordinarily there are better reasons for re-
maining. Because often —

Who flees the wolf meets with the bear.

However, there are circumstances in which it is
right to take flight. But the whole tenor of the Psalm
indicates this was not the time. We should never
walk away from duty or unpopularity or peril just
for the sake of safety. And David didn't.

The Psalm contains the only sure answer to the
question of fear — faith. The writer's faith was not
in the mountain but in the Lord who made the mountain. The One higher than the mountain "is in his
holy temple," reigning and ruling, declared David.
Thus there was no need to fear Saul.

David believed the Lord's scrutinizing eyes give
the Just Judge the knowledge to try the wicked and
the righteous, to rain punishment on the wicked and
bestow favor on the righteous (vers. 4-7). This faith
kept David from running away.

If the Foundations Be Destroyed

IF the foundations be destroyed, what can the righteous do? —11:3

David's fearful friends were wrong in suggesting that he flee; but they were right in suggesting that society must have its pillars or fall.

If the past has any lesson at all for the present, it is: you can't build stronger than your foundation. History's pages are marked with individuals and nations that tragically fell because their supports were too weak.

If the foundations of society are destroyed, mankind drops lower and lower. When the people replace religion with irreligion, morality with immorality, justice with injustice, industry with indolence, and service to man with exploitation of man, that league of people is already declining.

Laws alone will not prop up a society. We must have more than a community of puppets on legal strings. The strongest control of the citizen is from within the heart by moral and religious principles. Almost every downfall of men and nations has been an inside job — weakness within.

David's friends recognized him as a pillar in society, but some others as burdens. Every person belongs to one category or the other, a support or a burden. Quite a sobering thought.

> *Give us Men —I say again,*
> *Give us men!*
> *—Bishop of Exeter*

This Is Their Cup

THE Lord trieth the righteous: but the wicked and him that loveth violence his soul hateth. Upon the wicked he shall rain snares, fire and brimstone, and a horrible tempest: this shall be the portion of their cup. —11:5, 6

You have heard this before: "This is your cup"; and the negative: "This is not your cup." However, only a few people are aware that the metaphor is in the Bible, found a few times in Psalms and in other places.

In the text, their cup was filled with the bitter dregs of hate and violence, the drink they had prepared. It was their making and they had to drink it. For as you brew, so must you drink.

God does not tolerate a lawless world, but does respect man's volition. Man was not made to be a pushbutton mechanism, but rather a self-determining creature who must make the decisions and live his life.

However, in the interest of motivating man, God reproves to improve and punishes to reward. The God of Justice permits man to brew his cup, but he must drink it.

In this particular case, the cup consisted of: (1) *Snares* — difficulties in which they would be entangled. (2) *Fire and brimstone* — God's punishment. (3) *A horrible tempest* — literally, a breath of horrors.

Here are two lessons for us: Our cup is good or bad to the last drop, depending on how we prepare it; and when it is made, we must drink it.

Help, Lord

HELP, Lord; for the godly man ceaseth; for the faithful fail from among the children of men. They speak vanity every one with his neighbor: with flattering lips and with a double heart do they speak. —12:1, 2

Help! This is the cry of millions around the globe. You hear the anguish in divorce courts, in bankruptcy courts, in unemployment lines, in sick rooms and around the flower-decked mounds in the silent cities of the dead.

Help! This is the cry of one in distress. It is proof of inadequacy. If the distressed were big enough, strong enough and smart enough to solve his problem, why beg for assistance? Thus a million cries for help is audible proof of man's weak humanity, that it is not within frail and ailing man to supply all his needs.

The poet expressed the reasons for his helplessness: "The godly man ceaseth." "The faithful fail." "They speak vanity," vain and empty words instead of truth. They have double hearts — one for the words, another for the hidden aim. This was discouraging.

Whatever the cause, the forlorn feeling comes to all. When it does, let's say more than, "Help"! Let's say, "Help, Lord." May we address the powerless feeling to Him who is the ablest to help, as David did; for humans can go only so far and do only so much. And now let us remember —

God helps them that help themselves.
—Benjamin Franklin

Who Is Lord Over Us?

WHO have said, With our tongue will we prevail; our lips are our own: who is Lord over us? —12:4

The question indicates rebellion. Nobody, not even God, is allowed to tell them what to believe and how to live. They are determined to be the sole masters over themselves. Mighty big talk! How brave are some people in fair weather; but, oh, how pale they turn at the clap of thunder.

The revolting spirit is often the main cause of one's turning to atheism. He drives himself into infidelity by his desire to be free of any restrictions or rules. The proposition that the Lord exists implies that He is over man. This means rules for man, and rules are sure to be broken occasionally. Man's falling short of the precept may produce guilt feelings and fear; but instead of overcoming the discomfort with faith and resolution, some seek relief in no faith and no pattern. By deciding that God is a farce and the Bible is a fable, they find consolation in becoming freethinkers. Believing there are no Divine requirements to meet, they feel they can never commit any Divine violations to distress them.

Playing god by deciding there is no God is a self-deception that brings self-destruction.

> *Blind unbelief is sure to err,*
> *And scan his work in vain;*
> *God is his own interpreter,*
> *And he will make it plain.*
>
> *—William Cowper*

Despondency Turns to Assurance

How long wilt thou forget me, O Lord? for ever? how
long wilt thou hide thy face from me? —13:1

One thing sure — David was very human. His emotions sometimes varied between despair and hope. As we behold his despondency spells, we sorrow with him. We have been through some of it, too. No person can stay on top of the world all the time.

David complained that God had forgotten him (ver. 1), but He hadn't. It just seemed that way.

Neither had the Lord hidden His face from David (ver. 1). The persecution had blurred his view. Sometimes in a storm we cannot see very far, but the object is over there.

David took counsel in his heart to solve his problems (ver. 2). He tried — plan after plan was formed, but to no avail. Their collapse brought daily sorrow.

It seemed unfair that his enemies would be exalted over him (ver. 2). They didn't deserve the honor. But another day would dawn, and the winner might not be today's victor. For victory belongs to him who won't stay down.

Now David takes heart. His faith is equal to the occasion. He prays (vers. 3-5). He beseeches Jehovah, "Lighten mine eyes." Put brightness in my eyes. Revive me. Cheer me up. Oh, how often all of us need to pray this prayer.

His outlook changes: He trusts in the Lord's mercy and salvation, and sings because of the Merciful Giver's bounties. Faith triumphs over doubt.

The Blindest Foolishness

THE fool hath said in his heart, There is no God. They are corrupt, they have done abominable works, there is none that doeth good. —14:1

A fool convinces himself of what he wishes. A denial of the existence of God is the most foolish foolishness. It leaves too many unanswered questions to be smart and scientific:

— *How could there be creation without a creator?* Spontaneous generation has never been proved.

— *How could there be life that never came from life?* Science says that life can come from only life.

— *How could there be design without a designer?* There is too much to assume everything is an accident.

— *How could there be law (law of gravity, law of production, etc.) without a law-giver?* We have many laws. If God didn't give them, who did?

The only way to explain our world is to start with a self-existent First Cause. Something or some being had to exist in the beginning from which everything else has come. Note this syllogism:

Something cannot come from nothing (admitted fact).
But something is (does exist).
Therefore, something always was.

This proves it. And that something that always was is God. Isn't it much more sensible to start with a living, powerful Being *as the First Cause* than to start with lifeless, powerless matter?

Depravity Follows Disbelief

THE Lord looked down from heaven upon the children of men, to see if there were any that did understand, and seek God. They are all gone aside, they are all together become filthy: there is none that doeth good, no, not one. —14:2, 3

After mentioning atheism in verse one (considered in the previous essay), the poet next discusses depravity, a natural consequence of disbelief: No God, no ruler; no ruler, no law; and no law, no restraint.

But this is not as pleasant as it might seem to some. For it leaves the pricking conscience with no healing balm, the briny tears with no blessed comfort and the weary steps with no assuring direction.

It strips the race of a common unity, a common purpose and a common goal. Atheism permits no wise plan to live through man. And apart from a regenerating influence, his steps are always downward. Paul emphasizes this in the Roman Epistle in which he quotes from this Psalm and elaborates, as follows:

THEIR throat is an open sepulchre; with their tongues they have used deceit; the poison of asps is under their lips: Whose mouth is full of cursing and bitterness; their feet are swift to shed blood: Destruction and misery are in their ways: And the way of peace have they not known: There is no fear of God before their eyes. —Romans 3:10-18

Belief in God does make a difference!

Have They No Knowledge?

HAVE all the workers of iniquity no knowledge? who
eat up my people as they eat bread, and call not upon
the Lord. —14:4

The question expresses wonder at the folly of evildoers. Their witless shortsightedness bewilders thinking people. Don't they know better? Do they think
they can escape the reaping?

FOR they have sown the wind, and they shall reap the
whirlwind. —Hosea 8:7

The unknowledgeable state of atheism is incredible.
Workers of iniquity should learn from observation
and experience. As they endure pain, suffer sorrow,
surrender in defeat and fret with frustration, they
should perceive that an Eternal Refuge to which man
may fly is too necessary not to be true.

As seen in the text, those who reject God reject
His people — attack them, eat them up. They try to
confirm themselves by condemning the godly. They
point to good people's inconsistencies, mock at their
shortcomings and make sport of their weaker moments. And often this is unfair, for the example is
harder than the precept. You can preach a perfect
gospel, but you cannot live a sinlessly perfect life.
The spirit of man is willing, but the flesh is weak.
This was true of Abraham, David, Peter and Paul.
So there is no comfort here for the critic in pointing
to a believer whose life falls below his goal. The dis-
believer should know this! And much, much more!

Question of Divine Acceptance

LORD, who shall abide in thy tabernacle? who shall
dwell in thy holy hill? —15:1

This is life's most basic question. Who is acceptably
religious? Who is permitted to abide in God's tabernacle? Who can have fellowship with Him? The answer is found not in census but in character, not in
rhetoric but in right, not in mere profession but in
many proofs. The answer — a classic on real religion
— embraces ten practical particulars, as follows:

1) The upright: "He that walketh upright" (ver. 2).

2) He who is right with God and man: "And
worketh righteousness" (ver. 2).

3) The truthful: "And speaketh the truth" (ver. 2).

4) One who guards his tongue: "He that backbiteth
not with his tongue" (ver. 3).

5) The person who treats his neighbor properly:
"Nor doeth evil to his neighbor . . ." (ver. 3).

6) The individual who regards men according to
a moral standard: "In whose eyes a vile person is
contemned" (ver. 4).

7) He who honors the righteous for what they are:
"But he honoreth them that fear the Lord" (ver. 4).

8) The one who keeps his word or contract, despite
its pain: "He that sweareth to his own hurt, and
changeth not" (ver. 4).

9) The man who does not oppress others in his
greed: "He that putteth not out his money to usury"
(ver. 5).

10) And he who cannot be bribed (ver. 5).

A Plea for Preservation

PRESERVE me, O God: for in thee do I put my trust.
—16:1

This petition expresses a keenly felt need of man, ever present through the ages. This urgency was heavy on the heart of David when he went forth to meet the champion warrior Goliath. Likewise, it was self-preservation that prompted Naaman to make a trip to a foreign country in search of recovery from his leprosy. And, wishing to escape the wrath of Herod, Joseph took Mary and Jesus down into Egypt. And it was this ever-abiding feeling to be preserved that prompted Peter to draw the sword in Gethsemane.

In the text we hear the pleadings of a man who put his trust in God. He was sure his own wisdom, unaided by Divinity, was too faulty to cope with life's vicissitudes. He knew his own hands, unsupported by the hand of God, were too feeble to triumph over the world's constant opposition.

And David's extremity is an example of man's ever constant need of help. So each of us says:

— Protect me from my enemies: Enemies I have caused who refuse to be reconciled. Enemies without cause who have picked me as the object of their tormenting anger.

— Keep me from my friends who mean well, but whose influence can be so hurtful.

— Spare me from myself (Romans 7:15), for there is no destruction so tragic as that which is self-inflicted, and no darkness like one's putting out his own light.

Two Attachments

O MY soul, thou hast said unto the Lord, Thou art
my Lord: my goodness extendeth not to thee [I have
no good beyond thee, A.S.V.]; but to the saints that
are in the earth, and to the excellent, in whom is all
my delight. —16:2, 3

After pleading for his preservation and after expressing his trust in the Lord (ver. 1), David stated
(1) his closeness to God and (2) his affinity to God's
people. The two go together. An association with
God brings a person into the society of God's children,
which is pleasant and profitable.

Concerning God, he said, "I have no good beyond
thee." He was saying, "My good is not independent
or separate from thee. I have no source of good of
any kind — salvation, safety, happiness or hope — but
in thee." He found in Jehovah all that the concept
of deity implies.

Relative to God's people, David declared, ". . . in
whom is all my delight." He cited this as evidence
of his feelings toward the Heavenly Father — since
he delighted in God's children he evidently delighted
in God. In the fellowship of God's people he enjoyed
the sweetest bond and the easiest living. Among them
he found kindred hearts with whom he shared mutual
beliefs and common aspirations. If like appeals to
like—and it does—then his fondness for godly people
shows that he belonged with them. For where your
affection is, there you gravitate.

Remember — your attachments are telling on you.

Multiplied Sorrows

THEIR sorrows shall be multiplied that hasten after
another god: their drink offerings of blood will I not
offer, nor take up their names into my lips. —16:4

Compounded heartaches — and David specifies their
cause: hastening after another god. If your god is
false, your life can hardly be true.

In this case, the sufferer brings the agony on himself, causes the grief that envelops his life, creates
the very foundation that feeds his tears. The way
of the transgressor is hard. This is why sin is forbidden.

> *Sin is not hurtful*
> *Because it is forbidden,*
> *But it is forbidden*
> *Because it is hurtful.*
>
> —*Benjamin Franklin*

Whatever joy sin offers, it must be viewed as fleeting. The transgressors may appear to have the whole
world in their hands—glory, honor, wealth and speed.
But just over the hill are widening pitfalls, boulders,
blinding darkness and multiplying sorrows. This is
the unimpeachable witness of experience, observation
and history. Remember — all's bad that ends bad.

In view of this danger, David resolved to shun the
peril of idolatry: not even to mention the names of
false gods, which was forbidden (Exodus 23:13). For
familiarity has a tendency to take away the repug-
nance and horror of that which is wrong.

Cast Into a Pleasant Situation

THE lines are fallen unto me in pleasant places; yea,
I have a goodly heritage. —16:6

The "lines" mentioned in the text were employed
to measure or survey land, to denote one's possession.
David's portion had fallen into pleasant places. He
had a "goodly heritage." But more than the land, he
had the Creator of it. He had the Possessor as well
as the possession. He declared, "The Lord is the
portion of mine inheritance" (ver. 5).

May we, too, reflect upon the advantageous circumstances into which we have fallen. Born in America,
the land of the free, we have:

— *Free politics*. One can vote as he pleases.

— *Free education*. A poor child can become a scholar.

— *Free religion*. Each can worship according to
his own interpretation.

— *Free opportunity*. A peasant can become a prin-
cipal in the endeavor of his choice. The country is
wide and the only limit is the sky. There is nothing
wrong with it that man has not caused and that man
cannot cure.

Fortune has smiled on America. It is here that
the poorest is the wealthiest, when measured by the
standards of many other countries.

And now let us bear in mind —

This generation of Americans has a rendezvous with destiny.
—Franklin D. Roosevelt

Hope Beckons

THEREFORE my heart is glad, and my glory rejoiceth: my flesh also shall rest in hope. For thou wilt not leave my soul in hell; neither wilt thou suffer thine Holy One to see corruption. —16:9, 10

My flesh shall rest in hope. David's hope or expectation extended to the "flesh" as well as to the "soul." Here we see his confidence in a bodily resurrection. The Old Testament writers did teach the resurrection of the body. They did believe the dead would come forth incorruptible. Another instance: "Thy dead men shall live, together with my dead body shall they arise" (Isaiah 26:19).

Thou wilt not leave my soul in hell. The original word is *Sheol,* meaning the abode of the dead, symbolized by the grave. Thus the word "hell," as used here, does not mean a place of punishment but rather a resting place for the dead.

Neither wilt thou suffer thine Holy One to see corruption. This is another expression of hope. The statement is expressly applied in Acts 2:27 to the Saviour. It undoubtedly was meant to designate the Lord, even though it had an application in David.

The Saviour is "the resurrection and the life" (John 11:25), and the victor over the grave for all mankind.

THEN shall be brought to pass the saying that is written, Death is swallowed up in victory.
—I Corinthians 15:54

The resurrection is a necessary part of religion. As the journey gets shorter, there must be at the end a new beginning. For humanity will not settle for obliteration.

A Prayer of David

Hear the right, O Lord . . . give ear unto my prayer,
that goeth not out of feigned lips. —17:1

The leading points in the prayer follow in the Psalm:

A sincere appeal to God to do what is right: "Behold the things that are equal" (ver. 2), fair, just and right.

An acknowledgment of what God had done for him (ver. 3): "Proved mine heart." "Visited me in the night." "Tried me" and found nothing.

An assertion of what he had done for himself (vers. 3, 4): "Purposed that my mouth shall not transgress." "By the word of thy lips I have kept me from the paths of the destroyer."

A plea for more help based on Divine assistance and human endeavor: "Hold up my goings . . . that my footsteps slip not" — the perils were many. "Keep me as the apple of the eye" — an object of favor. "Hide me under the shadow of thy wings."

A description of the wicked (vers. 10-12): "Inclosed in their own fat" or prosperity. "Speak proudly." "They have now compassed us." "Like as a lion that is greedy." They are cruel and persistent.

A plea that the great Vindicator would defend the wicked (vers. 13, 14): "Disappoint him, cast him down: deliver my soul." Appointment comes to those who do right, disappointment to those who do wrong.

An expression of the only hope that satisfies (ver. 15): "I shall be satisfied, when I awake, with thy likeness" (ver. 15). Immortality!

Kept by the Word

CONCERNING the works of men, by the word of thy lips
I have kept me from the paths of the destroyer. —17:4

The *works* spoken of in the passage are the doings
of men. In this instance, their conduct was evil and
hurtful. The author had kept himself from their sinful paths: not through an all-sufficiency of his own
but rather through the word of the Great Keeper.

What a sublime tribute to the efficacy of the Word.
He gave a similar ovation in 119:11: "Thy word
have I hid in mine heart, that I might not sin against
thee."

From the Word he received direction, and wise
living necessitates wise instruction. Without guidance
it is easy for one to lose his way. It is important
that we keep an eye on the road signs, and it is as
equally important that we remember the destroyer
changes the signs. He erects guideposts that point
the wrong way. Man must be wary. We need to
examine the signs in the light of the whole counsel
of God (Acts 20:27), remembering —

The devil can cite Scripture for his purpose.
—William Shakespeare

The Word had strengthened the poet in time of
peril. It is very vital that there be a protective power
in the heart of man to guard him in time of temptation, so that he will not be tempted above that he is
able to bear (I Corinthians 10:13).

As a practical lesson, give God's word a chance.

A Pitiful Portion

FROM men which are thy hand, O Lord, from men of the world, which have their portion in this life, and whose belly thou fillest with thy hid treasure: they are full of (satisfied with, A.S.V.) children, and leave the rest of their substance to their babes. —17:14

These men sought their reward strictly in this fleeting life, while David sought his in God. Observation confirms they were wrong. There are scattered all along the shores of time the live-for-the-moment people, wrecked on the cruel rocks of "eat, drink and be merry, for tomorrow you die." This is all they sought and this is all they got — a pitiful portion.

Those give-me-my-portion-now people centered their lives around the prosperity and pleasures of this world, and thus were aptly described as "men of the world."

In the affairs of the world, they were successful. They prospered in their purpose. Their stomachs were filled. They had all the stuff and pleasure that money could buy. And after all their worldly needs were taken care of, there was left an inheritance for their children.

But this was their only reward. They had nothing! absolutely nothing to look forward to beyond this life! Since their plans and purposes were solely connected to this world, it was only natural that their lot consist in only what this world has to offer—vanity.

Solomon summed up for us the materialistic life —

VANITY of vanities; all is vanity. —Ecclesiastes 1:2

Satisfied Then

As for me, I will behold thy face in righteousness: I shall be satisfied, when I awake, with thy likeness.
—17:15

In the realm of material things the heart of man keeps saying, "It is not enough." "He that loveth silver shall not be satisfied with silver; nor he that loveth abundance with increase: this is also vanity" (Ecclesiastes 4:10). Every material thing turns to "vanity and vexation of spirit" (Ecclesiastes 1:14). The whole human family testifies that the longings of man are satisfied in only that which rises above materialism. Yet —

> *How often do we labor for that which satisfieth not.*
> —*John Lubbock*

David realized that the deepest cravings and sweetest joys would be fulfilled in perfect satisfaction when he awoke in the incorruptible and immortal likeness of his Creator. He evidently believed that he would be given a glorious body like that of his Lord, a body suited to an everlasting habitation; and that over there he would dwell forever in a state where service is never blemished, where peace is never disturbed and where happiness is never marred.

Accordingly, then the only satisfaction one enjoys in this world is in pursuing the course that leads to the resurrected, blissful state. In this pursuit there is the single, earthly satisfaction everybody wants and only the few find. David found it. And so can we.

God in Seven Epithets

I WILL love thee, O Lord, my strength. The Lord is my rock, and my fortress, and my deliverer; my God, my strength, in whom I will trust; my buckler, and the horn of my salvation, and my high tower. —18:1, 2

In an unrivaled production of praise, the writer uses seven epithets in describing and lauding God:

My strength. The psalmist knew where his strength lay—in God. Without God he would have succumbed; with Him he had been victorious.

My rock. My cliff. When the storms beat the hardest, he found God a rock, a solid rock, a cliff of shelter.

My fortress. A place of defense and protection. There is no safety like Fort Divine.

My deliverer. Most of us, like David who faced the giant Goliath, have had our own giants (differing only in kinds and sizes), and we, too, have been delivered.

My buckler. The original word is the same one used in 3:3 where it is translated *shield,* a shield buckled to the arm. Life is a warfare, and to win you need God on your arm when you raise it in defense.

The horn of my salvation. Jehovah was to the writer what the horn is to an animal, the means of defense.

My high tower. Or *refuge,* that being the translation of the word in 9:9. Truly, "The name of the Lord is a strong tower: the righteous runneth into it, and is safe" (Proverbs 18:10).

How great God is!

Worthy of Praise

I WILL call upon the Lord, who is worthy to be praised:
so shall I be saved from mine enemies. —18:3

God is worthy of exaltation beyond human expression. No language is adequate to fully express the praises due Him. But in our feeble way we unreservedly say: *To Thee, O God, belongs all the praise, for in Thee is all the merit.*

For God is merciful.

Sinlessly perfect.

Completely just.

Longsuffering to all.

The giver of every good and perfect gift, seen and unseen, thousands upon thousands.

No respecter of persons, though He does respect faith and character.

Loves the world, the whole world, everybody in it.

He extends His grace to all. No exceptions.

His ability and power are so unlimited that with Him on your side you have the majority.

And so we, too, extol His name and sing within our souls:

Worthy of praise is God our Redeemer;
Worthy of glory, honor and pow'r!
Worthy of all our soul's adoration,
Worthy art Thou! Worthy art Thou!

—Tillit S. Teddlie

Reasons for God's Help

HE delivered me from my strong enemy, and from
them which hated me: for they were too strong for me.
—18:17

Why is it that God helps one and doesn't help another? His justice is not subject to question, so there
must be reasons. The eighteenth Psalm tells us why:

1) David asked for help: "In my distress I called
upon the Lord, and cried unto my God" (ver. 6).
This proves his faith and humility, that he believed
in God and that he was not too proud to ask Him
for assistance.

2) Jehovah delighted in him: "He delivered me,
because he delighted in me" (ver. 19). Of course,
there was basis for this pleasure.

3) The writer was rewarded "according to his righteousness"; recompensed "according to the cleanness"
of his hands (ver. 20). God is always on the side of
right, and this is where David was.

4) He had "kept the ways of the Lord," and had
"not wickedly departed from" Him (ver. 21). David
could say, "I did not put away his statutes from me"
(ver. 22). He had not substituted human commandments for the Divine ones. Neither had he followed
opinion instead of faith, nor convenience in preference
to conviction. He was a stickler for the Word. He had
faults, but supplanting Scripture with a make-believe
religion of convenient views was not one of them.

5) He trusted in God (ver. 30). And he was not
disappointed. No one ever is!

God Lent a Hand

THOU hast also given me the shield of thy salvation: and thy right hand hath holden me up, and thy gentleness hath made me great. —18:35

In the chapter David gave a recapitulation of what God had done for him. It is a forceful exposition of Divine sustentation and vindication of the righteous, a masterpiece of encouragement to all who trust God.

God scattered David's enemies: "Yea, he sent out his arrows, and scattered them" (ver. 4).

He drew him out of many waters, calamities troubles: "He drew me out of many waters" (ver. 16).

The Lord was his stay, support or prop: "But the Lord was my stay" (ver. 18).

God lighted his candle — gave him power to shine: "For thou wilt light my candle" (ver. 28).

With God's help, no troop could stop him and no wall could hold him back: "For by thee I have run through a troop; and by my God have I leaped over a wall" (ver. 29).

The Lord's gentleness had enhanced him: "Thy gentleness hath made me great" (ver. 35).

The Just One enabled him to overcome his opposers: "Thou hast subdued under me those that rose up against me" (ver. 39).

God avenged him: "It is God that avengeth me" (ver. 47).

All of this shows that man should regard Jehovah as a personal God who is always concerned with the welfare of His children and ever ready to help.

The Heavens Attest to God

THE heavens declare the glory of God; and the firmament showeth his handiwork. Day unto day uttereth speech, and night unto night showeth knowledge. There is no speech nor language, where their voice is not heard. Their line is gone out through all the earth, and their words to the end of the world. —19:1-4

Hundreds of millions of stars hang in the heavens, but they are not stuck up there in some haphazard, irregular manner. They are grouped together in universes like our own, and operate on a perfect timetable. To say this is an accident is as ridiculous as to say that the New York Telephone Directory is the result of an explosion in a printing plant.

The firmament goes on and on. No end has been found to it. And if space can go on and on, so can the next life, so can eternity.

Since every effect must have a cause, those heavenly bodies lift a voice to man, testifying to a cause which says, "God exists." The message goes "to the end of the world." Consequently, no tribe has ever been found that does not believe in super-human power.

Years ago a French infidel strutted and bragged that infidels would tear down the churches and destroy everything that reminded the people of God. A poor peasant replied, "But you will leave us the sun, the moon, and the stars; and as long as they shine, we shall have a reminder of God."

Though time may dig the grave of creeds,
And dogmas wither in the sod,
My soul will keep the thought it needs—
Its swerveless faith in God.

The Efficacy of the Scriptures

THE law of the Lord is . . . . —19:7-11

While the works of nature testify to deity (vers. 1-4), they do not tell us how to live, how to worship and what to expect in destiny. In meeting these needs, God has given His inspired word, called in this Psalm "the law of the Lord."

In singing its praises, the writer declares it is:

— "Perfect, converting the soul." Complete. Adequate to accomplish the purpose intended.

— "Sure." Fixed and definite in contrast with the shifting and uncertain precepts of men.

— Capable of "making wise the simple." Enlightens.

— "Right." Correct, conforming to duty and justice.

— Proficient in "rejoicing the heart." Its gracious instruction lends beauty, faith, hope and joy to man.

— "Pure." Holy. Faultless.

— "Enduring for ever." Heaven and earth shall pass away, but not God's word (Matthew 24:35).

— "True and righteous." Nothing false in it.

— "More to be desired are they than gold." Priceless.

— "By them is thy servant warned." They caution us.

— "In keeping of them there is great reward." The keeper of the Scriptures shall be blessed.

What a Book! Vast and wide as the world, rooted in the abyss of creation, and towering up behind the blue secrets of heaven. Sunrise and sunset, promise and fulfillment, birth and death, the whole drama of humanity all in this Book.

—Heinrich Hein

Power to Convert

THE law of the Lord is perfect, converting the soul:
the testimony of the Lord is sure, making wise the
simple. —19:7

The word "conversion" is one we freely use in everyday conversation. We speak of converting water into
ice, and we know what that means. We talk of converting a forest into a field, and a log into lumber,
and in each case we know there is a changing or
making-over process.

Conversion simply means a changed or new life.
It is an essential part of religion. Unless our religion
makes some changes in us, then it has failed us — or
we have failed it. One hundred percent conversion
requires a threefold change:

1) A change of heart. That part of man with which
he understands, believes, loves and obeys, must be
changed from a lack of knowledge to understanding,
from unbelief to belief, from hate to love and from
rebellion to obedience.

2) A change of life. One must start living dif-
ferently.

3) A change of state. He must be changed from a
child of the world to a child of God. This is effected
by the new birth.

The power to bring about the conversion of the soul
is the law of the Lord. In a similar wording, Peter
said: "Being born again . . . by the word of God, which
liveth and abideth for ever" (I Peter 1:23).

Let it —
Rule your heart.

Errors

WHO can understand his errors? cleanse thou me from secret faults. Keep back thy servant also from presumptuous sins; let them not have dominion over me: then shall I be upright, and I shall be innocent from the great transgression. —19:12, 13

If there is a law of God and there is (vers. 7-11), then to omit it or go beyond it is an error. So, after discussing the statutes of God, it was natural that David would turn his attention to this soul-searching question: *Who can understand his errors?* The law is broad, making it possible for imperfections to be all the more numerous (119:96). Furthermore —

The longer thread of life we spin,
The more occasion still to sin.
—Herrick

Appropriately, he asked: Who can understand or discern his mistakes? All of them? Who can number every unholy thought, impure word, selfish act, unkind deed, blind deception and omission of positive duty? Only Him who has the all-seeing eye, and that's the One whose mercy man needs.

And David besought it, asking God to cleanse him from secret faults, errors hidden even to himself.

In the same vein of a conscious need, he further entreated God to restrain him from *presumptuous* sins. The original word means *swelling, inflated,* therefore pride and arrogance. He mentioned presumptuous sins in contrast with secret faults, the willingly committed sins in contradistinction to the unknown. When cleansed of one and spared from the other, this would make him upright and "innocent from the great transgression."

Words and Meditations

LET the words of my mouth, and the meditation of my heart, be acceptable in thy sight, O Lord, my strength, and my redeemer. —19:14

David's plea for acceptance suggests that he was well aware that man's thoughts, words, deeds and acts of worship may be accepted or rejected by Him before whom we live. Man who was given the volition to do right must of necessity be endowed with the freedom to do wrong; therefore he ever faces the matter of heaven's approval or disapproval.

The converted soul longs for Divine acceptance. He is anxious to please God, not man, not self. His constant prayer is, "Not my will, but thine be done."

The thoughts and words of man are indicative of the real person he is. "For as he thinketh in his heart, so is he" (Proverbs 23:7). And "out of the abundance of the heart the mouth speaketh" (Matthew 12:34). Out of the heart come the issues of life, presenting decisions, courses, the good and the bad. Thus no man is better than his unfeigned words, and no man's free words are loftier than his meditations.

The text surely lends purpose to this volume — a year of daily meditations. For man is lifted by pondering the higher and nobler things of life.

I think, therefore I am.
—Rene Descartes

A Prayer for the King

THE Lord hear . . . . —20:1-9

The twentieth Psalm was composed for the occasion of David's going to war. It was designed to be used by the people in expressing their feeling toward their king and the impending military action. They petitioned:

— "The Lord hear thee [David] in the day of trouble." And this was one thing he had plenty of — trouble! trouble! trouble!

— "The God of Jacob defend thee [David]." In God's hand is the surest defense. To moralize a little, may Americans never forget this.

— "Remember all thy [David's] offerings, and accept thy [David's] burnt offerings." His worship told of his worthiness. And until this day, sincere worship continues to speak in the behalf of the worshiper: The people see it [as they saw David], and God remembers it [as He remembered David]. Blessed is the country that has such a ruler.

— "Grant thee [David] according to thine [David's] heart, and fulfil all thy [David's] counsel." Grant his wishes. May his purposes be executed.

— "Save, Lord." Save the ruler.

— "Let the King [God, King of all Kings] hear us when we call." Now and in the future. They were anticipating more prayers — and more answers. And so should we.

FEAR God. Honor the king. —I Peter 2:17

Trust in God Versus Weapons

SOME trust in chariots, and some in horses: but we will remember the name of the Lord our God. They are brought down and fallen: but we are risen, and stand upright. —20:7, 8

In this military prayer, prayed by David's loyal subjects, let us consider their trust in God.

Placing their hope in God, they said they would set up their banners in His name (ver. 5). In going to war, all nations have their standards or banners. And the one David's army would unfurl would be in the name of God. Under it they would rally.

Their confidence was in the saving strength of God's right arm rather than in military equipment. They felt a greater urgency to have God with them in battle than to be well armed with armaments. In what must have been an unpopular view among fearful doubters, they mentioned in the prayer the mistaken view of some nations' trust in chariots and horses. And the Psalm continues by voicing the hard truth of disappointment for those who trust in weapons: "They are brought down and fallen; but we are risen, and stand upright."

While man uses weapons in warfare, it is God who has the power to schedule the timing, stage the events, and multiply their effectiveness. No one knew this better than David; for he had gone forth to meet the giant Goliath, taking only a sling and some stones.

Effective arms require good hands, smart minds and strong hearts — and God on your side.

After the Victory

THE king shall joy in thy strength, O Lord; and in thy salvation how greatly shall he rejoice! Thou hast given him . . . . —21:1, 2

The twenty-first Psalm, being a companion to the twentieth, is one of thanksgiving and rejoicing, following the victory. One is a military prayer, the other a victory prayer. It proves God answers the supplications of His children. That God answers prayer is one of the most basic and heartening promises repeated in the Scriptures. If He doesn't, why do we pray?

Their petitions had been granted. In their thanksgiving they mentioned that the Most High had given their king "his heart's desire"; had not withheld "the requests of his lips"; had given him a golden crown; that the blessings were good; had granted him life and "length of days for ever and ever" (referring perhaps to a continuance in his posterity, and in the full sense especially to Christ); that his glory was great; and that honor and majesty had been laid upon him.

It is easy to pray before a battle, but what is our attitude after it is won? These people rejoiced. They were grateful. Victory did not ruin them. Some people are wasted in defeat, while others are wasted in victory. Some can stand failure easier than they can stand success. But these people who remembered God in crisis did not forget Him when it passed. Victory comes too hard not to be grateful.

They Intended Evil

FOR they intended evil against thee: they imagined a
mischievous device, which they are not able to perform.
—21:11

The second portion of this Psalm is addressed by
a victorious people to their triumphant king, assuring
him of future successes.

It sings of the "intended evil" against him by enemies
who "imagined a mischievous device which they were
not able to perform." It wasn't an incident of unin-
tentional harm, but rather a case of deliberate evil
which they were not big enough to execute. Heaven
found ways to frustrate their evil purposes and laid
an awesome paralysis upon their wicked hate.

> *The roughshod rider turns out to be*
> *the rider of the pale horse.*
>
> —*Anonymous*

They were put to flight. Indeed, they were destined
to fail before they started. For the best-laid plans
are doomed to miscarry when God wills they fail. And
if they had won, they still would have lost. For no
one wins, in the long run, in his intention to harm
another.

Though they failed in their mischief, they were still
guilty. In measuring guilt, the intent is equivalent
to the act. St. Bernard said, "Hell is full of good intentions," but remember — hell has its share of bad
intentions, too.

The Messiah

My God, my God . . . . —22:1-31

Some have thought the twenty-second Psalm referred to David, others to the Israelitish people. But all the circumstances were never fulfilled in either, eliminating its application to them. However, there is in it an exact description of the Passion.

Furthermore, the Jewish writers had the conception of a coming person, called the Messiah. He would bear their burdens, lift them up and give them hope. He was their hero. So it was natural for David to sing of that One's coming. And it is interesting and faith-creating for us to observe the closeness between the Psalm and the incidents in the life and suffering of Christ, which we shall do in three dissertations:

— "My God, my God, why hast thou forsaken me" (ver. 1)? These are the words Jesus uttered on the cross (Matthew 27:46).

— "Why art thou so far from helping me, and from the words of my roaring" (ver. 1)? In its fulfillment, we read, "Jesus . . . cried again with a loud voice, yielded up the ghost" (Matthew 27:50).

— "O my God, I cry in the daytime, but thou hearest not: and in the night season, and am not silent" (ver. 2). Jesus prayed incessantly, but His most intense prayer was in the night (Matthew 26:36-45).

— "Our fathers trusted in thee" (ver. 4). Here He identified Himself with man (Luke 19:10).

(*Continued*)

The Messiah

A continuance of the Messianic Psalm:

— "A reproach of men, and despised of the people" (ver. 6). Isaiah issued the same prophecy: "He is despised and rejected of men" (Isaiah 53:3).

— "All they that see me laugh me to scorn: they shoot out [open] the lip, they shake the head . . ." (ver. 7). This was fulfilled in Christ: "And they that passed by reviled him, wagging their heads" (Matthew 27:39).

— "Saying, he trusted on the Lord that he would deliver him: let him deliver him, seeing he delighted in him" (vers. 8, 9). The account of fulfillment is exact: "Likewise also the chief priests mocking him, with the scribes and elders, said . . . He trusted in God; let him deliver him now, if he will have him" (Matthew 27:41-43).

— "But thou art he that took me out of the womb" (ver. 9). God had brought Him into the world, begetting Him by the Holy Spirit (Matthew 1:18).

— "Many bulls have compassed me: strong bulls of Bashan have beset me round. They gaped upon me with their mouths, as a ravening and a roaring lion" (vers. 12, 13). The bulls of Bashan were large and mean, which is an allusion to the cruel and fierce men who persecuted Christ (Matthew 27:29, 30).

(Continued)

The Messiah

More on the Messianic Psalm:

— "My tongue cleaveth to my jaws" (ver. 15). His mouth was dry, the effect of intense thirst. It was fulfilled when Jesus said, "I thirst" (John 19:28).

— "They pierced my hands and feet" (ver. 16). This they did to Jesus (John 20:24-28).

— "They part my garments among them, and cast lots upon my vesture" (ver. 18). This was literally fulfilled (Matthew 27:35).

— "Neither hath he hid his face from him; but when he cried unto him, he heard" (ver. 24). The fulfillment is certain. For when Jesus died, "the earth did quake, and the rocks rent; and the graves were opened" (Matthew 27:51, 52). Visible signs that God heard!

— "And all the kindreds of the nations shall worship before thee" (ver. 27). In giving a universal plan, Jesus said, "Go ye therefore, and teach all nations" (Matthew 28:19).

— "For the kingdom is the Lord's (ver. 28). Christ called it His (John 18:36).

— "They shall come, and shall declare his righteousness unto a people that shall be born, that he hath done this" (ver. 31). A perfect description of the work of His disciples (I Corinthians 15:1).

Obviously these many plain predictions were fulfilled in Jesus. Surely this Psalm adds credibility to the inspiration of David and to the Divinity of Christ.

The Lord Is My Shepherd

THE Lord is my shepherd, I shall not want. He maketh me to lie down in green pastures: he leadeth me beside the still waters. He restoreth my soul: he leadeth me in the paths of righteousness for his name's sake. Yea, though I walk through the valley of the shadow of death, I will fear no evil: for thou art with me; thy rod and thy staff they comfort me. Thou preparest a table before me in the presence of mine enemies: thou anointest my head with oil; my cup runneth over. Surely goodness and mercy shall follow me all the days of my life; and I will dwell in the house of the Lord for ever. —Psalms 23

This is the best known and most often quoted Psalm. In all literature its popularity has no equal. Its beauty is unmatched. Its comfort has no rival. This Psalm has been on the lips of countless numbers as they confidently walked through the valley of the shadow of death. Its precious words stand engraved today on a million marble shafts in the peaceful cities of the dead.

This beautiful, methaphorical hymn embraces the complete needs of man: The Lord's leadership. A life free from want where the pastures are green and the waters are still. A restored soul. Paths of righteousness. No fear of death. Comfort. The shepherd's constant presence. Protection from enemies. The Shepherd's approbation. Goodness. Mercy. A glorious certainty. And the hope of immortality.

Nothing could be dearer in life or death!

(*Continued*)

The Lord Is My Shepherd

A continuance of the Shepherd Hymn:

Picture ourselves in the Orient where the sun is hot and the earth is scorched. There life is a struggle with the elements.

We see hungry sheep that need help. The shepherd calls and the sheep muster their last ounce of strength to follow. They know not the path ahead, but they know the shepherd.

The journey commences amidst choking dust. As they go, the shepherd avoids the treacherous rocks that cause stumbling and the hidden holes that entrap spindling legs. He bypasses the thorns that reach out to cut. At last they arrive in the valley of plenty where the grass is green and the waters are still.

The wild animals are kept at a distance. They only howl. They dare not come any closer. For the good shepherd is present.

Now the day is far spent, and the sheep are in need of more mercy. He beckons. Together they head toward the fold provided by his grace. When they arrive he anoints every head with oil and gives to each a cup of cold water. As the night closes in he bars the door. The sheep sleep in peace. Blessed sheep.

David who had been a shepherd boy sums up the pastoral scene by ascribing to himself this poetic hope: "And I will dwell in the house of the Lord for ever." Blessed man.

The Rightful Owner

THE earth is the Lord's, and the fulness thereof; the world, and they that dwell therein. For he hath founded it upon the seas, and established it upon the floods. —24:1, 2

God is the Creator and Proprietor of the whole world. All creation is vested in Him. He has the right to use it and dispose of it as He pleases. He can sweep it away by flood or fire. It is His.

The ground of ownership is given in the text: *He hath founded it . . . and established it.* His by right of creation. This is the first thought presented in the Bible — and the most basic: "God created the heaven and the earth" (Genesis 1:1). Accept this and you are ready for more lessons and broader horizons.

How deceived we are in our attachment to materials. We call them ours when they are not. The wealthiest and most powerful holder is but a tenant who may at any moment receive notice to vacate. And with the notice comes the revealing question in Luke 12:20: "Whose shall those things be, which thou hast provided?" In our extreme pursuit of possessions, this appropriate question can give our lives a new meaning by causing us to relax some of the grip on that which must be given up sooner or later anyway.

ONE generation passeth away, and another generation cometh: but the earth abideth for ever.
                                        —Ecclesiastes 1:4

Who Shall Stand in His Holy Place?

WHO shall ascend into the hill of the Lord? or who shall stand in his holy place? He that hath clean hands, and a pure heart; who hath not lifted up his soul unto vanity, nor sworn deceitfully. —24:3, 4

Through the ages humanity has asked the question in the title. The hill of the Lord was Mount Zion, for it was a place of worship. Who can stand there? Who can worship acceptably?

The answer is simple in rhetoric. A more beautiful and comprehensive outline of terms could not be crowded into such few words. A higher standard of practical religion cannot be found:

Clean hands. Kept clean by the power of God. For if our hands are not cleansed by Him, no soap will wash away the stain.

A pure heart. The worth of service and worship depends on the motives. Worship from a wicked mind is vain (Proverbs 21:27).

Has not lifted up his soul to vanity or falsehood. Not carried away by false standards and erroneous appeals.

Nor sworn deceitfully. True. Sincere. No falsehood-spinner. No shadow-chaser.

> *Faithfully faithful to every trust,*
> *Honestly honest in every deed,*
> *Righteously righteous and justly just,*
> *Religiously religious—'tis his creed.*

Such a person is acceptable in God's holy place.

Who Is This King of Glory?

LIFT up your heads, O ye gates; and be ye lifted up, ye everlasting doors; and the King of glory shall come in. Who is this King of glory? The Lord strong and mighty, the Lord mighty in battle. —24:7, 8

The twenty-fourth Psalm was composed perhaps to celebrate the removal of the ark of the covenant to its appointed place in Jerusalem. Such a sacred entrance into the city called for a special hymn of praise, covering three major thoughts: (1) An ascription of praise to the owner and ruler of the world. (2) The person worthy to engage in this holy act. (3) A responsiveness on the glory of God.

As they entered Jerusalem, carrying the ark, they in hymnal form asked the gates to lift up that the King of glory might come in.

It seems a portion of the singers asked in poetic verse, "Who is this King of glory?"

Then other singers replied in rhythmic beauty, "The Lord strong and mighty, the Lord mighty in battle."

Fundamental knowledge is what we have in the Psalm, glorious acknowledgment and real dedication.

To be practical, each needs to ask himself the same question, "Who is this King of glory?" His answer will lift him high, or pull him low.

Let Me Not Be Ashamed

O MY God, I trust in thee: let me not be ashamed, let not my enemies triumph over me. —25:2

May I have no occasion for shame, that's the prayer.

When one starts to build and is unable to finish, he feels ashamed. Others will say, "This man began to build, and was not able to finish" (Luke 14:30). So, Lord, help me to plan wisely and to work diligently.

When one trips and falls, he feels ashamed. Falling is humiliating. Therefore, Lord, give me a good footing (26:12), and may I watch my step.

When one loses control of himself, he is later sheepish. Indeed, Lord, help me to keep myself in subjection (I Corinthians 9:27).

Begging is shameful (Luke 16:3). Lord, may there be no occasion for it. Give me health and opportunity that I may make a living.

May I not be ashamed of my religion. "If any man suffer as a Christian, let him not be ashamed" (I Peter 4:16).

May I never be "ashamed of the testimony of the Lord" (II Timothy 1:12). When it is derided, may I waver not.

Lord, though I'm asking not to be ashamed, may I ever be ashamed when shame sits on my brow.

For there is hope of salvation where there is shame.
—Latin Proverb

Sin Without Cause

YEA, let none that wait on thee be ashamed: let them be ashamed which transgress without cause. —25:3

What David desired for himself, he desired for others — that they be not ashamed (vers. 2, 3). But he could not pray this for those who "transgress without cause."

Transgress without cause — what does it mean? The interpretations vary. One commentator states, "It brings into view a prominent thought in regard to sin, that it is without cause," meaning there is never a cause for it. But another says, "Those who transgress [or rebel] without reasonable cause."

Surely there is no cause for sin that makes sin righteous. But there are extenuating circumstances that cry out for understanding and mercy. One of which is a lack of knowledge. Ignorance of the law does not change a violation to compliance, but it does attest that the infraction was of the mind and not of the heart.

Here is a Biblical example: "Whom therefore ye ignorantly worship . . ." (Acts 17:23). The worship was wrong, but there was a cause — ignorance; not a cause that turned idolatry into truth, but a cause for their doing it.

Everything must have a cause.
—Chinese Proverb

Whatever "transgress without cause" means, let's keep our intentions pure that our deeds be well-meaning.

Lead Me

LEAD me in thy truth, and teach me: for thou art the God of my salvation; on thee do I wait all the day.
—25:5

One of the greatest needs of man is capable leadership. He needs to be led — not misled. However, the one and only unerring direction is found in God and His inviolable truth.

David recognized his need of guidance, its true source, and sang of it. And so do we, as expressed in this popular hymn:

> *Lead kindly Light, amid the encircling gloom,*
> *Lead thou me on:*
> *The night is dark, and I am far from home;*
> *Lead thou me on.*
> *Keep thou my feet; I do not ask to see*
> *The distant scene — one step enough for me.*
> *—J. H. Newman*

Unless we are led by the light of truth, we are left to grope and stumble in darkness. Being well aware of this, the psalmist pleaded for leadership in truth, effected by teaching.

"The paths of the Lord are mercy and truth" (ver. 10) — where mercy is extended and truth is kept. Those who walk the higher paths are those who "keep his covenant and his testimonies." Every person who follows Him does it by virtue of heeding Him. So if we want Divine leadership, we have a responsibility to move at His command.

Forget the Sins of My Youth

REMEMBER, O Lord, thy tender mercies and thy loving-kindnesses; for they have been ever of old. Remember not the sins of my youth, nor my transgressions: according to thy mercy remember thou me for thy goodness' sake, O Lord. —25:6, 7

This was the prayer of the writer: Forget! forget! O Lord, the sins of my youth. And God will; for when He forgives sin, He remembers it no more forever (Hebrews 10:17).

David asked God to remember and to forget — remember His own Divine mercies and kindnesses, but forget David's youthful sins. The psalmist apparently thought the former had a bearing on the latter, which it did and does. For if it were not for the Lord's mercy and goodness, man would be compelled to bear his guilt forever.

Such a prayer was very human. And how very human was the man who prayed it. And we, too, bear the stamp of the same clay. Not any of us would be willing to dig up the follies of youth, breathe life into those skeletons and parade them down the street. We rather beg: Let them lie. Forget them. Don't deal with me according to what I have been, but rather according to what I have become; and especially according to what Thou art: the God of mercy and kindness, good and upright. This is our prayer to the God who is —

Good to forgive: Best to forget.
—Robert Browning

At Ease

WHAT man is he that feareth the Lord? him shall he teach in the way that he shall choose. His soul shall dwell at ease [lodge in goodness]; and his seed shall inherit the earth. —25:12, 13

The man spoken of in the text finds a resting place in contrast with the restlessness of the man who has lost his way. In the school of the human heart he does well in the following courses:

— Fear of God and trust in Him. The psalmist stipulates this as a condition of ease (vers. 12, 13). This is a protector against worry and tension.

— The unashamed life (ver. 2). Wrong may grant a temporary satisfaction, but right gives a permanent peace.

— The leadership of God (ver. 3). Many are disturbed because of the pull of many ways. They shall never find peace until they obtain unity of direction.

— Meekness (ver. 9). No creature smarts so much as the proud. Pride knows no rest.

— Eyes that see the Lord (ver. 15). The self-centered eye has no ease, only frustration gone mad.

— Forgiveness (ver. 18). The soul feels free in the life where pardon has broken the shackles of guilt, granting a freedom freer than the birds, as expressed by Thomas Parnell:

> *My days have been so wondrous free,*
> *The little birds that fly*
> *With careless ease from tree to tree,*
> *Were but as bless'd as I.*

Assurance Against Slipping

JUDGE me, O Lord; for I have walked in mine integrity: I have trusted also in the Lord; therefore I shall not slide. —26:1

The very thoughts David mentioned in the Psalm would protect him from sliding. Let us ponder them, for we need the safety and assurance they give:

Integrity: "I have walked in mine integrity" (ver. 1). Integrity is truly the basis of all stability. When you walk in the path of uprightness, you encounter fewer slippery places. Make your word sacred. Prove it by performance, not just promise.

Trust: "I have trusted also in the Lord" (ver. 1). Trust in Jehovah energizes our steps and keeps us moving.

Truth: "I have walked in thy truth" (ver. 3)—God's infallible way. The truth needs no shift, thus those who imbide it have no need to change positions. Only truth marches with the future.

Association: "Will not sit with the wicked" (ver. 5). Evil associations corrupt good morals. Wrong company has been the undoing of many people.

Worship: "So will I compass thine altar" (ver.6). You become like the object you worship.

Even places: "My foot standeth in an even place" (ver. 12). On level ground he was less apt to lose his balance. The stumbling blocks were fewer. Watch where you stand, which is determined by what you stand for.

By meeting these conditions we don't slip, we advance.

Tell All the World

THAT I may publish with the voice of thanksgiving, and tell of all thy wondrous works. —26:7

What was it he wanted to tell? "All thy wondrous works." They are many. Creation is God's handiwork. Providence is His control of matters for the good of His people. Love is His gift to all, to even those who hate Him. His word is a guide to a people who without it would not know which way to go. The sunshine and the rain are but two of a thousand earthly blessings. How great they are.

Why did he want to tell it? He said it was because of thanksgiving. His telling the story would be an expression of gratitude.

What man tells,
Tells on him.

It told on Paul. He stated that God had done so much for him that he owed something in return, that he was a debtor to make known the gospel (Romans 1:14).

To whom was David thankful? To God. The works were wondrous, but the Worker was greater than the works.

Tell it, but to whom? The people. David's concern for them was a factor. He loved them enough to share the good news with them.

How grateful are we? Are we willing for it to be measured by what we declare?

I Love to Go to Church

LORD, I have loved the habitation of thy house, and the place where thine honor dwelleth. —26:8

In modern language, David's sentiment was, "I love to go to church." This is the sentiment of millions today, expressed by regular attendance. Millions more are in regular absence, evidencing they don't like to go.

It was a delightful experience for David, of which he said, "How amiable are thy tabernacles, O Lord of hosts!" (84:1). It was so enjoyable and profitable that he sang: "For a day in thy courts is better than a thousand" (84:10). It was no irksome ritual.

The psalmist was committed to worship. He declared, "I will compass thine altar" (ver. 6). His mind was made up. He knew what he was going to do. The pain that some people go through each week, not knowing whether to go or not go, is torturous. A once-for-all, irrevocable decision to attend worship would save them from a weekly, tormenting experience of indecision.

A telephone caller inquired of the minister of a church in Washington where the President attended: "Do you expect the President to be in church Sunday?" "That," replied the minister, "I cannot promise, but I do expect the Lord to be there, and that should be incentive enough for a reasonably large attendance."

FOR where two or three are gathered together in my name, there am I in the midst of them.
—Matthew 18:20

Whom Shall I Fear?

THE Lord is my light and my salvation: whom shall
I fear? the Lord is the strength of my life; of whom
shall I be afraid? —27:1

The writer's fearless life was an extraordinary accomplishment due to his belief that God was with him.
" For thou art with me," is his previous explanation
(23:4).

He did not fear *darkness*, for he believed the Lord
was his light (ver. 1). Most of our ills are due to a
lack of enlightenment.

Neither was he afraid of *condemnation*, because he
was assured his salvation was in the Lord (ver. 1).

Nor did he fear *weakness*. He believed that with
the Lord's help he would be strong enough to meet
every eventuality (ver. 1).

Neither did he flinch before his *enemies*, for his
experience had been that when they came upon him
the Great Protector caused them to stumble and fall
(ver. 2).

Nor did he fear *trouble* of any kind, because he felt
that when it came God would hide him in His own
dwelling place (ver. 5) ; shelter and protect him.

This glorious valor was a growth, a bravery that
fed on itself and on God's promise (ver. 14). So there
is hope for all of us to become braver.

> *The chivalry*
> *That dares the right and disregards alike*
> *The yea and nay o' the world.*
> *—Robert Browning*

This One Thing I Desire

ONE thing have I desired of the Lord, that will I
seek after; that I may dwell in the house of the Lord
all the days of my life, to behold the beauty of the
Lord, and to inquire in his temple. —27:4

It was an intense desire. A gripping aspiration. So
major and singular was this longing that David called
it the "one thing have I desired of the Lord." With
an overwhelming yearning he said he would seek after
it. He knew that a person seldom gets what he doesn't
seek.

What was it that meant so much to him? The one
thought that overpowered all others? The one desire
that gave the greatest purpose to living? Was it eating? No. Health? No. Entertainment? No. Recrea-
tion? No. Yet all of these are worthwhile. It was
worship, dwelling in the Lord's house and beholding
His beauty, inquiring of Him. That was it. What
the poet placed first, some place last. An absence from
worship was to him an insufferable privation. He
longed to be there, to offer sacrifices of joy and
thanksgiving (ver. 6). It was a privilege he loved
(26:8).

There is no association like that of being by the
Lord's side, in His house. There our eyes easier see
"the King in his beauty." There the musings on the
glories of Jehovah freely and fully pace the soul.
There we nourish our spiritual hunger.

> *O why do we feed on husks when there is
> bread in the Father's house?*

Saved From Fainting

I HAD fainted, unless I had believed to see the goodness of the Lord in the land of the living. —27:13

The psalmist admits that he has had a rough time
of it. He had some close calls. Life hadn't been a
bed of roses. He had been tested and tried, subjected
to firey ordeals, but he had gotten through.

What was it that buoyed him, that gave him strength
to endure when otherwise he would have fainted? It
was faith. His own heart condition of unrelenting
confidence supported him. This quality is called "the
good fight of faith" (I Timothy 6:12). It keeps you
from turning and running in battle. Where the faith
is great, the trials are less. If he had quit believing,
the good life of perservering, meeting all adversities
and overcoming them, would have been over.

So it is absolutely necessary that we protect ourselves from fainting, that we guard ourselves from a
powerless existence. One day at church a man in the
pew fainted. There was no need to pass him a song
book, he couldn't sing; nor call him to pray, he couldn't
pray; nor to speak to him, he couldn't listen. In this
state, life was no more than breathing.

We must avoid fainting; and the way to do this is
to increase our faith, which is accomplished by giving
the Word a chance in our hearts:

FAITH cometh by hearing, and hearing by the word of
God. —Romans 10:17

Smooth Words Spoken to Get You

DRAW me not away with the wicked, and with the workers of iniquity, which speak peace to their neighbors, but mischief is in their hearts. —28:3

Later David added this thought concerning the deceiver: "The words of his mouth were smoother than butter, but war was in his heart: his words were softer than oil, yet were they drawn swords" (55:21).

And Jeremiah had this to say, "One speaketh peaceably to his neighbor with his mouth, but in heart he layeth his wait" (Jeremiah 9:8).

And Samuel gave these two examples:

AND when Abner was returned to Hebron, Joab took him aside in the gate to speak with him quietly, and smote him there . . . . —II Samuel 3:27

AND Joab took Amasa by the beard with the right hand to kiss him. But Amasa took no heed to the sword that was in Joab's hand: so he smote him therewith . . . . —II Samuel 20:9, 10

The possibility of being taken by smooth-talking deceivers has ever been a danger. Their words hide their intents. Behind the kindest words, soft as butter, sweet as sugar, the hand clutches a concealed dagger. Deceitful lips press a kiss on your cheek, but a circling hand rams a dagger in your back — or slips the hand into your pocket. Thus until you know a person, it is wise to insist that he only throw the kisses at you, that you may stay beyond the reach of the dagger or the lift of the wallet.

According to Their Deeds

GIVE them according to their deeds, and according to the wickedness of their endeavors: give them after the work of their hands; render to them their desert.
—28:4

This is a prayer that the people be rewarded according to their deeds. *Render to them their desert.* This is in keeping with the will of God, which means that it was not improper. However, if the motive had been wrong — prayed out of malice and vindictiveness — it would have been evil in spirit, though it was correct in content. It seems that righteous indignation entered into the prayer, which is not wicked. If the time comes when a man ceases to become indignant at evil, he has lost his concern for the outcome of the struggle between right and wrong.

The concept of justice in all civilization is that men must account for their deeds. Responsibility requires it. Fairness says this is the way to play the game. If man could sow idleness and reap plenty, or scatter gossip and harvest goodwill, or disseminate hate and gather love, it would be extremely unfair. It is an equitable and just law of nature and of human behavior that everything and everybody be rewarded in kind. The three laws of sowing and reaping are: you reap what you sow; you reap later than you sow; and you reap more than you sow.

> *The tissue of the life to be*
> *We weave with colors all our own,*
> *And in the field of destiny*
> *We reap as we have sown.*
>
> *—John Greenleaf Whittier*

Like a Thunderstorm

GIVE unto the Lord, O ye mighty, give unto the Lord glory and strength. —29:1

In the twenty-ninth Psalm we have one of the grandest and most awe-inspiring descriptions of a thunderstorm. It was used to praise the glory and strength of God, and to encourage and comfort the people. The hymn ascribes glory to God seven times in the expression, "The voice of the Lord":

1) "The voice of the Lord is upon the waters: the God of glory thundereth" (ver. 3). Indeed, God speaks in the quiet, running brook, but thunder is more expressive of his might.

2) "The voice of the Lord is powerful" (ver. 4).

3) "The voice of the Lord is full of majesty" (ver. 4). It is grand and magnificent, filled with splendor.

4) "The voice of the Lord breaketh the cedars" (ver. 5). It is similar to the power that passes from the cloud, breaking up trees.

5) "The voice of the Lord divideth the flames of fire" (ver. 7). Like a flash of lightning, every utterance of God flashes with brilliance and strikes with force.

6) "The voice of the Lord shaketh the wilderness" (ver. 8). The storm shakes our world, which is only a small comparison of the power of God's word.

7) "The voice of the Lord maketh the hinds [deer] to calve" (ver. 9). This they do because of their fear.

We ascribe to God the same praise. And though the storm rages without, we are at peace within.

Worship in the Beauty of Holiness

GIVE unto the Lord the glory due unto his name;
worship the Lord in the beauty of holiness. —29:2

We appreciate the beautiful, the elegant, the grace-
ful, the adorable: the majestic mountain, the blue
ocean, the singing tree, the green grass, the red rose,
the flying bird, the good looking child and the handsome adult. But the most adorable beauty is *the
beauty of holiness*. It is more charming and refined
than any other beauty, because it is human and inward. Holiness is truly a masterpiece of beauty within the individual, developed by the individual, with
the help of God. A major achievement.

Peter taught in a familiar quotation that holiness
is a likeness to God: "Be ye holy; for I am holy"
(I Peter 1:16). This expresses the highest idea of
holiness — human character copied after the character
of God. It is the likeness of God thriving in the heart,
beaming from the eyes, breathing from the lips, preach-
ing in behavior and worshiping in a beauty unexcelled.

In Old Testament times nothing was spared to
establish the idea that worship must be pure and
holy: a sacrifical victim without spot and blemish;
precious vessels; unleavened bread; altar of whole
stones; clothes washed clean. While all of this was
outward, it had the effect of emphasizing the need of
a pure inward state — *the beauty of holiness*.

> *More fit for the kingdom, more useful I'd be,
> More blessed and holy, more, Savior, like Thee.*
>
> —*P. P. Bliss*

Kept Alive

O LORD my God, I cried unto thee, and thou hast healed me. O Lord, thou hast brought up my soul from the grave: thou hast kept me alive, that I should not go down to the pit. —30:2, 3

David had been ill, critically ill. While on the brink of the grave he prayed unto God. The prayer was heard: "Thou hast healed me." He attributed his recovery to God: "Thou hast kept me alive."

David's experience has been the experience of countless numbers. They have walked down the slippery path and stood lingering at death's door. Yet they were pulled back when it seemed but natural for them to go on. A power stronger than medicine did it. Up from the grave, as it were, they sang praises unto God and exclaimed that they would give thanks unto Him forever, as David did (ver. 12).

Illness has its compensations. It can open deaf ears and unlock closed eyes. It teaches us that the thread of life is brittle. Health is no longer presumed. Friends are more highly esteemed than ever — they stood by with sympathy and kindness. Having a more accurate view of what really counts in life, we resolve to better use whatever days may lie ahead for us. We are thoroughly convinced that we had been caught up in too much ado with unimportant things. We realize that God kept us alive for some worthwhile purpose. The suffering was not in vain.

The chamber of sickness is the chapel of devotion.
—Anonymous

Joy in the Morning

WEEPING may endure for a night, but joy cometh in the morning. —30:5

The passage refers to the troubles and heartaches which the psalmist had suffered. He was so human. And he suffered so humanly.

No pain or trial seems short at the time. Weeping endures for the night, and it seems it will never pass. But every night has its ending. Every spell of darkness is finally scattered by the light of a new day. This we need to remember in the gloom of the night. And at the dawning there is joy, jubilation, singing — *joy cometh in the morning.* A morning free from sorrow. The tears have dried. The eyes see a new unblurred outlook. The ears hear a new call, or an order back to old responsibilities. The heart now beats with a new hope. The steps once again march with certainty. The world keeps turning, and we have climbed back on.

Life has its night and day, uphill and downhill; so whatever comes, whenever it comes, we must search our souls to find strength to live through it.

Let us take courage in the blessed fact that the affliction, whether short or long, is but for a moment in comparison with eternity, and that it has its compensation:

FOR our light affliction, which is but for a moment, worketh for us a far more exceeding and eternal weight of glory. —II Corinthians 4:17

My Mountain Stands

AND in my prosperity I said, I shall never be moved.
Lord, by thy favor thou hast made my mountain to
stand strong: thou didst hide thy face, and I was
troubled. —30:6, 7

There had been a time in David's life when he felt
too self-secure. It was at an interval of prosperity
in which he experienced comparative peace and ease.
Seeing nothing to alter his state, he said, "I shall
never be moved"; that is, I shall never be visited with
calamity or affliction. He just took it for granted
that his prosperity would last, as most people do.
When one enjoys good health, grand success, many
friends and what appears to be safe investments, it
is easy to suffer the allusion that tomorrow will be
the same as today.

Poor David. He saw his mountain come tumbling
down. The reason — it had been resting too much on
self and not enough on God. If our mountain stands,
it must have a stronger base than human tact, skill
and industry — it must rest on God. And when it
doesn't and when it tumbles, we see the folly in counting on materialism. Then as we pick up the pieces,
we put our dependence where it belongs — in God.
Then—and only then—is our mountain strong enough
to stand when trouble comes and danger strikes. David
later acknowledged this: "thy favor has made my
mountain to stand strong."

Erect your mountain. Raise it high. Let God help
you build it tumble-proof.

Have Mercy

HEAR, O Lord, and have mercy upon me: Lord be thou my helper. —30:10

One of the repeated pleas of David was, "Have mercy upon me." His plight required unmerited favor —mercy. He needed a benefaction of which he was not worthy. He needed an accommodation that could come only through the goodness of the Compassionate One.

The cowboy needs mercy when he is thrown from the bronc. The heartless logic of justice will not suffice, such as: "After all, he climbed on. He made the decision which precipitated his fall. It's his fault. Let him patch himself up." Hold on — have a heart. He needs mercy, not the applications of a rigorous justice.

If we were to rid ourselves of all mercy and follow nothing but a strict justice, it would dehumanize humanity. It would invite upon us a coldblooded harshness that would convert society into a tribe of brutes.

In view of all our shortcomings, the one thing we don't want is full justice, devoid of all mercy. We don't want it in society. We don't want it at the Judgment. What we want is mercy. And it is most heartening to know that God will grant it. But the mercy we would have Him show to us, we must show to others.

Who will not mercy unto others show,
How can he mercy ever hope to have?
                    —*Edmund Spenser*

Total Commitment

INTO thine hand I commit my spirit: thou hast redeemed me, O Lord God of truth. —31:5

These words were exceedingly important at the
time David sang them, but they increased in distinction and popularity when Jesus repeated them on the
cross (Luke 23:46). That pinpointed them with a
special significance. Perhaps David was not thinking
— as Jesus thought — of a final entrustment of his
spirit into the hands of God, but rather of a solemn
placement here on earth of his whole self, body and
soul, into the keeping of God.

Additionally, David said:

MY times are in thy hand. —ver. 15

The passage recognizes the sovereignty of God: His
prerogative to rule and bless, man's to trust and obey.

This commitment is appropriate at all times:

— In life, for David pledged it.

— In death, for Jesus uttered it.

We, too, need to be involved in this total dedication.
To cope with a world of troubles and dangers, we
need a faith in God that expresses itself in a living
commitment and in a resigning trust. Then we can
work in the day without fear, sleep in the night
without worry, and wake up in the morning without
dread. Every night is a beautiful dream. And every
dawn is a pleasant awakening.

Opportunity

THOU hast set my feet in a large room. —31:8

The author sang that God had given him a large room, plenty of space for movement and action — opportunity. He was not confined. He was not shackled or hindered in any way. He was given what we all need — opportunity.

When God gives you a large room, that implies an obligation to use it. For every right carries a responsibility.

Those who try to get the most for the least are not in the room of opportunity; they have already stepped into the hall of disaster.

The world does not owe us a living. It was founded to give us room. It is up to us to work it. Remember — the ant and the grasshopper had the same opportunity.

Life is full of possibilities. But to take advantage of them, most of us have to begin in a small way. Though the job is humble, it is a good place to begin to apply your industry, skill and honesty. These approaches are the best training and preparation for advancement.

Grab the opportunity; for such a chance, when taken seriously, leads to fortune.

There is a tide in the affairs of men,
Which, taken at the flood, leads on to fortune.
—William Shakespeare

In Trouble

HAVE mercy upon me, O Lord, for I am in trouble: mine eye is consumed with grief, yea, my soul and my belly. —31:9

David had his troubles. But this is the common lot of man. He spoke of:

Enemies who set a net for him (ver. 4). But if enemies can be the net-setters, God can be the net-breaker.

Adversities (ver. 7). There were setbacks. But they can be turned into forward marches, and therein lies the distinction.

Failing strength because of iniquity (ver. 10). We bring this upon ourselves. Sin weakens.

A reproach to his neighbors (ver. 11). They refused to associate with him.

His being forgotten like a dead man (ver. 12). He was forgotten in circles where he was once well remembered. This is the sad lot of the dead.

Slander (ver. 13). "Lying lips." The bigger a man is, the more anxious little people are to blacken him.

Counsel to take away his life (ver. 13). This just makes more enemies, for every man has some friends.

Haste (ver. 22). Too hasty in assuming that he had been cut off from God. For God heard his supplication.

So a very practical lesson in the Psalm is: *Learn patience in trouble.* Just because God does not act as fast as we desire does not mean that He is not watching over us.

Covered Sin

BLESSED is he whose transgression is forgiven, whose sin is covered. Blessed is the man unto whom the Lord imputeth not iniquity, and in whose spirit there is no guile. —32:1, 2

The sin referred to in the text is sin that has been covered with forgiveness and is no longer imputed to the sinner. It is past sin — iniquity no longer active in the heart of the offender.

There are many wrong ways to try to cover sin:

1) Hide. Adam and Eve tried this (Genesis 3:1-8).

2) Shift the blame to another. Adam blamed Eve. And Eve blamed the serpent.

3) Run away. Jonah took a ship and went to sea (Jonah 1:1-4), but God kept up.

4) Criticize the righteous. "And why beholdest thou the mote that is in thy brother's eye, but considerest not the beam that is in thine own eye" (Matthew 7:3)?

5) Persecute the reprover. The sinners Stephen rebuked sought relief by killing him (Acts 7:54-60).

6) Bring in false witnesses. If one is guilty, all the witnesses in the world cannot swear him innocent.

7) Measure self by a weaker person. Say, "I am not as bad as so and so." Maybe not. But it doesn't cover sin. It is unwise: "They, measuring themselves by themselves, and comparing themselves among themselves, are not wise" (II Corinthians 10:12).

There is only one right way to cover sin — get forgiveness!

Peace Through Confession

WHEN I kept silence, my bones waxed old through my roaring [groaning, A.S.V.] all the day long. For day and night thy hand was heavy upon me: my moisture is turned into the drought of summer. I acknowledged my sin unto thee, and mine iniquity have I not hid. I said, I will confess my transgressions unto the Lord; and thou forgavest the iniquity of my sin. —32:3-5

In David's silence or non-confession he found no rest. Conscience-smitten, troubled, agonizing in soul, his "bones waxed old"; that is, his strength failed and it seemed that the weakness of old age was upon him.

There was conviction of sin, but no confession. Trying to hide sin in his life, unwilling to confess it, refusing to seek pardon, life became hard for him. While his mouth kept silent on sin, his heart groaned with anguish. Pressure built up within him, but he refused to pull the valve of confession. As it wore on, he felt more distressed. His remembrance of guilt seemed to be the pressing hand of God upon him. When it became intolerable he confessed his sins. Forgiveness lifted the weight. Then peace came.

What the psalmist suffered is the experience of millions. In an effort to obtain ease from a painful guilt, yet unwilling to seek pardon, they try to find it in becoming amusement worshipers, bar flies, business pushers, honor chasers, or big givers. After suffering futility and disappointment, maybe they will go on to seek release in the Divine way — as David did — and peace shall come.

When God May Be Found

For this shall every one that is godly pray unto thee in a time when thou mayest be found. —32:6

"In the time of finding out sin" is the rendition in the margin of the American Standard Version. This is the propitious time. The text does not mean there are set times when God is disposed to give ear and grant mercy to sinners, whereas at other times He is too busy or unconcerned to be approached by the penitent. No! This is not what it means at all.

The real time of mercy with God is when the sinner submits himself to the will of God.

Now is the accepted time; behold, now is the day of salvation. —II Corinthians 6:2

The time is *now* with God, if the time is *now* with man. But the psalmist later explained that it is not the time for God or man, if man's heart is hardened: "Today if ye will hear his voice, harden not your heart, as in the provocation" (95:7,8).

David's experiences of agony in sin and ecstasy in forgiveness, discussed in the previous essay, is an encouragement to all others in similar circumstances. He counsels the religiously inclined to find themselves that they may find God. This was the order with the Prodigal Son: he found himself, and then found his father (Luke 16:17-20).

Don't Act Like a Mule

BE ye not as the horse, or as the mule, which have no
understanding: whose mouth must be held in with bit
and bridle, lest they come near unto thee. —32:9

Israel had always been stiff-necked, obstinate and
stubborn, like an unruly mule or horse. It is proper
for a mule to act like a mule and a horse to behave
like a horse, but it is highly improper for a man to
conduct himself like either. The ways of a mule are
acceptable for a mule, because he has no understanding. But for a man it is indefensible.

> *God made him, and therefore let*
> *him pass for a man.*
>   *—William Shakespeare*

A mule is controlled by reins. But man's higher
nature requires that his obedience be free and cheerful. It must come from his mind — not bit and bridle.

A mule has no conscience, and there is no appeal to
him with moral and spiritual law or reason. And when
man's conscience becomes completely seared over, then
he loses this faculty of restraint — this human distinction — and takes on the image of a brute. God
never intended this.

God fashioned us to live like men. Our role is exalted and privileged: "a little lower than the angels."
Let us not change it.

God's Word Is Right

For the word of the Lord is right; and all his works
are done in truth. —33:4

This is a glorious tribute to the infallible word of
God. It is right! Of course, it has been accused of
being wrong, but the wrong was in the eyes that beheld it and the ears that heard it and the heart that
considered it — not in the Word itself. "The law is
holy, and the commandment holy, and just, and good"
(Romans 7:12).

God's word is in exact agreement with right. His
nature would not allow Him to give one word that is
wrong. This is good enough reason for accepting the
Word — it came from God.

He gave it not to inform, guide or comfort Himself.
He needs none of these. He gave it to help man, and
the man who sins against it wrongs his own soul
(Proverbs 8:36).

And the person who thinks the Bible is dry on the
inside should at least withhold the criticism until he
gets the dust off the outside.

The Bible has been here too long to become out-
moded. The things that are right and practical are
here to stay, like the Bible and the multiplication
table — they are not in danger of becoming obsolete.
Our fathers needed the Word. We need it. Our posterity shall need it. And feeling this essential want,
we sing —

> *Give me the Bible,*
> *Write on my heart every word.*

Made by the Lord

By the word of the Lord were the heavens made; and all the host of them by the breath of his mouth. He gathereth the waters of the sea together as a heap: he layeth up the depth in storehouses. —33:6, 7

You have seen articles with such stampings on them: "Made by Toys, Inc." "Made by Artificial Flowers Co." But when you look at creation you see the inerasable stamping —

Made by the Lord.

This label is written all over the heavens (19:1). It is stamped everywhere on earth.

Moses ascribed creation to God (Genesis 1, 2).

Paul attributed the universe to Divine power: "...by whom he also made the worlds" (Hebrews 1:2).

Thus *creation by the Creator* is a primary and fundamental teaching of the Bible. This is rational. For there had to be a beginning point sometime and somewhere by a self-existent First Cause.

One evening Napoleon with a group of French officers were on the deck of a ship in the Mediterranean, returning from an expedition to Egypt. In a discussion of God, the officers were unanimous in their atheistic expressions that God does not exist. They then turned to Napoleon who stood alone in deep thought and asked him, "Is there a God?" Raising his hand and pointing to the starry firmament, he simply replied, "Gentlemen, who made all that?"

The Blessed Nation

BLESSED is the nation whose God is the Lord; and the people whom he hath chosen for his own inheritance.
—33:12

The blessed nation is a godly nation; hence religion is indirectly a form of patriotism. Some don't see it this way, but civil lawmakers have thought that religion added stability and greatness to a nation, and for this reason have given it tax-exempt status.

Religion has the leavening influence of diffusing truth, purity and virtue, which strengthen the nation.

The Bible teaches work, sacrifice, thrift and self-restraint, all of which are essential in lifting up a society.

Godliness is the guardian influence which has protected many from criminality. It is the rescuing power which has broken crime's grip on many others.

One thing history is sure of —

RIGHTEOUSNESS exalteth a nation: but sin is a reproach to any people. —Proverbs 14:34

> *A nation never falls but by suicide.*
> *—Ralph Waldo Emerson*

National history is but the history of many individuals. So after all is said and done, we determine the nation's rise or fall. Each day we furnish the material for the history books.

At All Times

I WILL bless the Lord at all times: his praise shall
continually be in my mouth. —34:1

At all times! And they do come. But no circumstance should cause us to withhold our praise to the
Lord. If our extolment of Him continues regardless
of what happens, it proves that the praise is no sur-
face whim but rather a deep-seated conviction of the
heart, a faith that refuses to be shaken.

You should bless Jehovah at all times: When you
are glad and when you are sad. When little ones are
born and when old ones die. When your purse is full
and when it is empty. When fortune smiles and when
it frowns. When victory awards you and when defeat appalls you. When health radiates you and when
illness racks you. When you are applauded and when
you are condemned. When friends stand by and when
they walk away. In youth and in age. In public worship and in private meditation. Praise Him. All you
people. At all times.

I have been in contact with thousands of people in
a multiplicity of circumstances, but I have never seen
the time when I thought praise to God was to be
omitted.

Whatever the time is, it is essential that you keep
your reasoning and your perspective. A closeness with
God will safeguard this.

By all means, praise to Jehovah is for such a time
as this!

Together

O MAGNIFY the Lord with me, and let us exalt his name together. —34:3

The text suggests that believers exalt the Lord's name together. If we are born-again children of the same God, why shouldn't we magnify his name together?

Since believers have a common cause and a mutual goal, it is only natural that they worship and work together. The Scriptures teach it:

NOT forsaking the assembling of ourselves together.
—Hebrews 10:25

WE then as workers together with him . . . .
—II Corinthians 6:1

Togetherness lends strength to each. "Two are better than one" (Ecclesiastes 4:9).

Unity generates warmth for all. "How can one be warm alone" (Ecclesiastes 4:11)? Fellowship among the children of God is like several sticks laid together on a fire, whereby one kindles another. It is easy, however, for the fire in one stick, separated from the others, to go out.

The hermit has fewer provocations to do wrong, but he also has fewer urges to do right.

> *'Tis the Almighty's gracious plan,*
> *That man shall be the joy of man.*
> —*From the Scandinavian*

This Poor Man

THIS poor man cried, and the Lord heard him, and saved him out of all his troubles. —34:6

Wealthy, but poor. There are lots of poor rich people. They have lands that stretch beyond the eyes, stocks that bulge bank boxes, bonds that bind cities and states, oil wells that flow and skyscrapers that mark the concrete jungles — but they are poor. Riches are not always what people think they are; neither is poverty. Being without money can be a problem, but being with money can be a bigger problem.

Powerful, but poor. David was king, but he had enough responsibilities to make him the object of pity — poor king.

There is but one measuring rod to determine whether one is rich — is he rich in joy and hope? The Master Teacher said the rule of measurement is not in earthly possessions: "For a man's life consisteth not in the abundance of the things which he possesseth" (Luke 12:15).

David, suffering persecutions and reverses, was poor because he felt desolate, forsaken and crushed. Any man who thinks he's poor is poor.

Additionally, one is poor, if he: (1) Cannot enjoy what he has. (2) Is not content. (3) Is short on good works. (4) Has no self-respect. (5) Has no real friends. (6) Has lost the zest for living. (7) Has little joy. (8) Has lost his health. (9) Has no Divine comfort. (10) Has no eternal hope.

A Quest for Good Days

WHAT man is he that desireth life, and loveth many days, that he may see good? Keep thy tongue from evil, and thy lips from speaking guile. Depart from evil, and do good; seek peace, and pursue it. —34:12-14

Good days! And David gave in the text a plan to find them, a program which calls for both positive and negative living:

— "Keep thy tongue from evil." This is negative: avoid all falsehood, deceit, slander, gossip and vituperation. Refrain from hasty words. Never speak without knowledge.

— "Depart from evil." Another negative approach: do no wrong; engage in no vice; follow no evil. *Don't* is a necessary word in the field of happiness.

— "Do good." Just refraining from evil is not enough. You must actively and positively do good to others for your life to be blessed with good days.

> *Life is a mirror, if you smile upon it,*
> *it smiles back again on you.*
>
> *—James T. Field*

— "Seek peace and pursue it." Peace is not a passive matter — you have to work for it. Do something yourself to be at peace with your neighbor and the world.

Hundreds of years after David gave this outline for peace, Peter quoted it (I Peter 3:10, 11). It works. Summed up, well spent days are good days.

For No Cause

For without cause have they hid for me their net in a pit, which without cause they have digged for my soul. —35:7

The complaint in the text is one of which David sang repeatedly in Psalms: "Hate me without a cause." "Fought against me without a cause." "Persecuted me without a cause." He had not wronged them. Envy and hate, however, need no cause to harm another. They are cause enough to incite the evil.

The injurer always hates his victim.

Whom they have injured they also hate.
—Seneca

This was what caused some to hate David — not what he had done to them but what they had done to him. Solomon stated the same principle of evil behavior: "A lying tongue hateth those that are afflicted by it" (Proverbs 26:28). The person who lies about you feels compelled to do more lying to make you look like what he says about you — persecution without provocation.

Envious people never like the ones they envy. The begrudging *have-nots* hate the prosperous *haves*. They resent you not for what you are but for what you have — dislike without cause.

There are those who praise the people who are failures and condemn the people who are successes. They are trying to equalize their position by knocking down those above them — injury without cause.

False Witnesses

FALSE witnesses did rise up; they laid to my charge things that I knew not. They rewarded me evil for good to the spoiling of my soul. —35:11, 12

In suffering from fabricated charges David met a fate that is not uncommon to good people.

Be thou as chaste as ice, as pure as snow,
thou shalt not escape calumny.

—William Shakespeare

The calumniators made accusations against David of which he had no knowledge. The lie peddlers went before King Saul and privately accused David of seeking the king's hurt (I Samuel 24:9).

Their lies forced David to become a fugitive and wanderer, which separated him from friends and desolated his soul.

The detractors rewarded David evil for good. Saul admitted this guilt: "Thou hast rewarded me good, whereas I have rewarded thee evil" (I Samuel 24:17). Helping undeserving people is like casting pearls before swine that later turn and rend you.

The false witnesses committed a sin God especially hates (Proverbs 6:19). And why shouldn't He? For it is mean, heartless and devoid of conscience.

"Thou shalt not bear false witness" is such an essential ethic in society that God included it in the Ten Commandments (Exodus 20:16). Centuries have passed, but its need has not lessened.

But As for Me

BUT as for me, when they were sick, my clothing was sackcloth: I humbled my soul with fasting; and my prayer returned into mine own bosom. I behaved myself as though he had been my friend or brother.
—35:13, 14

As seen in the previous essay, the psalmist experienced the sharp darts of lying tongues. Now he contrasts his conduct with theirs. "But as for me," he declares. And this is the only life any person can live — his own.

His kindness was especially shown when it was needed most — in their illness. This is always the time for the good man to come through — when he's needed. When they were sick he showed the deepest distress by donning sackcloth, a customary emblem of mourning. Furthermore he fasted, which was a common custom associated with mourning. Fortunate is the person who has anybody in all the world who cares enough to pray for him.

David behaved toward the traitor as though he had been his friend or brother. This says much. For friends or brothers extend to each other more than ordinary considerations. A stronger bond makes for stronger helpfulness.

Though occasionally our former favors are rewarded with evil, let us take comfort in that a greater reward cannot be denied us — the conscience of doing right.

A good deed has a witness in the heart.

Not Deterred by Mockery

WITH hypocritical mockers in feasts, they gnashed upon me with their teeth. —35:16

Mockers. More than mockers. Hypocritical mockers. The people that David had formerly aided drew around them at the feasts the buffoons and clowns — artists in jest and ribaldry — who made David the butt of their salty ridicule and coarse derision.

> *Mockery is the fume of little hearts.*
> *—Alfred Tennyson*

When reason is against a man he resorts to ridicule. It gives joy to little minds that need no evidence of truth. It was a low, backhanded stroke to turn public opinion against David. They intended to incite the rabble, which is not difficult; for they, without thinking, are ever ready to join in a cry and a march.

What the mockers did was not friendly joking in an atmosphere of goodwill. They gnashed upon him with their teeth, which is a Biblical expression of an angry desire to harm. It exhibits itself as low and cheap.

Lest we be dismayed, may we keep in mind that mockery in the end mocks the sport it feeds on. All of us have work to do and are obligated to do the best we can; so let us not be deterred by the sneers of those who grovel in ridicule.

Self-flattery

For he flattereth himself in his own eyes, until his
iniquity be found to be hateful. —36:2

All of us need to be realistic in assessing self. No
person should underrate himself. It is self-defeating
to assign yourself to a role beneath your ability.
Neither should one think more highly of himself than
the facts permit (Romans 12:3).

The egotist in the text made the grievous blunder
of overrating his judgment of what is right. It set
him on a course of conduct that became hateful and
odious. This is what happens when a man disregards
the standards of God and civilization to follow his
own rules. Yes, it's his life, but it's not his society,
and what he does affects the whole.

The basic error of the man who makes his own
rules is his exalted confidence in himself to map a
course without any assistance from God or anyone
else. Like a little god he sits on a creaky throne he's
not qualified to occupy and wears a shaky crown with
this inscription, "Nobody tells me anything." By sup-
posing whatever he wants to do is right he gives himself the latitude of an outrageous conduct as wide
as any whim he possesses. With this creed his sins
compound and become more obnoxious.

Who venerates himself, the world despises.

Departure From Wisdom and Goodness

THE words of his mouth are iniquity and deceit: he hath left off to be wise, and to do good. He deviseth mischief upon his bed; he setteth himself in a way that is not good; he abhorreth not evil. —36:3, 4

He hath left off to be wise and to do good. This is one of the saddest statements in all the Bible. Here is a man who once followed the way of wisdom and goodness, and then left it off. He can't plead ignorance, for he once knew to do right. Neither can he argue that he can't do better, for he has. He is without excuse.

Perhaps his word was once good — now it is deceitful.

Probably he once prayed in bed — now in bed he meditates on mischief.

There was a time when he abhorred evil — now he abhors nothing.

Banish wisdom, discard honor, and
man sinks lower and lower.

But it doesn't occur suddenly. It's gradual.

The moral is for us to guard against the things which cause us to drift from right. But if we already have drifted, remember it was not due to the wind but to the set of the sails; and now we can reset the sails and be brought back again.

Wings of Protection

How excellent is thy loving-kindness, O God! therefore the children of men put their trust under the shadow of thy wings. —36:7

The psalmist frequently used the impressive metaphor of wings: "Hide me under the shadow of thy wings" (17:8). "Yea, in the shadow of thy wings will I make my refuge" (57:1). "Because thou hast been my help, therefore in the shadow of thy wings will I rejoice" (63:7).

Wings indicate a solicitous concern and a tender summons. The analogy is striking. Just as little birds seek safety under the wings of the mother-bird, poor helpless man finds refuge under the care of his Creator. The only sure place for assistance is under those wings.

Refuge! From the plots of men. From the strife of enemies. From the bitterness of tongues. From the baseness of exploiters. And from the ill advice of friends.

There are so many opposing powers to crush and defeat. Had we not been protected by those invisible wings we would have been trampled many times. Thus humanity continues to cry out —

OH that I had wings like a dove! —55:6

Cheer up, God has some: wings stronger than the wings of a dove; the only wings we dare to trust; the only sure wings of the future. Use them. Use them for protection. Use them for flight.

Don't Envy Evildoers

FRET not thyself because of evildoers, neither be thou envious against the workers of iniquity. —37:1

Envy is discontent and pain at the comparative prosperity or excellence of another. Some people compare themselves with more successful or gifted people and, lo, the feeling begins to build up — especially when we behold the wealth of the wicked. However, there are many reasons why this is sheer folly:

1) "They shall soon be cut down" (ver. 2). The longest success of the wicked is brief in comparison with eternity.

2) They flourish for a while and pass away (vers. 35, 36). No prosperity goes with them.

3) "The wicked shall perish" (ver. 20) — an unenviable fate. We should no more envy them than we do the man in the electric chair.

4) They destroy themselves, fall on their own sword (ver. 15).

5) "A little that a righteous man hath is better than the riches of many wicked" (ver. 16). Ill-gotten money is no cause for envy.

6) If you could, you wouldn't alter nature's law which sends rain on the just and on the unjust (Matthew 5:45), whereby the wicked is allowed to prosper.

7) Envy stirs up evil passions; agitates a sense of inferiority; wastes time; embitters life; and questions the justice of God. It remedies no ill; only aggravates an internal malady, causing one to rot on the inside until it destroys him (Proverbs 14:30).

The Heritage of the Meek

BUT the meek shall inherit the earth; and shall delight themselves in the abundance of peace. —37:11

Jesus used this passage in giving the beatitudes:
"Blessed are the meek: for they shall inherit the
earth" (Matthew 5:5). Others have also taught it.
The smartest and wisest have seen its value.

The meek are humble, gentle and mild, in contrast
with the wicked who are proud, haughty and arrogant.

Contrary to popular opinion, meekness is not weakness. Moses was the meekest man of his day (Numbers 12:3), but he was not weak. He had the courage
to go against Pharoah, and the valor to lead the
children of Israel.

Just common sense tells us which group is more
apt to inherit the earth — the good things it has to
offer, like goodwill, friendship, love and peace. The
meek can occupy the earth in quietness and tranquility,
whereas the proud are caught up in the disturbances
of jealousies, contentions and strifes. The meek "shall
delight themselves in the abundance of peace" — peace
with God, peace with themselves and peace with others.
Their disposition does not excite vengeance nor stir
up wrath, but rather makes for harmony by holding
out the olive branch. Truly —

It's wiser being good than bad;
It's safer being meek than fierce;
It's fitter being sane than mad.

—*Robert Browning*

Pay Your Debts

THE wicked borroweth, and payeth not again: but the righteous showeth mercy, and giveth. —37:21

The text suggests the established view of economics that the righteous, following a way of life which makes for prosperity, are more apt to be in a position to lend and to give.

Some borrow with no intention of repaying — and this is wicked. Others borrow with no prospect of repaying — and this is also wicked, for willingness alone settles nothing. Others borrow with the idea they are honest, and that if the time should ever come when they have more than they need and do not have to sacrifice or put themselves out any, they will repay — and this, too, is wicked. So here are some *don'ts* in borrowing:

— Don't be reckless about borrowing.

— Don't be careless about paying.

— Don't hold yourself flawless if the debt pinches.

— Don't think that words pay debts.

— Don't let your creditor have a better memory than you.

— Don't let it be habit forming.

— Don't think that if you owe Jones a hundred dollars and God forgives you that it pays Jones.

Remember — it is better to live in less comfort than to live in more debt than you can pay.

Taught by the Years

I HAVE been young, and now am old; yet have I not
seen the righteous forsaken, nor his seed begging
bread. —37:25

I have been young, and now am old. This is a
solemn place in life. The journey on earth is almost
ended. Here is an old man who through the years
has seen the plan of God bless man. Experience has
taught him much. In fact, he had to live a long time
just to learn how to live — to live in more trust,
peace and expectation. This is one of the good things
about age — experience. The years teach what you
could never master in youth from books.

He knows best who has experienced it.

Now what was the specific lesson the psalmist had
learned from the passing years? That religion is an
advantage to man; that God's wings of protection are
not withdrawn from His children; that even in material matters the people of God are more consistently
blessed than aliens; and that he had not seen the
children of the godly begging bread.

It is an economic fact that the religion of God blesses
materially as well as spiritually. It teaches industry,
prudence and thrift, and promises the care of God
for His own. Begging is usually the result of a course
contrary to the Scriptures. It is ordinarily brought on
by extreme misconduct. Religion teaches man to depend on God and himself, while beggary teaches him
to depend on the handouts of others.

An Example in Sickness

THERE is no soundness in my flesh . . . . —38:3

The thirty-eighth Psalm gives the account of a very sick and threatened man. This good man's conduct in time of severe illness and torturing pain should be a welcome example to God's children who face similar suffering. When the body is wracked by pain and friends forsake and enemies threaten, this Psalm is exceedingly relevant and especially helpful.

Note the condition of the sufferer: His flesh was without soundness, no vigor, no strength (ver. 3). His wounds stank and made him repulsive (ver. 5)— maybe boils, maybe bed-sores. There was a burning inflamation in his loins, which was loathsome (ver. 7). Feebleness gripped him, and his condition produced "roarings" or groanings (ver. 8). He experienced palpitation as strength waned (ver. 10). And his sight was failing (ver. 10).

His condition was aggravated by friends and kinsmen who turned away from him (ver. 11), and by enemies who took advantage of his sickness to bring false charges against him (ver. 12).

His sickness sharpened his memory and caused him to suppose that it was the result of his sin and foolishness, an effect not uncommon among sufferers.

Yet the writer never despaired of faith. He freely confessed his sins and asked God for help.

In time of sickness the soul collects itself anew.
—Latin Proverb

Hold That Tongue

I SAID, I will take heed to my ways that I sin not with
my tongue: I will keep my mouth with a bridle, while
the wicked is before me. —39:1

I will. This was a resolution on the poet's part.
A necessary one. For we improve ourselves only
through concerted effort. He resolved not to sin with
his tongue. This was truly a mouthful — a mouth he
would keep full rather than unload on others.

> *The tongue offends and the ears get the cuffing.*
> —*Anonymous*

This is the biggest job any person ever had. But
don't blame the tongue, blame the heart that controls
it (Matthew 12:34).

However, he expected to keep the resolution through
two efforts: First, he would take heed to his ways.
Second, he would bridle his tongue. He was determined to say nothing, lest he say something that might
harm the cause of religion (ver. 2). This was a big
order to give himself.

Does this mean it is as bad to think a thing as it
is to say it? No! It is worse to give expression to
the sentiment. A wise man holds in his words for
the proper time (Proverbs 29:11).

David's resolution to hold his tongue was a noble
intent, and one that has our sympathy today.

A Burning Heart That Had to Speak

My heart was hot within me; while I was musing the
fire burned: then spake I with my tongue. —39:3

Though the psalmist had resolved to remain totally
silent in his affliction, refusing even to speak good,
he found it an impossible restriction. The silence was
like a fire that burned within him. When the fire
became too hot he had to speak. But not to man who
wouldn't understand or who might misrepresent him.
He spoke to God who is intellectually wise and merci-
fully kind.

And this is what he said: 1. He requested a deeper
insight to the measure of his days and frailty (ver.
4), which is a natural reaction in illness. 2. Said that
"every man at his best state is vanity" (ver. 5).
3. Mentioned that riches are heaped up for someone
else to gather (ver. 6). 4. Declared that he expected
relief from God alone (ver. 7). 5. Requested deliverance from his transgressions and that he be spared
the reproach of the foolish (ver. 8). 6. Stated that
he made no complaints because God did it (ver. 9).
7. Believing that his suffering was God's disciplinary
action, asked that the hand of discipline be removed
from him (vers. 10, 11). 8. Implored God to hear his
prayer (ver. 12). 9. Besought God to spare him that
he might recover his strength (ver. 13).

When you can open your mouth this way and to this
One, it is good to speak. David broke his silence, but
not his resolution — "that I sin not with my tongue."

Lessons From Man's Frailty

LORD, make me to know mine end and the measure of
my days, what it is; that I may know how frail I am.
—39:4

The thirty-ninth Psalm is often read at funerals.
It offers some timely and needful lessons on:

— The frailty of man. "Thou hast made my days
as a handbreadth; and my age is as nothing before
thee" (ver. 5). In measurement of time, life is just
a *breath* — and often a gasping one. But it is hard
for us to learn this lesson. While we know others
are passing, we think we are here to stay. But to
stay — we can't; for we are only walking shadows.

Out, out, brief candle,
Life's but a walking shadow, a poor player
That struts and frets his long hour upon the stage,
And then is heard no more.
—William Shakespeare

— The vanity of man. "Verily every man at his best
state is altogether vanity" (ver. 5). Life is burdened
with allusive attainments, useless trifles and worthless wonders. Our days are crowded with the hustle
and bustle of cares that don't care for us, that have
no real meaning and no lasting purpose. Edmund
Burke, the eloquent statesman, gave this memorable
comment on the passage: "What shadows we are,
and what shadows we pursue."

— The separation of man from all earthly treasures.
"He heapeth up riches and knoweth not who shall
gather them" (ver. 6). This gives much to ponder.

More Lessons From Man's Frailty

BEFORE I go hence. —39:13

From what is called a funeral Psalm, we continue:

— The hope of man. "My hope is in thee" (ver. 7). Not in self for man is too powerless. Not in riches for they can do only so much and go only so far. Not in friends for they often turn fickle. But cheer up. God is alive! In Him there is hope. In Him we rise in this material sphere until we break the mortal barrier and then it's — immortality.

— The deliverance of man. "Deliver me from all my transgressions" (ver. 8). From sin. From its slavery. From the discontent it produces within us. From the reproaches it brings on us. From the forebodings it hangs over us. And from the guilt it presses on our brow.

— The sojourn of man. "I am a stranger with thee, and a sojourner" (ver. 12). Every critical illness is a reminder that we are strangers and sojourners swiftly moving to our permanent home. And every bereavement reemphasizes the thought.

— The plea of man. "O spare me that I may recover strength, before I go hence, and be no more" (ver. 13). He asked to be spared for a better time to go. This is a common plea — "spare me." But why? To correct errors? To retrieve follies? To do more for God? Maybe you have already been spared. If so, use the spare time in the noblest manner.

A New Song

AND he hath put a new song in my mouth, even praise
unto our God. —40:3

The sweet singer of Israel was given a new song,
one that came forth freely and naturally from an internal compulsion that felt the need to express itself.

It was a song of deliverance. "Out of a horrible
pit." "Out of the miry clay" (ver. 2). Deeper and
deeper he had sunk in the pit of misery and the mire
of sin until he reached the frightful state of "innumerable evils . . . more than the hairs of mine
head" (ver. 12). But up from the pit he came, out
of the mire he ascended, with an appreciation of his
deliverance that inspired him to sing.

He sang of personal progress (vers. 2, 3). He had
been "in the pit," then on his knees and then "on the
rock." When weighed down by sin, he was lifted up
by prayer and firmly established on the Rock of Ages.

It was a song of praise (vers. 3, 5). Recognizing the
worthiness of God, David burst forth in a new song.

He sang of obedience (vers. 6-8). This passage
was later applied by an apostle to the Messiah (Hebrews 10:5-7), so David was speaking as a type of
Christ. The compliance is cheerful and from the heart,
which are essential requisites of true obedience.

If our training here on earth gives rise to a new
song, it is only a little foretaste of the song of Moses
and the Lamb we shall sing in the sweet bye and
bye (Revelation 15:3).

Acceptable Obedience

I DELIGHT to do thy will, O my God: yea, thy law is within my heart. —40:8

True obedience is not ritualistically giving gifts and offering sacrifices: "Sacrifice and offering thou didst not desire" (ver. 6). Yet God commanded sacrifices. But apart from a spirit of free and loving obedience, they are not desired at all.

Obedience begins with open ears: "Mine ears hast thou opened" (ver. 6). A characteristic description of the disobedient is: they "stopped their ears" (Acts 7:57). But the obedient listen.

Cheerful submission is demanded: "I delight to do thy will" (ver. 8). What one delights in is determined by what he believes and how he feels. Obeying the letter without the spirit does not meet the Divine requirements.

And lastly, acceptable obedience must be from the heart: "within my heart" (ver. 8). Hundreds of years after the Psalm was written an inspired apostle applied this portion of it to the Messiah (Hebrews 10:6-9). The Messiah's spirit was that of unreserved compliance: "not my will, but thine, be done." As He said, if the heart is not in the compliance, its only reward is the applause of men (Matthew 6:2). But when the heart is in our profession, we don't pick out the commands we would like to obey, rejecting all others. None is slavish! All are delightful!

Making Your Bed Soft

THE Lord will strengthen him upon the bed of languishing: thou wilt make all his bed in his sickness. —41:3

Whichever way you make your bed you have to lie on it. But with God's help it can be made soft. *Thou wilt make all his bed in his sickness:* literally, thou will turn it, turn its cushions and make it comfortable. God does it, but conditionally. The condition is that one considers the poor, regards and assists those in poverty, sickness, humiliation, defeat and all others in any other affliction (ver. 1).

We cannot do good without being made better by it. Every act of pity raises us in self-respect and power. Furthermore, there is the blessing which comes from the needy, many of whom will never forget us. Their confidence, gratitude and prayers might prove to be the figurative bed upon which we may someday lie. Besides this, we do have the promise of God to soften our bed.

HE that hath pity upon the poor lendeth unto the Lord; and that which he hath given will he pay him again.
—Proverbs 19:17

The great basis of religion is compassion. And God is asking us: "Shouldest not thou also have had compassion on thy fellow servant, even as I had pity on thee" (Matthew 18:33)?

I Have Sinned

I SAID, Lord, be merciful unto me: heal my soul; for I have sinned against thee. —41:4

David's confession of sin has been the admission of many. Some were sincere, others pretentious.

Pharoah said, "I have sinned this time" (Exodus 9:27). But he didn't mean it. Under the temporary shock of a plague, he confessed his guilt; but when the plague was removed, he returned to his true self.

Balaam confessed, "I have sinned" (Numbers 22: 34), and subsequently changed his course.

Achan admitted, "Indeed I have sinned" (Joshua 7:20). He took forbidden spoils when Jericho fell. When confronted by Joshua, he owned up to it.

Saul acknowledged, "I have sinned" (I Samuel 15: 24). He confessed when Samuel rebuked him for not destroying the Amalekites.

Job confessed, "I have sinned" (Job 7:20) — the humble admission of a bankrupt, afflicted man who was deeply religious.

Judas stated, "I have sinned" (Matthew 27:4). Unable to live with his sin, he committed suicide.

The Prodigal Son confessed, "I have sinned against heaven, and in thy sight" (Luke 15:21). He saw his mistake and penitently corrected it, returning home to his father.

May we be sincere in confessing our shortcomings — to ourselves and to others. It is essential to the reformation of life and the restoration of the soul.

The Betrayal

YEA, mine own familiar friend, in whom I trusted, which did eat of my bread, hath lifted up his heel against me. —41:9

This quotation from the Psalm had a fulfillment in the betrayal of Christ by Judas. Jesus said that it did:

I SPEAK not of you all: I know whom I have chosen: but that the Scripture may be fulfilled, He that eateth bread with me hath lifted up his heel against me.
—John 13:18

However, there are scholars who feel that the passage had a double meaning: First, that it referred to Ahithophel, an official counsellor of David who defected from David and joined the conspiracy led by Absalom (I Samuel 15:12, 31; 16:15-17:1). Second, that it had a fuller and truer application in the treachery of Judas. It is contended that "David was in much of his life a type of Christ, so the treachery of his trusted counsellor would be a foreshadowing of the treachery of Judas."

After the betrayal, despair possessed Judas and he chose to die at the end of a rope rather than to live with his guilt. So he hanged himself. He didn't sell Christ, he sold himself. Now Jesus lives in glory, Judas in infamy.

With a kiss of treason, Judas made a mockery of loyalty and rent the apostleship with the unkindest cut of all. To think upon it, stirs our blood and renews our determination to make ourselves of sterner stuff.

So Panteth My Soul

As the hart panteth after the water brooks, so panteth my soul after thee, O God. — 42:1

The poetic singer begins this Psalm with an analogy: As the deer pants after the water in the brook, so pants his soul, he declares, after God. The panting of the deer is indicative of its thirst for water, and the panting of the soul is expressive of its thirst for God. The soul craves its Creator.

> *The thirst that from the soul doth rise*
> *Doth ask a drink divine.*
>
> *—Ben Johnson*

David uses similar language in chapter 63:1: "My soul thirsteth for thee in a dry and thirsty land, where no water is." Often we feel that our little world is struck with drought and there is nothing on earth to quench our thirst. True! But beyond the earth of materials there is a Slaking Power, a Living Fountain, God! And every soul that drinks of Him is satisfied. He is the source of life.

Isn't it strange that humanity is dying of thirst when man has free access to the Ever-flowing Fountain?

Thank God for the intense yearning. It is inborn in our nature. Now let us quench the profound longing by drinking! Today! And forever!

A Diet of Tears

MY soul thirsteth for God, for the living God: when shall I come and appear before God? My tears have been my meat . . . . —42:2, 3

Tears are a meat that feed the soul in various circumstances. In sorrow. In ecstasy. In pain. In fear. In helplessness. They can ease a hunger that bread never satisfies.

All tears are not the same in every person's eyes. With David — they were related to his absence from worship services and to the taunting he took from vilifiers who asked, "Where is thy God?" As the deer pants for water, his soul panted for God. But his adverse circumstances made it impossible for him to attend the house of God. As he looked back on former days when he freely went with the multitude to public worship (ver. 4), the privation of the privilege pierced his heart and the tears flowed. They were the tears of a spiritual desire. He hungered to be in the house of God; and when he couldn't go, his soul was fed by his tears.

A little rain blesses man, and so do tears.

> *Would we know the meaning of happiness,*
> *Would we feel that the day was bright,*
> *If we'd never known what it was to grieve,*
> *Nor gazed on the dark of night?*

Here is a man who had the heart to go to worship, but not the opportunity. How different from many today who have the opportunity, but not the heart.

Overcoming Despair

WHY art thou cast down, O my soul? and why art thou disquieted in me? —42:5

At times all of us have our disquieting moments in which we lose heart and feel that fate has cast us into a losing role. From John Dryden's extreme melancholy we have this dismal view:

> *When I consider life, 'tis all a cheat;*
> *Yet, fool'd with hope, men favor the deceit;*
> *Trust on, and think tomorrow will repay.*
> *Tomorrow's falser than the former day;*
> *Lies worse, and while it says we shall be blest*
> *With some new joys, cuts off what we possest.*

Even a strong man like David felt the pain of despair. So what he did to cure it is most helpful to us. In the remedy we find such words as *God, hope, praise, remember* (vers. 5-9). He knew that God was the rock on which he could stand and be safe. His hope was in Him, that he "will command his loving-kindness in the daytime, and in the night his song shall be with me." Praising God changed his thought process from earthly woes to heavenly wonders. A remembrance of what his Lord had done at various places lifted his soul. For what God had done, God would do.

To be practical, when you feel depression coming on, seize these words: *God, hope, praise, remember.* As you dwell on them, it will fill your heart with optimism.

Plea for Deliverance

O SEND out thy light and thy truth: let them lead me; let them bring me unto thy holy hill, and to thy tabernacles. —43:3

It appears that the forty-third Psalm is a supplementary stanza to the forty-second. They bear strong resemblances in content and structure.

The author appeals to God to plead his "cause against an ungodly nation," and to deliver him "from the deceitful and unjust man" (ver. 1) — perhaps Absalom.

In recognition of the source of unfailing help, he prayed to God: "Send out thy light and thy truth: let them lead me." The word *light* here means favor. For instance, "the light of thy countenance" (4:6) means the favor of God's countenance. *Truth,* as used in the passage, refers to God's truthfulness. Exiled and cast into the darkness of trouble, he invoked God's grace and faithfulness to lead him back to his former privileges. As an exile banished from the holy hill and the tabernacles, his heart cried out to be led back to Jerusalem and to the altar of God, and there, he said, "will I praise thee, O God, my God."

> *O worship the King, all glorious above,*
> *And gratefully sing His wonderful love;*
> *Our Shield and Defender, the Ancient of Days,*
> *Pavilioned in splendor and girded with praise.*
>
> —*Robert Grant*

Our Fathers Have Told Us

WE have heard with our ears, O God, our fathers have told us, what work thou didst in their days, in the times of old. —44:1

Ancestors are mentioned, forefathers of whom the author was justly proud. He spoke of them with appreciation and respect.

The fathers from generation to generation had told their children of God: God's mercy, God's power, God's deliverance, how that He had driven out the heathen or the idolaters and given Israel the land of Canaan. The children were taught that their forefathers did not get the land "by their own sword," nor that they were saved by their own arm, but that the possession came through the favor of God (ver. 3).

This chapter of national history, one of interest and glamour, was told and retold through gratitude and commandment. The Law required the fathers to teach their children the history of the nation, and especially what God had done for them: "that thou mayest tell in the ears of thy son, and of thy son's son, what things I have wrought in Egypt . . ." (Exodus 10:2). The command recognizes the molding power of teaching. As the child is influenced, so lives the adult.

He who teaches a child —

> *Sees a world in a grain of sand*
> *And a heaven in a wild flower,*
> *Holds infinity in the palm of his hand*
> *And eternity in an hour.*
>
> *—Adapted, William Blake*

Yet They Did Not Forget

ALL this is come upon us; yet have we not forgotten
thee, neither have we dealt falsely in thy covenant.
—44:17

Many reverses came upon them. They were:

— Defeated (ver. 10).
— Plundered (ver. 10).
— Scattered (ver. 11).
— Reproached (ver. 13).
— Derided (vers. 13, 14).
— Martyred (ver. 22).

Yet they did not forget God. With a strong assertion they sang, "Our heart is not turned back, neither have our steps declined from thy way" (ver. 18). Pressured by the biddings of idolatry and afflicted by dreadful tortures for refusing to comply, yet they generally remained true to their religion. We can learn much from this. For God uses the past to teach the present. We should learn that apostasy does not come so often from privation and persecution as it does from affluence and popularity. Faithfulness is not dependent on wealth, popularity or affiliation with a prestigious group, but rather on faith and hope, which are begotten and strengthened by teaching.

By persevering you obtain the promised crown (Revelation 2:10). God help you to overcome.

> *It matters not how the battle goes,*
> *The day how long;*
> *Faint not! Fight on!*
> *Tomorrow comes the song.*

God Knows Our Secrets

SHALL not God search this out? for he knoweth the secrets of the heart. —44:21

In the context the sacred writer made the point that if there had been any alienation from God in the hearts of the people, God would have known it. This is repeatedly affirmed in the Scriptures (I Chronicles 28:9; Revelation 2:23).

The heart of each has its wall of concealment and veil of privacy. Every heart has its own secrets. And this is good. It would be bad, terribly bad! if every person could look into the heart of every other person and behold the privileged facts. Curious, intolerant and gossipy people would misuse the information.

But there is one who searches the heart and knows its secrets — God. No thought lies buried too deep in the heart of man for Him to see, nor flashes through too fast for Him to behold. But it is classified information, belonging only to Him and the person.

He searches the heart for the *intent* and sees the extenuating circumstances, which often put the deed in a more tolerable perspective, though cold and self-righteous critics come running with hammer and nails to crucify the person on what they call a cross of justice.

What goes on in the heart is often a mystery to the person himself, but God understands its workings better than man. I am glad He sees inside us! I am glad others don't!

A Bubbly Heart

MY heart is inditing [overfloweth with] a good matter:
I speak of the things which I have made touching the
King. —45:1

My heart is inditing a good matter: literally, it
means *bubbles with a good matter*. His heart was
bubbling over with things pertaining to the King of
Kings.

The world is drawn to the person with the bubbly
heart. That interesting exciting one gives you a sense
of being in the presence of life which lifts your soul.

When the heart starts bubbling, something is going
to happen: praise, propagation, outreach and achievement. Enthusiasm puts the sparkle in living, provides the drive for accomplishment. Without zealous
hearts no battles have been won, no wilderness con-
quered, no frontiers extended and no religion prop-
agated. The men and women with bubbly hearts have
kept the fires of progress burning when others would
have allowed the flames to fade into the cold gray
ashes of despair.

Every great achievement is the story
of a flaming heart.
—*A. B. Zu Tavern*

Hence one of the greatest needs in the modern
church is enthusiasm. The religion of God is not cold,
dull, lifeless. As an example: The minister brought
out a great truth and a visitor said, "Praise the Lord."
Immediately an usher touched his arm and whispered,
"You can't praise the Lord in this church." Why?
It might disturb the corpses sitting in the pews.

A Ready Writer

MY tongue is the pen of a ready writer. —45:1

The psalmist's heart was full of his subject — bubbling over — and he desired to express his thoughts in the warm overflowing emotion of a ready writer. Because he wrote, the world has this lovely and romantic Psalm.

God places extraordinary value on writing. He said: "I will write upon these tables" (Exodus 34:1). "Write thee all the words that I have spoken unto thee in a book" (Jeremiah 30:1). "But these are written that ye might believe" (John 20:31). The Bible itself is irrefutable proof that God greatly favors writing — and consequently reading.

> *Books give men great dreams to dream,*
> *Sun-lit ways that glint and gleam,*
> *Where the sages*
> *Tramp the ages.*
> *—William L. Stridger*

Many noble causes have died for the lack of a writer. *The pen is mightier than the sword.* Our society is maintained by a war of ideas.

For our own self-preservation we must not allow a nation of readers to become solely a nation of watchers. The trend is already having adverse effects. Surely the church should take the lead in promoting the writing and reading of uplifting pages. If the church would encourage its members to read something worthwhile everyday, the leavening results would exceed our fondest dreams.

The Bride and the Groom

UPON thy right hand did stand the queen in gold of Ophir. —45:9

Certainly I prefer Paul's interpretation of the forty-fifth Psalm. The application he made in quoting from it placed the Messianic stamp on it (Hebrews 1:8,9). In two main divisions it prophetically portrays Christ and His church in the figure of a marriage.

First, an address to the bridegroom: A man fairer than the sons of men (ver. 2); blessed with gracious speech (ver. 2); dressed as a warrior, for He has enemies (ver. 3); goes forth in majesty (ver. 4); wields His right hand with power (ver. 4); has the power to chastise enemies (ver. 5); His throne is forever (ver. 6); loves righteousness and hates wickedness (ver. 7); and anointed with gladness above His fellows (vers. 8,9).

Second, an address to the bride, the church: Bidden to hearken (ver. 10); to break with relationships that interfere (ver. 10); to worship the Lord (ver. 11); shall attract heathen nations (ver. 12); is glorious within (ver. 13); a virgin train shall follow the bride —probably symbolizes the Gentiles' following the Hebrews into the church (vers. 14,15); her fame shall not come from predecessors but from her own sons (ver. 16); and her name shall be remembered in all generations (ver. 17).

We need both. If we appreciate the groom (the Lord), we should appreciate the bride (His church).

River of God

THERE is a river, the streams whereof shall make glad the city of God, the holy place of the tabernacles of the Most High. —46:4

While the ocean fiercely raged and madly dashed against the mountains, seeking to undercut them (vers. 2, 3), the city of God, Jerusalem, was pictured with a peaceful and restful river spreading its beauty and fruitfulness throughout its course. This beautiful image was designed to portray a calm security in contrast with a chaotic world. Figuratively, the flowing river of Divine blessedness cools and calms hearts that otherwise would become fretful and feverish.

This unfailing assurance is especially needed today to soothe the sore, tattered nerves of a generation that has relied too much on earth-made tranquilizers and too little on heaven-made tranquility.

God's word provides a pure river with a thousand refreshing springs that can flow through your heart, diffusing the cool, self-composed effects. For such a blessing, run verses like these through your mind and trust them:

WHAT man is he that feareth the Lord? . . . His soul shall dwell at ease. —vers. 12, 13

COMMIT thy way unto the Lord; trust also in him; and he shall bring it to pass. —36:5

REST in the Lord, and wait patiently for him: fret not thyself. —36:7

The God Who Stills Us

BE still and know that I am God. —46:10

The forty-sixth Psalm was composed at a time when Israel was in great peril. Just what it was, we are not certain, but we are certain it is one of the most beautiful and reassuring of all the Psalms. It was the favorite of Martin Luther who often hymned it when troubles threatened. Its contents will lift our sinking spirits:

— "God is our refuge" (ver. 1).

> *Should storms of sevenfold thunder roll,*
> *And shake the globe from pole to pole,*
> *No flaming bolt shall daunt my face,*
> *For my God is my hiding place.*

— "Therefore will not we fear" (ver. 2). With God as our refuge nothing should scare us.

— "God shall help" (ver. 5). Though troubled waters rise and mountains tumble, there is the life-sustaining river of God that flows into the heart of man.

— "The Lord of hosts is with us" (ver. 7). Though the heathen rage and kingdoms fall, there is one immovable power that remains with us — the Lord.

— "He maketh wars to cease" (ver. 9). God's righteousness expels from the hearts of men the very things that produce war. For wars are first inward.

It is exceedingly wise that we stop and have a little time for stillness everyday. For it is possible to be still and make progress.

Clap Your Hands

CLAP your hands, all ye people; shout unto God with the voice of triumph. —47:1

This Psalm is a triumphal one, probably composed to celebrate some victory.

We are constantly engaged in conflicts, some we win, some we lose. When we win, it's time to clap hands and sing. Clapping the hands is no cold gesture, but rather the spontaneous coming together of the heart's ready servants — the hands. And singing is no senseless emotion, but the echo of the heart.

In an adaptation of the Psalm, let us also clap our hands and sing, for the reasons are the same:

The same God who was called *terrible* has not changed (ver. 2). The avenger of all wrongs!

God still has the prerogative to choose His people's inheritance (ver. 4). If Israel would praise Him for giving them an earthly land of death and sorrow, how much more we should praise Him for offering us the deathless land of endless joy.

God continues to reign over the heathen (ver. 8). They are not regarded as write-offs but as subjects, though they are disobedient. In time many may accept His grace.

He still sits "upon the throne of his holiness" (ver. 8). His government is not oppressive. He has no unjust demands. Every regulation is for the good of man.

You have cause to clap your hands and sing.

We Have Seen

As we have heard, so have we seen in the city of the Lord of hosts, in the city of our God: God will establish it for ever. —48:8

They had heard of God's deliverance of Jerusalem. Now they had seen it with their own eyes. They had listened with pride to the stories of how God had put the heathen to flight for Israel's sake. Now it has been confirmed in their own sight.

This assurance lifts the soul heavenward, bends the knees to pray, tunes the lips to sing and strengthens the heart to continue. This we know, He cares for us. So, in all trials and sorrows, let us to His bosom fly.

We, too, can say, "As we have heard, so have we seen." We were told that God answers prayer; now we know it: our prayers have been answered. We heard of the providence of God; moreover we have seen it actually work. We heard that the right way to treat enemies is to return good for evil; after trying it, we know it is best. We heard that God would provide for His children; the years have passed and now we say with David, "I have seen" (37:25).

What "we have heard" (indirect) and what "we have seen" (first hand) unite with telling effects to give us the skyward look.

Keep looking up —
The waves that roar around thy feet,
Jehovah-Jireh will defeat
When looking up.

Mark Well Her Bulwarks

MARK ye well her bulwarks, consider her palaces; that ye may tell it to the generation following. —48:13

The admonition was to pay close attention to the fortifications and breastworks protecting Jerusalem. Behold its safety.

That ye may tell it to the generation following. The object is to give the next generation a correct account that they may be inspired to believe the city cannot be vanquished, that within the city there is safety.

In a present-day application let us mark the ramparts of the New Jerusalem, the church, that we may see the defenses that make it strong and defensible:

Founded by the Divine Founder (Matthew 16:18); established on the solid rock that Christ is the Son of God (Ephesians 2:20) ; headed by the perfect head —Christ (Ephesians 1:22, 23); guided by all Scripture as its creed (II Timothy 3:16,17); peopled by the saved (Acts 2:47); everlasting — hades shall not prevail against it (Matthew 16:18).

The church is distinguished with Divine defenses which make it safe: impregnable bulwarks, everlasting fortifications. Its only human aspect is its membership (human beings, but saved ones); and this also is to the glory of God: a divine church for people, just as Jerusalem was the city of God for people.

Mark well the bulwarks of the church. Tell it to the generation that follows.

Choosing a Guide

For this God is our God for ever and ever: he will be our guide even unto death. —48:14

This resolve is worthy of emulation. It was definite. It was final — "unto death." Happiness requires some basic, once-for-all-time decisions that man be spared the worry and fret of wondering what to do. They made the most basic one of all — to follow God. A smart choice! For going to heaven requires you to follow the Guide that leads there.

They didn't know where the Guide would lead them, but they knew the Guide. So on they went. Such confidence was needed for the completion of the journey. Wagon trains that once rolled across the West moved only because those who followed put trust in their guide.

When all is considered, the lifetime resolution of Israel should be the natural and easy one for all of us.

> *When confronted with two courses of action, I jot down on a piece of paper all the arguments in favor of one — then on the opposite side I write the arguments against each one. Then by weighing the arguments pro and con and cancelling them out, one against the other, I take the course by what remains.*
>
> —*Benjamin Franklin*

If you, in selecting a guide to the promised land, will do as Franklin suggested, there is no question about the choice. And then when the journey has ended, how comforting it will be to have picked the Guide who knew the way.

Their Wealth Is Their Folly

THIS their way is their folly; yet their posterity approve their sayings. —49:13

The author presented some irrefutable arguments which show the folly of trusting in wealth and boasting in riches (ver. 6):

First, riches won't buy the redemption of a soul (vers. 7-9). Salvation cannot be bought in the market.

Second, the rich "perish, and leave their wealth to others" (ver. 10). It's only a temporary possession.

Third, their deception "is, that their houses shall continue forever," and that their lands are in their names — theirs (ver. 11). But they are only tenants.

Fourth, man abides not (ver. 12). Both the rich and the poor have appointments with death.

Fifth, and "when he dieth he shall carry nothing away" (ver. 17). Nothing! Absolutely nothing!

But to be factual and practical, let us remember: While money cannot buy redemption, it can aid the church; cannot fully support a family, yet it can feed, clothe and house them; cannot give an education, but can pay college tuition; cannot purchase health, but can pay the hospital bills; and cannot give life in the next world, but can pay the cost of leaving this one. Beyond this, wealth is not needed; and to chase it needlessly is labeled *folly*. For to be wealthy, unhealthy, unhappy, unsaved and dead is unwise.

The use of money is all the advantage
there is in having it.
> —*Benjamin Franklin*

Double Praise for a Single Error

THOUGH while he lived he blessed his soul, (and men
will praise thee, when thou doest well to thyself.)
—49:18

The rich man in the text praised himself. So did
others. All because he became rich. Double praise
for a single error. The fault, however, was not in
amassing riches but in overestimating their value.

The wealthy man "blessed his soul," blessed himself, praised himself. He regarded his affluence as
an accomplishment to be admired and envied. He
thought his standing on a pile of gold made him taller
than others, and that they should look up to him.
Of course, the accumulation of wealth does require
thought, sagacity, hard work, sacrifice, thrift and wise
investments. It doesn't come easily; if so, everybody
would be rich. But to make it the chief aim in life and
an end within itself is not praiseworthy. To allow the
big purse to give one the big head shrinks stature.

Wealth turns the heads of a lot of people — especially the ones who don't have it to the ones who do.
The *have-nots* applaud the *haves.* It is a sad commentary on our society that other accomplishments
more important go unnoticed. But our society uses
a ruler of gold to measure a man's success. Many a
person is blinded by the luster of that gold ruler
until finally it becomes cankered, and then he sees
that he misread it.

FOR when he dieth he shall carry nothing away.
—ver. 17

The Gift Without the Giver

I WILL not reprove thee for thy sacrifices or thy burnt offerings, to have been continually before me. —50:8

"The gift without the giver is bare," wrote James Russel Lowell. He also stated:

> *He gives only the worthless gold*
> *Who gives from a sense of duty.*

This was a common fault of many worshipers. For the Israelites to think the ritual of giving, irrespective of the spirit, met Divine approval was most appalling, and the Lord rebuked them for it: not for neglecting ceremonial sacrifices for they hadn't (as seen in the text), but because their spirit was wrong.

The Lord would not accept any sacrifice offered amiss (ver. 9). For "every beast of the forest . . . and the cattle upon a thousand hills . . . the fowls of the mountains, and the wild beasts of the field" were already His (vers. 10, 11). He needed nothing. He even asked if they thought He needed material nurture (ver. 13).

Next, the Psalm gives the basic instruction for acceptable worship: "offer unto God thanksgiving" (ver. 14). Material gifts could be given from the hands out, but thanksgiving and praise (which are to accompany giving) could come only from the heart.

In this materialistic age when the size of a gift is emphasized more than the spirit, we need to reread the Scriptures which teach that the giver should give *himself,* give *willingly,* not *grudgingly,* or of *necessity* (II Corinthians 8:6, 12; 9:7).

Teacher Teach Thyself

> BUT unto the wicked God saith, What hast thou to
> do to declare my statutes, or that thou shouldest take
> my covenant in thy mouth? —50:16

The fiftieth Psalm is one of the most instructive in
setting forth the necessity of a spiritual religion in
contrast with the mere observance of religious forms.

In the first portion of the chapter the more moral,
ritualistic worshipers are reproved; now in the second
division the more shameless transgressors are rebuked.
They claimed the privileges of the Divine covenant,
but ignored its duties (vers. 16-20). However, they
did not have the privilege to declare the statutes to
others until those ordinances meant something to
them, no right to open their mouth to men until they
first opened their heart to God (ver. 16).

While performing religious ceremonies with scrupu-
lous regularity, they committed the basest crimes:
They hated instruction which disqualified them as
instructors (ver. 17), for the best teacher is willing
to be taught. They cast their lot with thieves and
became partakers with adulterers (ver. 18). Their
tongues were used to propagate deception and de-
traction (ver. 19). They slandered their brothers
(ver. 20).

Centuries later Paul put the inconsistency in focus
by asking:

> THOU therefore which teachest another, teachest thou
> not thyself? thou that preachest a man should not
> steal, dost thou steal? —Romans 2:21, 22

The ever relevant lesson is: *Teacher, teach thyself.*

Thinking That God Is Like Man

THESE things hast thou done, and I kept silence; thou
thoughtest that I was altogether such a one as thyself: but I will reprove thee, and set them in order
before thine eyes. —50:21

Since the people in the text did not regard sincerity,
justice, purity and morality as essential, they supposed
God felt this way, too, and that He would be satisfied with the mere rites of religion. It met their
approval; so they thought it met His.

Thinking that God is like man is one of the most
common errors, and one of the greatest menaces to
religion. Men and women make their images of God
— not metal but mental — to conform to their own
views. They make God in the likeness of themselves,
corresponding to their likes and dislikes, beliefs and
disbeliefs, with all their prejudices, limitations, weaknesses and follies.

Men can hide from men; therefore they suppose
they can hide from God. Humans can be bribed; hence
they imagine God also can be bought. Since men
feel that they do not have to obey the laws of God,
they think He feels the same way. The masses are
impressed with pomp and ostentation; thus they assume it appeals to God. Whatever teaching they es-
pouse, they presume God favors the same.

> *The most common idolatry is the Specter of the
> Mirror in which one sees God as a colossal shadowy
> figure of himself, of course, with human frailties,
> passions and scanty virtues.*

Repentance

For I acknowledge my transgressions: and my sin is ever before me. —51:3

Three steps are essential in repentance:

First, a broken and bruised spirit caused by sorrow for sin. David experienced this heart feeling and offered it to God as a sacrifice: "The sacrifices of God are a broken spirit: a broken and a contrite heart" (ver. 17). God delighted in this rather than in burnt offerings, and was pleased with the latter only after the former was offered to Him (vers. 16-19). The emphasis is placed on what goes on in the inward man:

Behold, thou desirest truth in the inward parts. —ver. 6

No outward acts of religion will satisfy the Father unless they emanate from inward purity.

Second, confession. "For I acknowledge my transgressions" (ver. 3). This was David's free and open confession. It is very similar to his admission of guilt in 32:5: "I acknowledge my sin unto thee, and mine iniquity have I not hid." He did not try to conceal the fact that he was a sinner. Nor did he try to exonerate himself.

Third, reformation in life. This is the test of repentance, provided the amendments are prompted by grief for sin rather than for economic, social or political gains. The changed heart produces a change in living, as stipulated by John the Baptist: "Bring forth therefore fruits meet for repentence" (Matthew 3:8).

God's Judgment Is Justified

AGAINST thee, thee only, have I sinned, and done this
evil in thy sight: that thou mightest be justified when
thou speakest, and be clear when thou judgest. —51:4

David's sin, which is true of all people's sins, was
primarily against God. Of course, David knew that
he had wronged some humans and had hurt society.
His sin against Uriah and his family was low, treacherous and violent (II Samuel 11), but still the offense
derived its blackest blackness from the fact that Divine law had been transgressed. God gave the law
that David sinned against, and God — not Uriah —
would judge him. The chief heinousness of sin is not
in its devestating power to disgrace, or to bankrupt,
or to sadden, but in its disregard for the law of God.
Even the sins of David, adultery and murder, faded
into insignificance as wrongs against humans when
viewed as offenses against God. This is why David
said, "Against thee, thee only, have I sinned."

Without trying to vindicate himself, the psalmist
acknowledged that God was right and he was wrong.
He suggested that God was justified in all that He
said in the condemnation and punishment of sin; that
any sentence God might pronounce upon him would
be deserved; and that God should not be blamed. He
wanted Jehovah to stand clear in the eyes of the
world, free from all severity and rancor, in judging
him, which the Judge of all the earth must do.

In a world of sinners this attitude is hard to find.
May the same spirit be yours. And may it be mine.

After Forgiveness — What Then?

THEN will I teach transgressors thy ways; and sinners shall be converted unto thee. —51:13

In this chapter David penitently pleaded for forgiveness, that he be purged and made clean, whiter than snow. In his appeal for pardon, he promised to use his restored life to the conversion of man and to the praise of God.

First, he pledged to teach others: "Then will I teach transgressors . . . sinners shall be converted." Jesus enunciated the same principle of soul-winning in the Great Commission: He commanded the apostles to go teach and baptize and then teach the new converts to observe all things He commanded the apostles, one of which was to go teach (Matthew 28:19, 20). This is a most obsessive and lovely pursuit.

How beautiful are the feet of them that preach the gospel of peace, and bring glad tidings of good things!
—Romans 10:15

Second, he promised to praise God: "My mouth shall show forth thy praise" (ver. 15). His awareness of guilt had closed his lips too long. But with sins forgiven and conscience cleared, his mouth would open and his heart would flow with praise. A condemning conscience interferes with devotion and worship. It dries the heart and seals the lips, shutting off praise of God and teaching of sinners. But when a person is washed in the mercy of God and made whiter than snow, he can preach and pray and sing with a full heart.

Nothing to Brag About

WHY boastest thou thyself in mischief, O mighty man?
the goodness of God endureth continually. —52:1

When people applaud themselves for being evil,
they have much to brag about — if it were a laudable
matter. For they must be mighty wicked to commend
themselves for it.

Boasting is never good, and it is all the worse when
it is for being bad. But some are determined to have
something to brag about, even if it's their depravity.
They feel the need to excel, though it's in immorality
and criminality. Thus the world has its champions
in corruption: the boldest bank robber, the slickest
confidence man, the shrewdest forger, the sharpest
shoplifter, the filthiest mouth, the thirstiest drinker
and the cruelest heart.

Also, there are other braggarts of their shortcomings.

Did you ever hear a person boast about missing
church? And have you heard a person brag about
paying no attention to a sermon?

Likewise, there is the man who pats himself on the
back for cheating somebody.

And there is the person who extols himself for
telling somebody off.

Furthermore, there is the employee who blows his
trumpet about how little he works on the job.

On and on it goes, but not to one's glory.

An empty barrel makes the loudest noise.

More Love for Evil Than Good

THOU lovest evil more than good; and lying rather than to speak righteousness. —52:3

It is thought that Doeg was the one spoken of in the text (I Samuel 22:9-19). He loved the mischief of devouring words, preferring to use his tongue like a razor, slashing the innocent (ver. 2). Doeg lent support to the ungrounded suspicions of Saul that David was a traitor.

The explanation of Doeg's meanness is given in the seventh verse: "Lo, this is the man that made not God his strength; but trusted in the abundance of his riches, and strengthened himself in his wickedness." The key to the whole problem is Doeg's lack of trust in God and consequently his opposition to Him. This led to a trust in riches; and to obtain it, he became Saul's bought tool of brutality, for no doubt he was rewarded. His crimes sprang from his love of evil, which is the lowest form of degradation, described by Milton —

Evil, be thou my good.

How depraved! But what people love most points them to the way they go. There is always before us the conflicting loves — love of evil versus love of good — and one must prevail over the other.

The Root of Atheism

THE fool hath said in his heart, There is no God. Corrupt are they, and have done abominable iniquity: there is none that doeth good. —53:1

The fifty-third Psalm is a repetition of the fourteenth, with a few minor exceptions.

The Psalm describes atheism as foolish: "The fool hath said in his heart, There is no God." It is contended, however, that this is only a mere assertion and that to assert a proposition proves nothing. True. But neither do mere denials prove anything. However, this particular negative — no God — infers some unreal positives: No God — the world is an accident. No God — life sprang from lifeless matter. No God — man is strictly a fleshly being. No God — the Bible is a fraud. No God — heaven is a fable. No God — man's fulfillment is found in materialism.

As seen in the text, the thing that encourages atheism is personal corruption and iniquity: "Corrupt are they . . . there is none that doeth good." If they were doing good, God with His restrictions would not seem odious to them. Thus the Biblical explanation of infidelity is that it is rooted in man's moral nature, grounded in a defect of the heart. Not wanting to submit to God's will, a person finds the rejection easier if he assumes there is no God — and especially if he calls it intellectual or scientific.

The fool says, "There is no God"; but the wise man says, "There is." Label yourself.

Fearful for No Reason

> THERE were they in great fear, where no fear was:
> for God had scattered the bones of him that encampeth
> against thee; thou hast put them to shame, because
> God hath despised them. —53:5

The people of God became fearful where there was no fear. They were filled with consternation, because they felt the threat of being overthrown by the wicked. It was a cycle of decreasing faith and increasing fears. Hence the Great Protector reminded them that he had scattered the bones of an adversary and had put the enemy to shame. He refreshed their memory to abate their misgivings.

The passage addresses a common woe of man — fear, which often exists for no cause other than fear. Man's major fear is fear.

A wild, fearful imagination sees a storm in every cloud, a falling limb on every tree, a snake behind every log and a death in every illness. The scared person sees more dangers than the world could possibly hold.

O anxious people! O blind hearts! In what uncalled-for fear you spend these few fleeting years! Where is your faith? If we are living in the promises of God, we have nothing to fear. For —

> *God tempers the wind to the shorn lamb.*
> *—Henri Estienne*

So with renewed faith we say, *Farewell to fear.*

Praying in Troublesome Times

HEAR my prayer, O God; give ear to the words of my mouth. —54:2

In this short Psalm we have a most earnest prayer in time of dreadful trouble.

First, there is a plea for deliverance:

— "Save me, O God." From the oppressors.

— "Judge me." Vindicate me.

— "Oppressors seek after my soul." Seek my life.

— "They have not set God before them." Having no regard for God, they follow no rules but their own.

Second, there is an expression of confidence in the forthcoming help and a vein of gratitude for it:

— "God is mine helper." The only sure help.

— "The Lord is with them that uphold my soul." The Lord works with the helpers.

— "He shall reward evil unto mine enemies." They shall reap their wrongs.

— "I will freely sacrifice unto thee." He vowed a thanksgiving offering.

— "I will praise thy Name . . . for he hath delivered me." In his assurance and praise he treats the future as if it were the past.

> *Begin the day with God!*
> *He is thy Sun and Day!*
> *His is the radiance of thy dawn;*
> *To Him address thy lay.*
>
> *—Horatius Bonar*

Oh That I Had Wings

AND I said, Oh that I had wings like a dove! for then would I fly away, and be at rest. —55:6

The poet wanted to get away from it all, to "wander far off, and remain in the wilderness," get out of the city, get back to the quietude of nature.

He was very explicit of the agony that made him want wings: "I mourn." "The oppression of the wicked." "They cast iniquity upon me." "They hate me." "My heart is sore pained." "The terrors of death are fallen upon me." "Fearfulness and trembling are come upon me." "Horror hath overwhelmed me." "I have seen violence and strife in the city." Poor man.

No wonder he wanted to "fly away, and be at rest."

At times we, too, have the same urge. The pressures of a complex society are disquieting, and our soul cries out for the quiet wilderness life. We want wings to fly away, but this is unreal. Opposition must be faced. Responsibilities must be met. Furthermore —

> *You cannot fly like an eagle*
> *with the wings of a wren.*
> —*William Henry Hudson*

So maybe we had better stay put, fight it out and grow some stronger wings; by then we might want only temporary leaves to regain strength for a renewal of the struggles.

This Treachery Was Too Much

FOR it was not an enemy that reproached me; then I could have borne it: neither was it he that hated me that did magnify himself against me; then I would have hid myself from him. —55:12

David felt the rumblings of revolution about him. His own son Absalom whom he dearly loved had risen in revolt. Multitudes forsook David in support of the rebellion. He discusses in the Psalm one of the rebels in particular — a traitor — perhaps Ahithophel who was known as David's counselor (II Samuel 15:12). Today we would call him Prime Minister. His defection was one of the deepest disappointments and saddest sorrows the unhappy king was called upon to bear. While David trusted, "bloody treason flourished" over him. Anything else — he said he "could have borne," but this was too much for him. The turncoat was a man he had befriended; had trusted as a guide (friend); and had walked with him in fellowship to worship. It was a sore wound for David's heart. It outraged his sensibilities.

To place confidence — how bitter a thing it is when it crouches in treachery!

One of the necessary traits of a strong and wise character is loyalty — no selling a friend, not for money, not for glory, not for ambition. It's made of sterner stuff.

For the same reason David had his griefs we've had a few. You can hardly live (especially in public life) and not be Judas-treated.

Smooth Like Butter and Sharp Like a Sword

THE words of his mouth were smoother than butter,
but war was in his heart: his words were softer than
oil, yet they were drawn swords. —55:21

In a continuation of the theme on the treachery
of David's chief adviser, the Psalm states, "He hath
broken his covenant" (ver. 20). This was a covenant
of friendship with David in which they "took sweet
counsel together" (ver. 14).

> *Treachery lurks in honeyed words.*
> *—Danish Proverb*

The trust-breaker's words were masterpieces of deceit, excelling in smoothness like butter, surpassing
in softness like oil, and exceeding in sharpness like
swords. Lots of ability went to waste, because he
didn't have the character to be loyal.

While God sustains the righteous, He brings down
the wicked. In this case, their days were cut short
more than half (ver. 23). There was the suicide of
Ahithophel, the master deceiver; and the slaughter
of Absalom, David's rebel son, and many others.

> *Treachery, in the end, betrays itself.*

David's faith in a confidant was shattered; but, with
faith in God still in tact, he closes the Psalm on a
happy note of confidence: "I will trust in thee."

When friends stay and when friends betray, may
our confidence in God — "I will trust in thee" — ever
fill our hearts and keep us going.

O Thou Most High

MINE enemies would daily swallow me up: for they be many that fight against me, O thou Most High. —56:2

Most High. The original means *high, exalted,* and the translators understood the poet used it in reference to God in contrast to his foes. Other names and appelations bear out His Highness:

— God of Heaven (136:26). Universal God.
— Holy God (Joshua 24:19). Pure. Guileless.
— God of Israel (Exodus 24:10). Israel's God.
— Living God (84:2). Alive. Deathless.
— Merciful God (Nehemiah 9:31). Kind. Good.
— God of all Comfort (II Corinthians 1:3). Consoler.
— Eternal God (Deuteronomy 33:27). Timeless.
— Just God (Isaiah 46:21). Fair. Upright.
— Jehovah (83:18). I AM, the eternal living One.
— Father (John 6:37). Everything a father is.
— Creator (Ecclesiastes 12:1). Originator.
— Almighty (Job 8:3). Omnipotent.
— King (29:10). Supreme lawgiver.
— Saviour (Isaiah 45:15). Redeemer of the sinful.
— Rock (18:46). Solid support. Firm defense.
— Shepherd (80:1). Provider. Protector.
— Judge (Hebrews 12:23). Factual. Merciful.
— I Am (Exodus 3:14). I AM WHAT I AM.

Hallowed be His name. Speak it with awe. Indeed, we need a personal relationship with Him, but don't let it be common and flippant. For He is the Most High.

Praise His Word

IN God I will praise his word, in God I have put my
trust. —56:4

The Word is inexhaustible. It has a bottomless pro-
fundity; we can spend a lifetime digging and never
reach the bottom.

It is instructive: declares man's duties to God, and
man's obligations to man.

The power to protect is within it. Hide it in your
heart and you will be shielded from every vice.

It sustains a spiritually hungry world. Sweet bread
— that's what it is.

The revealing nature of the Word lifts it for exaltation. It makes known the Divine plan to snap the
shackles of sin from human feet that man be free.
Reveals the merciful hand that reached down from
heaven to wipe away humanity's tears that man be
comforted. Discloses the power over death by Him
who said, "I am the resurrection and the life" that
man be immortal.

Would you be moved by sublimity, read it, imbibe
it. Be true to it, and when music has lost its charm
and poetry no longer stirs your soul, the word of
God, having been your way in life, will be your stay
in death.

On the other hand, destroy man's confidence in the
Word, and you fill his future with darkness; you pull
the sun out of his life, and the brightness of human
hope is gone from his soul forever.

God Is on My Side

THIS I know; for God is for me. —56:9

The author believed God was for him, that He was taking his part. In the struggle between right and wrong, surely God is not neutral. His very nature dictates that He be on the side of right. Accordingly, if we are on the side of rectitude, then God is for us — this is how simple the matter of Divine partisanship is. God is no respecter of persons, but He is a respecter of faith, trust, obedience, uprightness and worship.

These are the reasons the God of Goodness was for the psalmist:

— "I believed" (116:10).

— "In thee do I put my trust" (7:1).

— "For I have kept the ways of the Lord (18:21).

— "I was also upright before him" (18:23).

— "I will worship toward thy holy temple" (138:2).

It simply comes down to this: God is on the side of him who is on His side. So a timely, soul-searching question is, "Who is on the Lord's side" (Exodus 32:26)?

> *Once to every man and nation comes*
> *the moment to decide,*
> *In the strife of Truth with Falsehood*
> *for the good or evil side.*
>
> —*James Russell Lowell*

Calamities

IN the shadow of thy wings will I make my refuge, until these calamities be overpast. —57:1

There is one thing about calamity — it passes. The psalmist mentioned this in the text. Elsewhere he stated, "the day of my calamity" (18:18) — day, something that ends. No night is so black but its lingering darkness gives way to the dawn of a new day. It did for David. It passed for Abraham. It spent itself for Joseph. And it will for you and me.

Another thing about calamities — they keep coming. Fate points them toward us and gives them speed. After one hits us, another starts gaining on us.

Fortune is not satisfied with inflicting one calamity.
—Pubilius Syrus

What we need is what David needed — strength to endure trouble while it lasts. For there is no calamity as great as the calamity of not being able to bear it. Bearing it makes you a genius.

Genius is capacity for taking trouble.
—Leslie Stephen

To be mentally and spiritually prepared for reverses, to stand up to trouble, we need to be undergirded by faith in the Almighty. "God is our refuge and strength, a very present help in trouble" (46:1).

Among Lions

My soul is among lions: and I lie even among them that are set on fire, even the sons of men, whose teeth are spears and arrows, and their tongue a sharp sword.
—57:4

The lions weren't beasts but "sons of men" who resembled lions: fierce, ferocious, savage men. When the author lay down for the night's rest, they were around him: beastly men, "set on fire," inflamed with hate, burning with anger. They had teeth like spears and arrows, and a tongue as sharp as a sword.

A cruel man is a two-legged, second-rate lion.

Yet, with these characters surrounding him, the psalmist was able to lie down and find repose. How did he do it? Trust. He slept under the shadow of the wings of the Lord (ver. 1). And with a fixed heart he declared, "In God have I put my trust: I will not be afraid of what man can do unto me" (56:11).

In a very short time our society has degenerated into a series of horrors. Walking the streets in our cities at night is unsafe. The parks, once harmless places of relaxation, have been turned into forbidden jungles of violence. And moving away is no solution, for the threat is spreading.

What is the answer? David's behavior is the solution. Take precautions to preserve yourself and trust God for the rest. Don't live in fear with every breath a dread and every night a nightmare.

Unjust Judges

Do ye indeed speak righteousness, O congregation?
do ye judge uprightly, O ye sons of men? Yea, in
heart ye work wickedness; ye weigh the violence of
your hands in the earth. —58:1, 2

Some questions were put to the congregation of
the sons of men, mighty ones, the judges. They were
asked in mocking irony: Do you speak righteousness?
Do you judge uprightly?

No! In their heart they devised wickedness and
carried out the violence with their unclean hands.
Their poison was similar to the poison of an adder.
Like poison spreads through the veins, the unjust decisions of corrupt judges were spreading through the
veins of a stricken society. Their obstinacy was "like
the deaf adder that stoppeth her ear . . . which will
not hearken to the voice of charmers" (vers. 4,5).
An adder was considered deaf because it was so hard
to charm. How true of self-serving Judges! No charms,
no arts, reach them. No persuasion, no eloquent logic,
robs them of their venom. Misusing their powers for
selfish ends, they "judge for reward" (Micah 3:9).

> *Thieves for their robbery have authority*
> *When judges steal themselves.*
> —*William Shakespeare*

God give us just laws; and for their execution, give
us honorable judges, men honorable in heart, men to
whom it is fitting that we say, "Your Honor."

Not His Fault

FOR, lo, they lie in wait for my soul: the mighty are gathered against me; not for my transgression, nor for my sin, O Lord. They run and prepare themselves without my fault: awake to help me, and behold. —59:3, 4

This was a trying time for the young hero. He was guilty of no treason, high crime or misdemeanor. But circumstances had placed him in the position where he was the object of the cruel envy of a proud king turned madman. Hence it became an obsession with King Saul to kill him.

The strife, the envy and hard feelings, was not the fault of David. It takes two to have peace, and he was only one. So in the Psalm he sang that the cruelty directed against him was not for any transgression or sin on his part. Not "my fault," he stated. In this matter he was absolutely innocent. He said in another Psalm:

FOR without cause have they hid for me their net in a pit, which without cause they have digged for my soul. —35:7

However, a common error is to assume that where there is estrangement and strife both are at fault; and a grosser assumption is that perhaps both are equally at fault. The former is not always true, and the latter seldom is.

Do everything you can to stay on friendly terms with everybody — "if it be possible," (Romans 12:18) — but sometimes with some people it is not possible.

Despondency in Defeat

O GOD, thou hast cast us off, thou hast scattered us, thou hast been displeased; O turn thyself to us again. —60:1

Apparently this Psalm was written following a defeat of the forces of Israel when they had been engaged in a war with Edom (II Samuel 8:13; I Kings 11:15, 16). The Psalm was composed before the fortunes of war turned in their favor, which they finally did, enabling them to occupy the country. But in their defeated state, despondency flows from the poet's pen:

— "Thou hast cast us off."
— "Thou hast scattered us."
— "Thou hast been displeased."
— "Thou hast made the earth to tremble."
— "Thou hast showed thy people hard things."
— "O God, which didst not go out with our armies."

Fortune is something that rides the tides, in and out. When it is going out, it is easy for despondency to overwhelm us. Indeed, it is natural to think upon defeat for a time; but as soon as we can we need to turn to positive thinking, which is the best antidote for depression. David did. In the Psalm's last verse despair blossoms into hopefulness through a dual faith: faith in self, faith in God. He said, "Through God we shall do valiantly: for he it is that shall tread down our enemies."

Now, God be prais'd, that to believing souls
Gives light in darkness, comfort in despair.
—William Shakespeare

Vain Is the Help of Man

GIVE us help from trouble: for vain is the help of man. —60:11

A man may turn against you and rend you. Your outstretched hand of goodness does not assure his gratitude. After entrusting him with your good name, he may prove to be a traitor; he may sacrifice your reputation for fear or favor; to the highest bidder he may let you go. The very people who were eager to do you honor when the crown of success looked so kingly on your brow may be the very first to nail you to the cross when failure comes.

Even if a man is true and loyal to the very end, he is limited in the assistance he can render. His advice may prove disastrous. His efforts to help may only worsen your plight. His hand may be too weak to sustain you. Sometimes he can do no more than sympathize. He is as powerless as you are.

The only absolutely unfailing source of adequate help is God, the One strong enough to help, the One *that never deserts you.* He is as constant as the rising and setting of the sun. He stands by when others forsake. And if fate drives you out into a cold, friendless world, He walks by your side and encourages you in every faltering step you take — to take another and another. And when the death scene comes, and helpless loved ones stand by weeping, He will take you by the hand and lead you into the better world. His help is the only help that fully suffices.

Have God and have all.

A Cry Unto God

HEAR my cry, O God; attend unto my prayer. —61:1

In centuries gone by, the sixty-first Psalm was often sung in worship services. It is short, beautiful and a suitable sentiment when trouble comes. Man has had his ups and downs.

David had enough troubles to break a man of lesser faith.

This life is not a pilgrimage on a gentle down-hill pavement, marked with signboards saying, "No Troubles," "No Sorrows," "No Efforts." So evidently the God who created us thought we needed some struggles that we may grow stronger. The great men whose illustrious names brighten the fading pages of history faced challenging difficulties, which brought out the heroic qualities within them. In their examples they give inspiration to the generations that follow.

Another thing we can be sure of — God has an open ear to the cries of believing children. "Hear my cry, O God," petitioned David. You may doubt others. You may doubt yourself. But never doubt God. He will attend your prayers. Disaster may push you to "the end of the earth." But God is near and you may still cry out:

Lead me to the rock that is higher than I.

No matter how distressing your hardships are, God is near. He is the Rock of Shelter. Cling to Him.

The Rock That Is Higher Than I

FROM the end of the earth will I cry unto thee, when my heart is overwhelmed: lead me to the rock that is higher than I. —61:2

This passage inspired E. Johnson to compose one of the great hymns sung today by worshipers throughout the world.

> *O sometimes the shadows are deep,*
> *And rough seems the path to the goal;*
> *And sorrows, how often they sweep*
> *Like tempests down over the soul.*
>
> *O sometimes how long seems the day,*
> *And sometimes how weary my feet;*
> *But toiling in life's dusty way,*
> *The Rock's blessed shadow, how sweet!*
>
> *O near to the Rock let me keep,*
> *Or blessings or sorrows prevail,*
> *Or climbing the mountain way steep,*
> *Or walking the shadowy vale.*
>
> *O then to the Rock let me fly,*
> *To the Rock that is higher than I;*
> *O then to the Rock let me fly,*
> *To the Rock that is higher than I.*

We fly to the Rock for a refuge, to reach a stronghold where safety may be found.

In man's low vale he is exposed to every threat. If he would have security, he must get higher. A Saviour no higher than man would never elevate him any. But the Lord is "the rock that is higher than I."

Prolong My Life

THOU wilt prolong the king's life: and his years as many generations. —61:6

May Thou prolong the king's life. Here David prayed for his own days to be lengthened.

Life is one of man's most precious possessions. In testing Job, Satan said, "Skin for skin, yea, all that a man hath will he give for his life" (Job 2:4). But he was wrong! Life is not as priceless as the soul. Not as valuable as honor. Not as great as God's cause. But it is more precious than gold. Hence man spends money to protect it, changes climates to keep it and prays God to lengthen it. For when it is gone, it is "as water spilt on the ground, which cannot be gathered up again" (II Samuel 14:14).

Life on earth means so much that one of the rewards God has offered is longer days: "Thou shalt keep therefore his statutes, and his commandments ... that thou mayest prolong thy days upon the earth" (Deuteronomy 4:40). And, coming to the New Testament, Paul repeated the promise of longer days to those who honor their parents (Ephesians 6:2,3).

Now for a longer life, let us live the approved way and pray to Him who watches over it. For, excepting the soul and honor, its value is as Goethe stated:

Nothing is worth more than this day.

Like a Leaning Wall or a Tottering Fence

How long will ye imagine mischief against a man?
ye shall be slain all of you: as a bowing [leaning]
wall shall ye be, and as a tottering fence. —62:3

David was secure on the rock: "He only is my rock"
(ver. 2). But his oppressors, having no foundation,
were like a leaning wall and a tottering fence. For a
little while such construction appears solid, but Father
Time disproves the hasty assumption. Time tries the
foundation; if it is weak, the wall starts bending or
the fence starts tilting, which aptly describes a life
with no foundation.

These leaning-wall, tottering-fence people had no
character on which to build. The Psalm says they
imagined mischief, consulted to do harm, delighted
in lies and spoke hypocritically (vers. 3, 4). Intel-
lectualism without heart, cleverness without goodness,
is a power only for mischief.

But when a strong character is the nature of a person, he is like an acorn that grows into an oak. Conditions may destroy the acorn, but they cannot divert
it as long as it survives. While it lives, it defies man
and beast, earth and sky, to produce an oak. Circumstances do not change its nature. So it is with a human being: a truthful, loyal character defies the circumstances to make the man. For what a person
becomes tomorrow he already is in character today.

Character is a man's guiding destiny.
—Heraclitus

Men of Different Ranks

SURELY men of low degree are vanity, and men of high degree are a lie: to be laid in the balance, they are altogether lighter than vanity. —62:9

The text speaks of *men of low degree,* mere sons of Adam, commonly called common men, creatures of a vain and empty state. But worse than this, he points out, are *men of high degree* who are a lie, a false illusion, *lighter than vanity,* lighter than the *men of low degree,* for they are lacking in substance.

The matter of true rank has become awfully confused. The person who is ranked the lowest in the eyes of the world may actually stand the highest in the sight of God. Worldly rank is only an empty bubble. God can change the degrees of men rather fast: "He hath put down the mighty from their seats, and exalted them of low degree" (Luke 1:52).

In God's sight, barring faith and accomplishment, no person is last or first — all rank the same. Real nobility is one of merit, something you make for yourself — with God's help.

> *Let none presume*
> *To wear an undeserved dignity.*
> *O! that estates, degrees, and offices*
> *Were not deriv'd corruptly, and that clear honor*
> *Were purchas'd by the merit of the wearer.*
>
> *—William Shakespeare*

Increased Riches

IF riches increase, set not your heart upon them.
—62:10

If riches increase — they may. If one enjoys health, works hard, practices thrift and exercises good judgment, his riches will increase.

Then there is the needed warning: *Set not your heart on them.* Wealth is not a thing to be trusted; for it has wings, and easily takes to flight (Proverbs 23:5). It is not something to love, for it is the root of all evil (I Timothy 6:9, 10).

But, of course, many have been pierced because they didn't have it. The have-nots have also been covetous, wanting what is not theirs, which is a form of idolatry (Colossians 3:5). They have been envious of successful people — another sin. They have borne false witness against industrious, saving people, accusing them of dishonesty and greed. Furthermore they have slapped the hand that provided their blessings.

For instance: To buy a house, a family had to borrow $30,000.00 from a savings and loan company, which it got from a depositor. Everytime somebody borrows money, somebody else had to save some.

Therefore let us recognize there are possible pitfalls concerning wealth: Those who have it may sin by trusting in it; and those who don't have it may sin by having the wrong attitude toward it and its possessor.

Sublime Superlatives

O God, thou art my God . . . . —63:1-8

A reflection on the superlatives in this Psalm gives insight to its popularity in private and public worship:

Most helpful relationship: "O God, thou art my God" (ver. 1). God is ours and we are His.

Most primary seeking: "Early will I seek thee" (ver. 1). It should come above all other seeking.

Thirstiest thirst: "My soul thirsteth for thee, my flesh longeth for thee in a dry and thirsty land, where no water is" (ver. 1). When your burning, parched soul can no longer endure and cries out for cool refreshment, it is then that you know what thirst is.

Grandest sight: "To see thy power and thy glory, so as I have seen thee in the sanctuary" (ver. 2).

Kindest kindness: "Because thy loving-kindness is better than life" (ver. 3). The favor of God is more valuable than life.

Most deserved praise: "My lips shall praise thee" (ver. 3). Jehovah is wholly worthy of praise.

Fullest satisfaction: "My soul shall be satisfied" (ver. 5). The sweetest contentment is found in a consecrated relationship with man's Creator.

Surest help: "Because thou hast been my helper" (ver. 7). There is no power to interpose and assist man like the Almighty.

Strongest support: "Thy right hand upholdeth me" (ver. 8). Sustained by the most powerful hand.

While I Live

THUS will I bless thee while I live: I will lift up my
hands in thy name. —63:4

All of us need to think about what we are going to
do while we live on earth.

Life is too sacred not to protect it. We need to set
up a few watches, as Jesus did (Matthew 26:36-38).

Life has too stern a teacher with too many necessary
lessons for us not to learn.

Man is too fallible to throw his life into the par-
adox of judging others.

Life can be too productive to be idle; too helpful to
be selfish; and too peaceable to mar it with strife and
vengeance.

Our days are too few and uncertain to waste.

Man's memory is too abiding to fill it with ghosts
to haunt his future.

> *Let every man in mankind's frailty*
> *Consider his last day; and let none*
> *Presume on his good fortune until he find*
> *Life, at his death, a memory without pain.*
>
> *—Sophocles*
> 495-405 B.C.

And life is too dependent on God to ignore Him.
The psalmist didn't. Neither should we.

Encouraged to Do Wrong

THEY encourage themselves in an evil matter: they
commune of laying snares privily; they say, Who shall
see them? —64:5

Mischievous people! They encouraged one another
in a sinister scheme to destroy David's popularity
and to promote open revolt: "They commune of laying snares privily." In a spectacle of depravity and
vice they agitated horrendous living by suggesting
that which is degraded and immoral. In an unwholesome relationship, marked with conceited claptraps,
they pushed their ill-spent lives down a corrupt path.

How vicious for people to encourage each other to
do wrong in any degree! But those bent on evil can
always find something wrong to suggest. It begins
even in youth. One boy dares another to fight the
third boy, or tells him he is afraid to throw a rock
through a window. On and on it goes — encouragement to do wrong.

We see it in mature life. Here is some common
rhetoric, not very eloquent, but very common: "I
wouldn't take that." "Why don't you get even?"
"Have a drink. Prove to everybody you're a man."
"Don't work, if you can get out of it." "Sure, it's
all right if you don't get caught." "You ought to get
her told." "Now don't get too conscientious."

Leaving the unwholesome, we close with a thought
upon the higher influence over each other:

AND let us consider one another to provoke unto love
and to good works. —Hebrews 10:24

Searching for Ways
to Wrong Another

THEY search out iniquities; they accomplish a diligent
search: both the inward thought of every one of them,
and the heart, is deep. —64:6

In a further description of the people in the previous
essay, they searched for iniquities — ways to harm
a righteous man. And they found. In their blackguard endeavors they accomplished well-framed devices. With "much of Madness, and more of Sin,"
they plotted and plotted to harm and harm, to have
their way. And maybe they did for a while. But the
story is not finished. Their rotten words became a
stench in the mouth, which caused others to ostracize
them. They became known as harmers — not helpers,
and harmers are not in demand. They swapped *man-
hood* for *doghood* to cringe and bite, but good people
don't want that kind of a creature around.

And now here is the Divine side of the story: God
interposed. God shot back — "But God shall shoot at
them with an arrow" (ver. 7). In their plan to wound
another, they got wounded. I have literally seen the
principle fulfilled — more than once.

David had not always done right, but he was better
than those who sought to harm him.

> *And now among the fading embers*
> *These have been some of my regrets;*
> *When I am right, no one remembers;*
> *When I am wrong, no one forgets.*

Lashed by Their Own Tongue

So they shall make their own tongue to fall upon themselves: all that see them shall flee away. —64:8

This was the backlash that whipped some people who misused their tongue. Words spoken to harm another reacted to harm the perverters.

In another view, the psalmist says, "Who whet their tongue like a sword, and bend their bows to shoot their arrows, even bitter words" (ver. 3). They aim at others, but arrows return. God shoots back and they are wounded (ver. 7). Cruel and slanderous words are compared to arrows, swords, spears, razors and serpent's teeth. They are sharp. They cut.

Why, oh why, do people use the tongue to harm? Because the heart harbors pride, uncharitableness, maliciousness, anger, envy and selfishness. The bitter tongue is the ready servant of the bitter heart. And when it finds bitter ears, there is an affinity that makes both work well.

A bitter word may make the rounds, cutting a deep wound, before it stops; and then it may linger in suspecting hearts for years to come. But in contrast to the damaging outrage afflicted, the perpetrator suffers the greater injury. The liar is known for what he is. The gossiper is wounded by his own reputation. The whisperer, in separating friends, loses friends. The slanderer stymies himself with incredibility. The false witness knows he's false.

What shame! What tragedy!

Satisfied Only in God

BLESSED is the man whom thou choosest, and causest to approach unto thee, that he may dwell in thy courts: we shall be satisfied with the goodness of thy house, even of thy holy temple. —65:4

The soul finds in God what meets its needs. Nothing else will. Everything else leaves a void.

Unanswered questions would leave man frustrated. Where did he come from? How did the world originate? The answer is God.

Though man is a little lower than the angels, he still is insufficient to guide himself. Only God completely fills a person's need for guidance.

Life has its perils. When the storms beat, man needs a rock for a refuge; and when the enemies' arrows are drawn, he needs a protector.

Being spirit, man has an urge to worship. This requirement for human satisfaction is seen in the text. The psalmist said that he would be satisfied in the holy temple.

Life without hope would take the sun from man's sky and the rainbow from his cloud. The longing question, "If a man die, shall he live again?" will not take *No* for an answer.

> *One question, more than all others,*
> *From thoughtful minds implores reply,*
> *It is, as breathed from star and pall,*
> *What fate awaits us when we die?*

Thanks be to the Most High, people that live unfulfilling lives can be satisfied — if they will seek Him.

Crowned With Blessings

THOU crownest the year with thy goodness; and thy paths drop fatness. They drop upon the pastures of the wilderness: and the little hills rejoice on every side. The pastures are clothed with flocks; the valleys also are covered with corn; they shout for joy, they also sing. —65:11-13

There is one crown everyone has been given — the crown of God's goodness. He sends the rain on the just and the unjust.

His paths drop fatness — productivity and plenty. The wilderness blossoms with His blessings. The little hills, touched by His artistic hand, rejoice in nature's charm. The green pastures are clothed with thriving flocks, created and sustained by the Great Provider — for man. The fertile valleys, crowded with corn ever so nourishing, respond to the gentle breezes and sing their own tune to the provisionary purpose of God.

He visits the earth and waters it. "The river of God" flows upon it (ver. 9).

His "showers of blessing" fall upon us. Every good gift is from Him.

Truly our world is blessed with God's benevolence.

Nature manifests His omnipotent care morning and night (ver. 8).

God knows, He loves, He cares,
Nothing His truth can dim;
He gives His very best to those
Who leave the choice to Him.

A Divinity Rewarding and Retributive

COME and see the works of God: he is terrible in his doing toward the children of men. —66:5

The works of God have ever inspired the poet's pen and the orator's tongue. They have filled eyes with astonishment and hearts with gratitude. The works of God! How magnificent! How breathless! How enduring! As stable as the hills, as moving as the earth! Warm like the sun, cool like the night!

His works are good and terrible, rewarding to His people, retributive to their enemies. It is not that God wants to harm anyone, but there are times when there is hardly a choice. To save his people, He has to subdue their enemies.

For an example, the composer cited the deliverance of Israel through the Red Sea (ver. 6). It's a thrilling story. When they came to the sea, pursued by the Egyptians, God sent a strong wind that divided the waters and dried the land, enabling the Israelites to go across with a wall of water on each side. But upon "the Egyptians the waters returned, and covered the chariots, and the horsemen, and all the host of Pharoah that came into the sea after them; there remained not so much as one of them" (Exodus 14:28).

The profaner will fight and have his day; but later God will have his say. Truly —

> There's a divinity that shapes our ends.
> —*William Shakespeare*

Iniquity Nullifies Prayer

IF I regard iniquity in my heart, the Lord will not
hear me. —66:18

Prayer has always meant much to the children of
God. It is a powerful avenue open to them, not open
to those who regard iniquity in their heart. "Now
we know that God heareth not sinners: but if any
man be a worshipper of God, and doeth his will, him
he heareth" (John 9:31).

When one cherishes sin in his heart, refuses to give
it up, then his prayers rise no higher than his lips.

But in a finer vein, one of the most impressive
statements on the changed life is, " ...ye were the
servants of sin ... " (Romans 6:20). They were sinners, but now they're not. This is the design and
purpose of religion — to raise one above sin, which
qualifies him to pray, unburdens him to live and pre-
pares him to die.

Be it said to the credit of the composer, God heard
him. "God hath heard me," he declared, "he hath
attended to the voice of my prayer" (ver. 19). The
reason — he did not harbor sin in his heart.

So here is a most essential, soul-searching question
for each to ask:

> *Is thy heart right with God,*
> *Washed in the crimson flood,*
> *Cleansed and made holy, humble and lowly,*
> *Right in the sight of God?*
>
> *—E. A. Hoffman*

God Be Merciful

GOD be merciful unto us, and bless us; and cause his
face to shine upon us. —67:1

It is proper to ask God to be merciful; for He is
"the Father of mercies, and the God of all comfort"
(II Corinthians 1:3). "Rich in mercy" (Ephesians 2:4).

How beautiful are the mercies of the Most High!
"Like the drops of a lustre, which reflect a rainbow
of colors when the sun glitters upon them, when turned
in different ways . . . so the mercy of God is one and
yet many; the same, yet ever changing; a combination
of all the beauties of love blended harmoniously together." — Charles Spurgeon

Man needs a great mercy. Just a little will not
suffice.

> *It must be great mercy, or no mercy;*
> *for little mercy will never serve my turn.*
> —*John Bunyan*

While God is filled with pity and is anxious to extend mercy, its reception is dependent on man. "And
his mercy is on them that fear him from generation
to generation" (Luke 1:50).

After righteousness has been followed and God has
been praised, man still needs mercy. If it were not
for mercy, there would be no Divine way for man to
pursue. A dying man was told, "You are going to
receive the rewards of your labors." He replied, "I
am going to receive mercy."

The More Productive Way

THEN shall the earth yield her increase; and God, even our own God, shall bless us. —67:6

The Psalm expresses a desire that the way of God might be known to all nations (ver. 2). It voices a wish that all peoples might recognize the hand of God in the affairs of men and nations, and that they rejoice in this acknowledgment (ver. 4).

The prevalence of true religion — praise for God and regard for man — would greatly bless the temporal interests of the peoples: "Then shall the earth yield her increase" (ver. 5). True religion encourages the proper use of human lives and natural resources. It frees man from an unproductive course to follow a productive one. It gives him inspiration and direction to accomplish the purpose for which he was placed here, stated to Adam and Eve: "Be fruitful and multiply, and replenish the earth, and subdue it" (Genesis 1:28); to conquer the earth — not each other; to harness nature — not one another.

Today much wealth and many lives are being consumed by those who would force their will and way on others, and, in a reactive way, by those who feel the need to protect themselves.

How different it would be, if all the nations rejoiced in God's way. Then all useless and hurtful labors could be directed in the production of food, clothes, houses, hospitals, schools, highways and other physical accomplishments that lend prosperity and pleasantness to life.

Emancipated

GOD setteth the solitary in families: he bringeth out those which are bound with chains: but the rebellious dwell in a dry land. —68:6

As seen in the Psalm, God settles the solitary in families or houses. He gives a home to the outcasts and wanderers. Perhaps it refers to God's settling the nomadic Israelites in Canaan.

"He bringeth out those which are bound with chains." He loosed their chains and set them free. But the rebellious were not included; they were forced to "dwell in a dry land" of their own making, parched with their own impenitence.

God's principles favor the rights of man — oppose tyranny and oppression. "The Lord raiseth them that are bowed down" (146:7). The mistreated and trampled have cause to take heart. The God of mercy is a helper of the helpless, a Father to the fatherless and a defender of the widows (ver. 5). His defense and protection especially cover those who need it most.

God's hand has moved with power to reshape the order of things for the good of His people. This is the encouragement the psalmist gave in the text.

Chains — the cruelest and most enslaving ones are not those made of iron but those forged by sin. Have you allowed God to set you free?

Not all are free who scorn chains.
—Gotthold Ephraim Lessing

The Word Worthy of Publication

THE Lord gave the word: great was the company of those that published it. —68:11

What word? Answers vary: "the word of command"; "the word of victory"; "the assurance of victory"; "the word to march."

The host that proclaimed it was the choir of women. In that day there were choirs of women who sang the ancient war songs. Men did battle, and the women "that tarried at home divided the spoil" (ver. 12). Whether in peace or in war, women should aid their men.

Whatever the Word in the text is, it came from the Lord; that gave it unusual distinctions. For it is:

— The revealer of God.

— The way of salvation.

— The staff of spiritual life.

— The protector from sin.

— The guide of ethics.

— The comfort of the sorrowful.

— The reprover of tyrants.

— The inspiration of poets.

— The hope of tomorrow.

> *There is but one question of the hour: how to bring the truths of God's Word into vital contact with the minds and hearts of all classes of people.*
>
> *—William E. Gladstone*

He Captured the Captives

THOU hast ascended on high, thou hast led captivity captive: thou hast received gifts for men; yea, for the rebellious also, that the Lord God might dwell among them. —68:18

Some believe the immediate application of the text was in the Lord's ascending into Mount Zion when the Ark of the Covenant was transferred and placed "on high" above all foes — no longer carried about at the head of the armies but located there as a symbol of triumph.

There are various commentaries of men on the text. And while I sometimes find the comments of men appalling, I always find Paul appealing; so I quote him:

WHEREFORE he saith, When he ascended up on high, he led captivity captive, and gave gifts unto men. (Now that he ascended, what is it but that he also descended first into the lower parts of the earth? He that descended is the same also that ascended up far above all heavens, that he might fill all things.)
—Ephesians 4:8-10

Thus it is evident that Paul used the language in Psalms to describe the work, the glory and the triumph of the Messiah. In Christian relevance, it refers to Christ's converting Satan's captivity to His own captives. The Lord came down from His dwelling place on high, and after leading "captivity captive" returned to His seat; that is, He came to earth, died on the cross and ascended to heaven in triumph over all foes. It was a glorious victory. Now the bond captives of sin become the free captives of righteousness.

Scatter Those Who Delight in War

SCATTER thou the people that delight in war. —68:30

This is a prayer concerning war and peace. Drive asunder the warmongers. Rid us of them. Peaceable people have ever prayed for peace (I Timothy 2:2).

In the silent city of the dead, as a folded American flag is handed to a broken-hearted father and mother with the words, "From a grateful nation," they sob and silently pray, "Scatter thou the people that delight in war."

A little boy who misses a father that will never come home looks at his picture and prays, "Scatter thou the people that delight in war."

Grandmother, old and almost gone, requests to be driven to the military cemetery, and there amidst a thousand ghastly crosses, cold and silent, is led to the grave of a grandson she loved more than life; and there, as she wipes the tears from dim and sunken eyes, she prays with thin and shrunken lips, "Scatter thou the people that delight in war."

Size up war as you will, but don't say there is glory in it. You can say it is science — a science of destruction.

A battle is a terrible conjugation of the verb to kill — I kill, thou killest, he kills, we kill, they kill, all kill.

—Thomas Carlyle

Reproach for Thy Sake

BECAUSE for thy sake I have borne reproach; shame hath covered my face. —69:7

The thing that provoked enmity on the part of several people toward David was his consecration to God and his blessings from Him.

Here was a man whose conduct was such a contrast to theirs that it shamed them. He stood so much taller than they that it pained them to look up to him. His superior ability made their mediocrity look weak. His high ideal of returning good for evil showed up their wickedness and humiliated them. The high position of king, given to him by the Lord, contrasted their lower station too much for them to like him. His success turned their vicious tongues loose.

I have seen this resentful and malicious spirit work among all classes of people — even among and toward preachers. It happens like this: A young man decides to preach the gospel, and he is lauded to the sky for the noble decision. All want to encourage him when they can look down and give him a hand. But he has talent that comes alive and energy that knows no end. He works hard and God blesses him. Whatever he touches prospers. Now many of the same people who enjoyed reaching down and giving him a hand are the first to climb a ladder and stab him in the back.

O envy! how you despise the successful, but most of all yourself.

A Flaming Zeal

For the zeal of thine house hath eaten me up; and the reproaches of them that reproached thee are fallen upon me. —69:9

The author's zeal for God's house was a passionate ardor within him. David showed this (1) when he took the tabernacle to Mount Zion (II Samuel 6:12-19); also (2) when he manifested a desire to build a permanent dwelling for the Ark of the Covenant (II Samuel 7:2); next (3) in the preparation and appropriation with all his might for the house of God (I Chronicles 28:11-29:2); and, unable to build it, (4) in the instructions he gave to his son Solomon to go ahead with the erection of it (I Chronicles 28:9, 10). His religious zeal drove him forward.

Now let us observe how the passage was later used:

First, when Jesus drove the money changers out of the temple, "his disciples remembered that it was written, the zeal of thine house hath eaten me up" (John 2:13-17).

Second, relative to enduring persecution, Paul quoted the passage from Psalms and applied it to Jesus: "For even Christ," he said, "pleased not himself; but, as it is written, The reproaches of them that reproached thee fell on me" (Romans 15:3). In this particular passage he taught that just as Christ endured the calumnies of those who calumniated God, we, too, should be willing to bear abuse for His sake.

We see from the lesson: zeal gives energy to pursue and strength to persist.

They Gave Him Vinegar and Gall

THEY gave me also gall for my meat; and in my thirst they gave me vinegar to drink. —69:21

What David called a galling and bitter experience was literally fulfilled in the Messiah, as recorded by New Testament writers:

THEY gave him vinegar to drink mingled with gall: and when he had tasted thereof, he would not drink. —Matthew 27:34

AFTER this, Jesus knowing that all things were now accomplished, that the Scripture might be fulfilled, saith, I thirst. Now there was set a vessel full of vinegar; and they filled a sponge with vinegar, and put it upon hyssop, and put it to his mouth. When Jesus therefore had received the vinegar, he said, It is finished: and he bowed his head, and gave up the ghost. —John 19:28-30

The persecutors continued their course of maliciousness, but Jesus finished his earthly course of righteousness. He could say, "It is finished": a sinless life; his ordeal for human redemption. But what could they say?

Today mockers can contemptibly hand a cup of bitters to the Lord's disciples. They can taunt them with vinegary derision and galling scorn. They can nail the Divine cause to a cross of disbelief and depravity, but what do they later say? And where do they turn?

Better Than Sacrifice

I WILL praise the name of God with a song, and will
magnify him with thanksgiving. This also shall please
the Lord better than an ox or bullock that hath horns
or hoofs. —69:30, 31

He did not say material sacrifice is unimportant or
unacceptable. He merely made a comparison. He compared formal giving to heartfelt thanksgiving and
chose the latter. He prefers the inward feeling of
the heart in preference to the precise offerings of the
hand; it is better than an ox or bullock that hath
horns and hoofs — a full grown one. And today praise
and thanksgiving are better than greenback and gold.

The Almighty has His own priorities! In this age
when money is so urgently needed in the church, let
us not forget there are things better than temporal
sacrifice:

— Thanksgiving. Stated in the text. Also, Paul
said, "Let us offer the sacrifice of praise to God continually, that is, the fruit of our lips, giving thanks
to his name" (Hebrews 13:15).

— Penitence. Mentioned in 51:16, 17.

— Mercy. "For I desired mercy, and not sacrifice"
(Hosea 6:6).

— Knowledge. "For I desired . . . the knowledge
of God more than burnt offerings (Hosea 6:6).

— Obedience. "Behold, to obey is better than sacrifice, and to hearken than the fat of rams" (I Samuel
15:22).

No one questions the propriety of sacrifice, but it's
not the whole of godliness.

Aha, Aha

LET them be turned back for a reward of their shame that say, Aha, aha. —70:3

They opened their mouth in derision, which evidently was a common sport of the wicked, often directed toward David (35:21; 40:15).

Having no argument, the fool resorts to ridicule. It gratifies the little mind and eases the anger, but it proves nothing.

The important thing is for us to live as we should and leave the reaction to others, whether it be applause or mockery. It is ours to act, theirs to react. Job, feeling this way, said, "Suffer me that I may speak; and after that I have spoken, mock on" (Job 21:3).

The grasshopper mocks the ant, but it changes nothing. When the winter comes, the little ant that stuck with his duty can say:

> *Where be your gibes now?*
> *—William Shakespeare*

What difference does it make to the little canary, if the old cat despises her singing? She can *meow* and *meow* all she likes, but the little singer still has her role to fulfill.

It is imperative that the child of God keep on working and singing to the glory of his Maker, paying no mind to the sneers of men. Let them laugh. For God will laugh last.

The Design of the Commandments

BE thou my strong habitation, whereunto I may continually resort: thou hast given commandment to save me; for thou art my rock and my fortress. —71:3

Thou hast given commandment to save me. In the commandments of the all-wise God the author of the Psalm found help and salvation. Of course, faith in the commandments lay at the bottom of his rescue.

In the struggles today with man's greatest enemy — sin — we need to recognize that God has given commandments to save us. And he who sins against them hurts himself (Proverbs 8:36). For every command of the Most High has been given to bless man: the one of restraint to Adam and Eve; the mandate to Noah to build an ark; the charge to Israel to cast off their slave chains; the Ten Commandments; and coming to the New Testament, the commands to obey the gospel, assemble for worship, respect civil law and be faithful — all are for the good of man.

Way back in Deuteronomy there is a classic statement on the purpose of the commandments:

AND the Lord commanded us to do all these statutes, to fear the Lord our God, for our good always, that he might preserve us alive, as it is at this day.
—Deuteronomy 6:24

Now that expresses it exactly: *for our good,* but more than that — for our good *always.* Keep them and good will be your fortune.

From My Youth

For thou art my hope, O Lord God: thou art my trust
from my youth. —71:5

God had been his trust and his hope from his youth
— a remarkable distinction. His defense was God.
His hope was God. In God he placed his trust.

This is what youth is seeking today: something
that gives meaning to life; something to trust; a confident relationship with a protector; hope for an otherwise dull life. Youth has to feel his way through a
maze of problems; and, in finding himself, he needs
a trust that does not waver.

Youth is a time of instruction, formation and growth.
Every hour of it trembles with destiny. It would be
tragic to twist and warp a life so soon begun as
youth. For its formation it should be given to God,
like clay is given to the potter, for His own shaping
and molding. The Scriptures bear out this suggestion:

O God, thou hast taught me from my youth: and
hitherto have I declared thy wondrous works. —ver. 17

Remember now thy Creator in the days of thy youth.
—Ecclesiastes 12:1

Unless real quality is ingrained in youth's fiber, the
years will expose him as ordinary stuff. Like cheap
cloth assumes a different appearance when washed,
he, too, will shrink and fade when later tested and
run through the wringer.

In Time of Old Age

CAST me not off in the time of old age; forsake me not when my strength faileth. —71:9

This seems to be a natural and common feeling when old age starts creeping up on people; and apparently it had started overtaking the writer, for he alluded to it again in verse seventeen, "When I am old and gray-headed." In each instance he requested, "Forsake me not."

But age has its compensations:

— Wisdom: "Days should speak, and multitude of years should teach wisdom" (Job 32:7).

— Judgment: "At 20 years of age the will reigns; at 30 the wit; at 40 the judgment," declared the wise old Benjamin Franklin.

— Experience that enhances faith and hope: "I have been young, and now am old; yet have I not seen the righteous forsaken, nor his seed begging bread" (37:25).

— Tolerance: On this behalf Goethe said, "One has to grow older to become more tolerant."

— Less pride and consequently less concern for what people think: It had this effect on Montaigne, as he stated, "I dare a little the more, as I grow older."

— The best of life:

> *Grow old along with me, the best is yet to be,*
> *the last of life for which the first was made.*
>
> *—Robert Browning*

Weakness Invites Attack

FOR mine enemies speak against me; and they that
lay wait for my soul take counsel together, saying,
God hath forsaken him: persecute and take him; for
there is none to deliver him. —71:10, 11

As seen in verse twenty, the writer had experienced
"great and sore troubles." His enemies took this to
mean that God was no longer with him and, therefore, he would be an easy captive. They thought it
was the opportune time to strike. Hit him when he
can't hit back. Pull him down when there is no one
to lift him up.

In this spirit of striking the helpless, Ahithophel
said, "Let me now choose out twelve thousand men,
and I will arise and pursue after David this night:
and I will come upon him while he is weary and weak-
handed" (II Samuel 17:1, 2).

Their eagerness to overrun the weak supports the
contention that weakness invites war, that aggressive
nations feel freer to attack the unprepared. In recognition of this overbearing spirit, George Washington
said:

*To be prepared for war is one of the
most effectual means of preserving peace.*

But the irreverent guessed wrong — God had not
forsaken the psalmist. In a vein of confidence and projection he sang, "For they are confounded, for they
are brought unto shame, that seek my hurt" (ver. 24).
Thus hardship does not prove Divine rejection. It can
be the chastening of the Lord.

A Father's Prayer for His Son

GIVE the king thy judgments, O God, and thy righteousness unto the king's son. —72:1

Many think this Psalm was written by Solomon,
but it seems more probable that it was authored by
David as a prayer for his son Solomon. Beyond its
application to its time, there is strong evidence it is
Messianic; for it accurately describes the state of
things under the reign of the Messiah.

It requests that the king's son administer justice
and righteousness to all (vers. 1, 2). This is the first
responsibility of government.

It implores God for peace (ver. 3). A reign of
quietness and security would allow the people to chase
their dreams with safety and joy.

It mentions the rights of the poor against oppressors (ver. 4). Regardless of one's station in life, he
has the right of governmental protection.

The prayer alludes to the fear of the Lord (ver. 5).
The most basic thing in law and order is the attitude
in the heart; and the greatest influence for uprightness is the fear of God, which starts man on his whole
duty (Ecclesiastes 12:13).

The reign is to be refreshing like gentle showers
on freshly mown grass (ver. 6). Liberty, freedom,
opportunity, protection — all permit this.

It is a prayer that the righteous flourish in the
abundance of peace (ver. 7)—under an excellent ruler.

Blessed Be the Name

AND blessed be his glorious name for ever: and let the whole earth be filled with his glory. Amen, and Amen. —72:19

> *All praise to Him who reigns above,*
> *In majesty supreme;*
> *Who gave His Son for man to die,*
> *That He might man redeem.*
> *Blessed be the name,*
> *Blessed be the name,*
> *Blessed be the name of the Lord.*
>
> *—W. H. Clark*

The aforegiven song is in keeping with the psalmist's admonition: "Sing unto the Lord, bless his name; show forth his salvation from day to day" (96:2).

He is the only one that doeth wondrous things: "Blessed be the Lord God, the God of Israel, who only doeth wondrous things" (ver. 18).

Because of His power over life and death, His name is blessed: "The Lord gave and the Lord hath taken away; blessed be the name of the Lord" (Job 1:21).

"Now unto the King eternal, immortal, invisible, the only wise God, be honor and glory for ever and ever. Amen" (I Timothy 1:17). May this sentiment of blessing and extolling His name frequent our lips forever.

A Narrow Escape

Bᴜᴛ as for me, my feet were almost gone; my steps had well nigh slipped. For I was envious at the foolish, when I saw the prosperity of the wicked. —73:2, 3

The writer, supposedly Asaph, had experienced a narrow escape. He acknowledged that his feet were almost gone, that his steps had well nigh slipped. The thing that underminded his security was doubt.

Doubt gripped him because he took his eye off God and looked to sinners. Envy swelled in his heart, crowding out faith. When he beheld the prosperity of the wicked, it seemed too unjust to reconcile with the acts of a just God. It was a painful experience that caused him to almost abandon his faith in the Almighty.

Later in the Psalm he confessed his mistake: "So foolish was I, and ignorant," like "a beast" devoid of reason, as stupid as a brute (ver. 22).

But in his deeper thought, while in the sanctuary, he found the answer. He had placed too much emphasis on the physical, not enough on the spiritual; and to judge the matter aright he would have to await the end (ver. 17) ; that the irreverent are in slippery places awaiting destruction (ver. 18) ; that their life is not what it seems — rather one of terrors (ver. 19).

It's the counterfeit of prosperity that costs the most.

> *Measure not the work*
> *Until the day's out and the labor done;*
> *Then bring your gauges.*
> *—Elizabeth Barrett Browning*

Does God Know?

AND they say, How doth God know? and is there
knowledge in the Most High? —73:11

This question has been asked through the centuries
by many in various circumstances. By those who
wondered why God did not intervene to alter the state
of affairs. And by those who lived in open defiance
to His restrictions.

To the sinner one of the most horrifying things is
that God knows; but to the obedient this is one of
the most consoling facts.

It is *what* God knows that makes the difference.
When one is aware that the God of heaven knows
evil about him, he may seek relief by turning toward
skepticism, or by convincing himself God is weak and
unknowledgeable. Thus his wish becomes his faith;
so he begins to question God's existence, or God's
ability to know. The fault is not in a lack of Divine
evidence but in the human heart. You can't blame
the seed when the soil is bad.

Man can wish and wish, but God can't be disposed
of by wishing He does not exist; neither will wishing hide anything from His sight. God always knows.

> *Blind unbelief is sure to err,*
> *And scan God's work in vain;*
> *God is His own interpreter,*
> *And he will make it plain.*
>
> *—William Cowper*

Say Nothing to Avoid Offense

If I say, I will speak thus; behold, I should offend against the generation of thy children. —73:15

The writer had come to grips with a perilous problem. His faith was shaken and almost abandoned after reflecting on the prosperity of the wicked in contrast with his own plagues (vers. 3, 14).

But to his credit, as seen in the text, he kept quiet about it rather than offend others. Whatever his own doubts were, he kept them to himself. He would not say anything that might lessen the believer's confidence in the Almighty.

However, most disbelievers are not content to hold their infidelity as a personal pain, but rather want to make all others miserable by robbing them of their faith.

> *Nobody talks so constantly about God as those who insist that there is no God.*
>
> *—Heywood Broun*

If God exists, there are many reasons to promote faith in Him. If he doesn't, why rob others of their hope?

Though the composer was temporarily reeling from doubts, he was approaching closer to greatness than he thought; for he had enough regard for the people to say nothing that might hurt them. This is a worthy example in every matter.

> *Surely human affairs would be happier if the power in men to be silent were the same as that to speak.*
>
> *—Benedict Spinoza*

Nearer My God

BUT it is good for me to draw near to God: I have put my trust in the Lord God, that I may declare all thy works. —73:28

It is good for me to draw near to God. Oh, how it fills my heart with acclamation!

Nearer, my God, to Thee,
Nearer to Thee!
E'en though it be a cross
That raiseth me;
Still all my song shall be,
Nearer, my God, to Thee,
Nearer to Thee.

Though like a wanderer,
The sun gone down,
Darkness be over me,
My rest a stone;
Yet in my dreams I'd be
Nearer, my God, to Thee,
Nearer to Thee.

Or, if on joyful wing
Cleaving the sky,
Sun, moon, and stars forgot,
Upward, I fly;
Still all my song shall be,
Nearer, my God, to Thee,
Nearer to Thee.

—Sarah F. Adams

This is the happiest association. The sweetest fellowship. For now. Forever.

Infamous Fame

A MAN was famous according as he had lifted up axes
upon the thick trees. —74:5

We have in this recording an outstanding example
of infamous fame. They had built up a recognition
for destruction. This is what they had done: Put Jerusalem in perpetual desolations (ver. 3). Plundered
the temple (ver. 3). Raised tumults (ver. 4). With
axes and hammers broke down the carved work —
maybe for the overlaid gold (ver. 6). Set fire to the
temple (ver. 7). Burned up the sacred meeting places
(ver. 8). Their object was to destroy Israel altogether
(ver. 8). In their brutality they violated things dear
to God and His people. They demolished the holy
with no more consideration than a woodsman with
his axe in the forest.

Their celebrity was founded on how bad they were.
Their distinction was their blackguardism. This is
the only attention they got — their degeneracy. Their
fame created itself out of something worse than nothing. For it is a thousand times better to live unac-
claimed in righteousness and finally rest in an unknown grave than to be a headliner in criminality.
When upright people are hurt and holy things are
desecrated, how barbarious is the soul.

> *Where none admire, 'tis useless to excel.*
> *—Lord George Lyttelton*

I anger to think it was fame!

For God . . .

For God is my King of old, working salvation in the midst of the earth. —74:12

With Jerusalem in ruins, the poet came up with their only recourse — God. For He who had done so much in times past would surely help them now:

— "Thou didst divide the sea by thy strength" (ver. 13). He had divided the waters of the sea for Israel's crossing (Exodus 14:13-22). For generations this had buoyed them when their spirits sank.

— "Thou breakest the heads of the dragons in the waters" (ver. 13). The dragon was a symbol of Egyptian power, but no match for the true God.

— "Thou breakest the heads of leviathan," crocodile (ver. 14). It represented Egypt's might, which was feeble compared to God.

— "Thou didst cleave the fountain and the flood: thou driedst up mighty rivers" (ver. 15), enabling them to pass over Jordan.

— "The day is thine, the night is also thine" (ver. 16). All things are under His control.

— "Thou hast prepared the light and the sun" (ver. 16). Blessings for man.

— "Thou hast set all the borders of the earth" (ver. 17). Natural boundaries.

— "Thou hast made summer and winter" (ver. 17). God fashioned the seasons. They are not an accident.

O God, our help in ages past,
Our hope for years to come.
—Isaac Watts

The Doves and the Hawks

O DELIVER not the soul of thy turtle-dove unto the multitude of the wicked: forget not the congregation of thy poor for ever. —74:19

Common expressions used today by the news media are *the doves* and *the hawks*. It may startle some to learn that they were borrowed from the Bible. The rhetoric *dove* is in the text and in the language of Jesus. And *hawk* is mentioned in this Scripture: "I will give thee unto the ravenous birds of every sort" (Ezekiel 39:4).

In the text Israel is compared to a pet dove, the mildest and softest of birds. A bird of gentleness. But there are other birds — hawks, falcons, birds of prey, attackers, known for their war-like spirit. At the least provocation they come flying in for the kill.

The warriors who tore down the holy things in Jerusalem were the hawks. They were as —

Inhuman as a hawk's cry.
—Robinson Jeffers

"Birds of a feather flock together." But the dove and the hawk are not of the same feather. They have different dispositions — and so do people.

Plead Your Cause

ARISE, O God, plead thine own cause: remember how
the foolish man reproacheth thee daily. —74:22

To put it in literal form, "Contend thine own contention." Maintain the cause that is Thine — and, of
course, Thy people's. Any attack on God's people is
actually an attack on Him. This is reason enough to
ask God to assert Himself.

The practical point for humanity is: plead your
cause. The ancients did in several ways, including a
request that God intervene.

For a cause to command the deepest loyalty it must
grip the heart as a moral matter. If you have a worthwhile cause, plead it — don't let it die — pray in its
behalf, speak to make it known, talk to sell it, sacrifice to support it and work to put it over.

Let us take courage — just average ability fully
used in a good cause can make one famous.

> *The humblest citizen of all the land, when clad
> in the armor of a righteous cause, is stronger than
> all the hosts of Error.*
> —*William Jennings Bryan*

He lives in fascination that has a valuable cause.
And beyond this —

> *He lives in fame that died in virtue's cause.*
> —*William Shakespeare*

Thanksgiving Repeated

UNTO thee, O God, do we give thanks, unto thee do
we give thanks: for that thy name is near thy wondrous
works declare. —75:1

Give thanks, give thanks — the repetition emphasizes the intense feeling in the heart. There is nothing wrong with repetition. Nature does it all the
time: the day and the night, the seasons, the rains,
the foliage and the flowers. Repetition is a way of
life for man: breathing, eating, sleeping, working;
and another of his repetitious activities should be the
giving of thanks.

It will increase our gratitude to meditate on our
blessings and express our feelings in song, as Israel
did. One of the world's favorites is:

> *O Thou fount of every blessing,*
> *Tune my heart to sing Thy grace;*
> *Streams of mercy, never ceasing,*
> *Call for songs of loudest praise.*
>
> *—Robert Robinson*

Everything grows by expression. Tell God you are
thankful. And when man blesses you, thank him. It
enhances lovability.

When Paul was in a storm-tossed ship, tossed to
and fro by a mighty hurricane, he "gave thanks to
God" (Acts 27:35). He certainly was not blessed at
the moment with all he wanted (for the storm was
raging), but he had the faith to see his blessings.
And he was thankful. When we can see our blessings
in the storm, we have made progress.

In His Hand Is Success or Failure

BUT God is the judge: he putteth down one, and setteth up another. —75:7

One of the strong supports of Israel was their faith in the presiding power of God. This Psalm expresses that conviction.

It suggests that the foolish "lift not up your horn [a symbol of strength] on high: speak not with a stiff neck" (ver. 5). Do not exalt yourself.

"For promotion cometh neither from the east, nor from the west, nor from the south" (ver. 6). Natural advantages can be thwarted and human alliances can be shaken by an overriding power. Exaltation can come from God alone. Prosperity depends more on Him above than on anything here below. Thus sometimes —

THE race is not to the swift, nor the battle to the strong. —Ecclesiastes 9:11

The most elaborate plans can fail while success can spring out of almost nothing. God can lift up one and humble another. He is the sovereign.

Believing this, then we must hold the view that neither success nor failure has to be final. Armed with this conviction, life takes on new dimensions. Therefore let us follow His counsel, do our best and trust Him for the results. This will give us the mental attitude for success; and with it will come high aiming, energetic pushing, powerful pursuing and undiminished hoping.

Drinking From His Cup

For in the hand of the Lord there is a cup, and the wine is red; it is full of mixture; and he poureth out the same: but the dregs thereof, all the wicked of the earth shall wring them out, and drink them. —75:8

This passage is in keeping with the previous one which states God "putteth down one, and setteth up another." He holds the cup from which man must drink.

The contents vary. There is the sparkling, red liquid mixed with spices to increase the quality — the better part. But there are the sediments the wicked must drink, wringing out the last murky drop. The containers were bags made of skins which lent themselves to wringing. The dregs were the strongest part of the mixture, representing the severest wrath of God (Job 21:20). This portion was handed to the wicked.

Life has its dregs for the rebellious: hardships, disappointments, smiting conscience, frustration, paralytic disbelief and hopelessness. And in those dregs the disobedient drown themselves in misery.

All of us, even Israel (Isaiah 51:17), have at times had to drink the distasteful. But one thing sure: we can renew our relationship with Him and ask for another cup.

The lesson from the dregs is a bitter one, but helpful if it teaches us to ask for another cup that we may appropriate it to our sweetest taste.

Forget the past, live the present hour,
Drink from God's cup, your blessed dower.

Rebuke

AT thy rebuke, O God of Jacob, both the chariot and the horse are cast into a dead sleep. —76:6

Rebuke is something errant man needs.

In the setting of the text the charioteers and the horsemen, two chief arms of the military, were cast into the sleep of death.

And there lay the steed with his nostril all wide,
But through it there rolled not the breath of his pride;
And there lay the rider distorted and pale,
With the dew on his brow, and the rust on his mail.

—Lord Byron

Sometimes God rebuked with *interposing actions,* as seen in the text. And there are other instances: The plagues were sent upon the Egyptians (Exodus 7-12). A storm was sent to stop the fleeing Jonah (Jonah 1:1-4). The persecuting Saul was temporarily afflicted with blindness (Acts 9:8,9).

Othertimes God rebuked with *reproaching words:* David felt the reproof of pointed rhetoric (II Samuel 12:1-7). Moses was rebuked in uncompromising terms, because he did not sanctify God in the eyes of the people (Numbers 20:11). The Pharisees were reprimanded in sharp language for their hypocrisy (Matthew 23). Peter was censured in kind words for his little faith (Matthew 14:31).

If we need rebuke, let's not "kick against the pricks." It would be foolish to break the mirror because it reveals the wrinkles. The pain of rebuke is in its need; and its helpfulness is in the correction it works.

Man's Wrath an Occasion for God's Glory

SURELY the wrath of man shall praise thee: the re-
mainder of wrath shalt thou restrain. —76:10

Man's wrath occasions the praise of God; affords an opportunity for the Divine character to display itself.

The principle is seen in everyday life: A rebellious child breaks the heart of his parents, but his obstinacy does allow their wisdom to manifest itself. A murderer or robber grieves society, but he does occasion an opportunity for the commonwealth to show its strength in the administration of protective laws.

Also in another sense, the wrath of man is used to God's glory. His universal purpose requires Him to overrule all evil to His eventual good. The Just One transmutes the rage of man into His praise. The intended malice is utilized to the unintended glory of God.

As examples: (1) The treachery of Judas was turned to human redemption. (2) Heathen nations were used to discipline God's people. (3) The persecutors in the first century were employed to scatter the believers and thus spread the gospel far and wide.

Let this suffice us still,
Resting in childlike trust upon his will,
Who moves to his great ends unthwarted by the ill.

—John Greenleaf Whittier

But let's not confuse right and wrong. Man's fury is still wrong though God uses it to accomplish His holy purpose. The deed must be judged for what it is.

Keep Your Vows

Vow, and pay unto the Lord your God: let all that
be round about him bring presents unto him that ought
to be feared. —76:11

God's people are addressed in the passage. In time
of great trouble they evidently made some vows to
Him. Vows, under the spell of aroused feelings, are
easy to make; and when some of the feelings wear
off they are easy to neglect. But a vow made in the
storm should not be forgotten in the calm.

Vows to God are not to be taken lightly:

BETTER is it that thou shouldest not vow, than that
thou shouldest vow and not pay. —Ecclesiastes 5:5

The God of all honor exhorts men not to defer in
keeping their vows, but rather to "pay that which
thou hast vowed" (Ecclesiastes 5:4).

Are you keeping your vows, the ones you made
when your life was spared, when baby was born, when
husband or wife lay at death's door, when you went
back to work?

Vows should hold us to the stronger moments when
we made them. Your vows are you; keep yourself
by keeping them.

IF a man vow a vow unto the Lord, or swear an oath
to bind his soul with a bond; he shall not break his
word, he shall do according to all that proceedeth out
of his mouth. —Numbers 30:2

Song in the Night

I CALL to remembrance my song in the night. —77:6

Here is a man in the grip of trouble who was trying to find some strength. Hence he remembered when he sang in the night — when he had a psalm that darkness could not silence. Life had its problems and the night its shadows, but he could still sing. There were favors to cheer him and brighten his view in spite of the darkness that engulfed him. Though the night was black, he saw blessings that opened his mouth with praise. And he recalled those nights with the fond hope that what *was* might become what *is*.

When the night is dark, look. Can't you see something to liven your heart? Sing on.

> *Sing on, ye joyful pilgrims:*
> *The time will not be long,*
> *Till in our Father's kingdom*
> *We swell a nobler song.*
>
> *Where those we love are waiting*
> *To greet us on the shore;*
> *We'll meet beyond the river,*
> *Where surges roll no more.*
>
> *Sing on, O blissful music!*
> *With ev'ry note you raise,*
> *My heart is filled with rapture,*
> *My soul is lost in praise.*
>
> —*Carrie M. Wilson*

A Diligent Search

I COMMUNE with mine own heart: and my spirit made diligent search. —77:6

Concerning the past and the present matter that lay before him, the author made inquiry which prompted him to ask the questions that follow (vers. 7-9):

— "Will the Lord cast off for ever?"

— "Will he be favorable no more?"

— "Is his mercy clean gone for ever?"

— "Doth his promise fail for evermore?"

— "Hath God forgotten to be gracious?"

— "Hath he in anger shut up his tender mercies?"

After making the search and communing with his own spirit, the author absolved God. He never indicted the Most High. He rather freely admitted: "This is my infirmity." Whether the infirmity in this particular usage was something to bear or something he caused, it still remains that God never brought it on; and if God is not to be blamed, then it follows that men's ills are the fruit of men's folly. It's all right to search for the source of your troubles, but be prepared for a little self-incrimination; for you may find them within yourself.

Like a Shepherd Lead Us

THOU leddest thy people like a flock by the hand of
Moses and Aaron. —77:20

In spite of some depressing circumstances connected
with the Psalm, it closes with a happy note on the
pastoral work of the Almighty. It brings sweet satisfaction to meditate on the heartening truth that God
is really the Shepherd of His people.

The sheep have their perils and need a shepherd
devoted to their care. They require direction and protection, food and water, assistance in sickness, and
a security that allows them to freely graze in the pastures by day and to soundly sleep in the fold by night.

The benedictions are many, though the conditions
are demanding. The tiresome journey to greener pastures is an ordeal, but a necessary one to obtain the
blessing. The restrictions of the fold are cramping,
but essential to the night's protection.

Flocks must be kept moving because of diminishing
food and changing seasons. Sometimes they are led
to the mountain top, but before winter starts in they
must be led back to the valleys. So we sing:

> *Savior, like a shepherd lead us:*
> *Much we need Thy tend'rest care;*
> *In thy pleasant pastures feed us,*
> *For our use Thy folds prepare.*
>
> *—Dorothy A. Thrupp*

Teaching From Generation to Generation

FOR he established a testimony in Jacob, and appointed a law in Israel, which he commanded our fathers, that they should make them known to their children: That the generation to come might know them, even the children which should be born; who should arise and declare them to their children. —78:5, 6

The writer states that from the past generation they had learned of God: "Our fathers have told us" (ver. 3). Furthermore, he declared that the fathers should teach the children, and the children, in turn, should arise and declare the Word to their children" (vers. 5, 6).

The Psalm gives these reasons for early teaching: (1) That they might know (vers. 5, 6). (2) "That they might set their hope in God" (ver. 7). (3) That they forget not "the works of God, but keep his commandments" (ver. 7). (4) That they be not "stubborn and rebellious" (ver. 8). (5) That they have a spirit "steadfast with God" (ver. 8).

A person bends more freely in youth. And what is learned well in early life becomes ingrained and a part of one's lasting being (Proverbs 22:6). Today's adults are yesterday's children who were taught — or not taught, and it shows in either case.

> *'Tis education forms the common mind:*
> *Just as the twig is bent, the tree's inclined.*
> —*Alexander Pope*

And it is the responsibility of parents to bend the twigs.

Deserters

THE children of Ephraim, being armed, and carrying bows, turned back in the day of battle. —78:9

The tribe of Ephraim was one of the large and leading tribes of Israel. They were well equipped and fully armed, but in the day of battle they turned back. They refused to stand with their brethren in the defense of the cause and the country. Favorably born, adequately armed, pledged to serve, yet when the day came to do battle they ran. What bravery in peace, what cowardice in war. What strength when it wasn't needed, what weakness when it was.

We never know our fiber until the crisis arises. The storm tests the structure and the zero hour the person.

To turn back when the going is rough, however, does not assign one to the role of a deserter forever. Peter is an example. Sometimes we rise above ourselves, other times we drop below our normal stance. This is largely what history is all about — those who fell below or climbed above, not those who stayed within the norm.

Our world is a battlefield. The war is one of ideas, morals and spiritual principles; and, like it or not, you are a soldier. Now this personal question: What kind are you? Like a child of Ephraim "who turned back in the day of battle?" Or like David who went out to meet the giant? You know the kind you should be. To run, when truth is attacked, is treason to humanity.

Compounded Sin

AND they sinned yet more against him by provoking
the Most High in the wilderness. —78:17

The cause of their multiplied sins was a lack of
faith in God (ver. 22). Though God "had commanded
the clouds from above, and opened the doors of heaven,
and had rained down manna upon them to eat, and
had given them of the corn of heaven," they still asked
such faith-lacking questions: "Can God furnish a
table in the wilderness? . . . can he give bread also:
can he provide flesh for his people" (vers. 18-24)?
The Most High had wrought streams out of the rock
and dropped manna out of heaven; He had led them
with a cloud by day and a fire by night (ver. 14);
still they doubted and "limited the Holy One" (ver. 41).

Their sin was all the greater because they had seen
and received all the more. There was a growing disbelief. Doubt is sure to "add sin to sin" (Isaiah 30:1).

"They tempted God in their heart" (ver. 18). In
a complaining and murmuring way they asked for
food more tasty, though they had manna, food fit for
angels (ver. 25).

Doubt compounds sin, increasing the payments that
must be met —

> *The sin ye do by two and two*
> *Ye must pay for one by one.*
> —*Rudyard Kipling*

But Flesh

FOR he remembered that they were but flesh; a wind that passeth away, and cometh not again. —78:39

The people of God were far from perfect. "How oft did they provoke him in the wilderness, and grieve him in the desert! Yea, they turned back, and tempted God, and limited the Holy One of Israel. They remembered not his hand . . ." (vers. 40-42).

"But he, being full of compassion, forgave their iniquity, and destroyed them not" (ver. 38). This is compassion's nature — full of pity, mercy and forgiveness. Without His forgiveness all would be doomed.

God's compassion looked beyond the deeds and beheld the fleshly nature and weakness of sinners. *He remembered that they were but flesh;* that they were human; that they were as weak as clay; that they were subject to temptation and error. He saw man as he is: no god, no angel, a fleshly creature whose spirit is willing, but whose flesh is weak (Matthew 26:41).

The God of compassion took all this into consideration — their flesh, their trials, their temptations — and accordingly forgave them. This gives us the true view of man and God. Man can sin, but God can forgive. Let us, therefore, not lose sight of the need of this realistic approach to living.

Teach me to live and find my life in Thee,
  Looking from my mistakes to the right way.
Let me not falter, but untiringly
  Press on, and gain new strength and power each day.

From the Pasture to the Throne

HE chose David also his servant, and took him from
the sheepfolds. —78:70

God sent Samuel the prophet to the house of Jessie
to anoint a king. They felt sure they had the very
one — Eliab. After looking him over, the prophet
agreed. "Surely the Lord's anointed is before him,"
he declared. A specimen to behold. But the God with
the better eyes refused to go along. He rather explained: "Look not on his countenance, or on the
height of his stature; because I have refused him:
for the Lord seeth not as man seeth; for man looketh
on the outward appearance, but the Lord looketh on
the heart" (I Samuel 16: 6-8).

Seven of the sons, one after another, passed before
Samuel and the Most High rejected them all. Could
there be an error? Are these "all thy children?" All
that have a chance, thought their father. But there
was another — the youngest who was keeping the
sheep. Well, they sent for him and, to their amaze-
ment, God said, "This is he." Though he was ruddy
and handsome, he was chosen for his heart.

Now for some moralizing: (1) When you measure
a man put the gauge to his heart. (2) Keep yourself
strong within and there's a chance for you.

> *Where I so tall to reach the pole,*
> *Or grasp the ocean with my span,*
> *I must be measured by my soul;*
> *The mind's the standard of the man.*
>
> *—Isaac Watts*

Praying Against Enemies

POUR out thy wrath upon the heathen that have not known thee, and upon the kingdoms that have not called upon thy name. For they have devoured Jacob, and laid waste his dwelling place. —79:6, 7

An attitude that has bothered some in their study of Psalms is the prayers against enemies. They have felt that they were vengeful and thus opposed to godliness. We do not wish to hide them, nor to stumble on them, but to learn the truth about them.

First, the spirit of resentment is natural in human beings when there is strong provocation. It comes easily when suffering is experienced, when honor is attacked and when religious issues dearer than life hang in the balance.

Second, bear in mind this was not a prayer of personal antagonism and revenge, but rather a plea against kingdoms or nations that had not called upon God. It was not necessarily imprecatory. It was rather an expression of intense care for the honor of God's name. Simply, it was a prayer that justice might be done which necessarily required reprimands to be meted out.

Third, it is a matter of easy logic to assume that whatever was proper for God to do was proper for man to pray. God's righteous judgment had been poured down on Israel's enemies many times. To commit the procedure to Him placed in His hand the *time* and the *how*.

Former Sins

O REMEMBER not against us former iniquities: let thy tender mercies speedily prevent us; for we are brought very low. —79:8

The American Standard Version renders the passage, "Remember not against us the iniquities of our forefathers."

One thing about sin: its effects remain around for a long time — to worry even the posterity of the sinner. That was true in this instance. The failures of their forefathers haunted them, though there was assurance the often-sinning Israel was just as often forgiven. *Forgiving* includes *forgetting*, which has always been hard for people to fully grasp. The Lord's covenant promises His forgetfulness of the sins He forgives: "I will forgive their iniquity, and I will remember their sin no more" (Jeremiah 31:34; Hebrews 8:10-12). Blessed assurance! What an uplift to be able to say, "Thou hast cast all my sins behind thy back" (Isaiah 38:17).

Their fear of punishment for the sins of their parents may have surfaced because of a feeling of their own guilt. However, if one is forgiven, he should have no guilt complex. It is to God's honor that we feel clean after being laundered in His mercy.

Furthermore, our fathers lived their lives and must answer for themselves. Now, as we live ours, let us think of our own responsibility, remembering, "The son shall not bear the iniquity of the father" (Ezekiel 18:20).

O for a Tongue That Praises

So we thy people and sheep of thy pasture will give thee thanks for ever: we will show forth thy praise to all generations. —79:13

In a conversation Peter Bohler had with Charles Wesley, he remarked, "If I had a thousand tongues I would praise Him with them all." Wesley loved the phrase and used it in writing the famous song, *O for a Thousand Tongues to Sing.* We shall give two of the verses:

> *Oh, for a thousand tongues to sing,*
> *My dear Redeemer's praise,*
> *The glories of my God and King,*
> *The triumphs of His grace!*
>
> *My gracious Master and my God,*
> *Assist me to proclaim,*
> *To spread through all the earth abroad*
> *The honors of Thy Name.*

Yes, if we had a thousand tongues, each should be dedicated to praising the name of God. This was the spirit of the psalmist.

As long as a person can see to praise and magnify the name of God, he can see his way clear to pass through a maze of trying, baffling vicissitudes. I have never known the daily praiser of God to lose his courage to pursue. A few setbacks? Yes. But in the end he triumphs. So may we, the sheep of His pasture, use the one tongue we have to praise Him forever more.

Pray All the Time

GIVE ear, O Shepherd of Israel, thou that leadest
Joseph like a flock. . . . —80:1

This simple but eloquent Psalm contains three distinct prayers, each concluding with the same thought: "Turn us again, O God, and cause thy face to shine; and we shall be saved" (vers. 3, 7, 19).

The *first* is a prayer that tenderly compares God's leadership to a shepherd that leads his flock. It beseeches Him to stir up His strength; to allow His countenance to shine upon them; and to save them. They needed to pray.

The *second* is also based on their troubles. They were a people so sorrowful they were forced to live on a diet of tears. They had strife with their neighbors and were a laughing stock in their sight. They needed to pray.

The *third* concerns God's former dealings with His people, represented by a vine that was planted, nurtured and made fruitful, but presently broken down and trampled. In this desolation they implore God to interpose, to behold and visit the needy vine, vowing to Him that if He alleviates their distress they will not turn back from Him. They needed to pray.

We have our problems, too, and the need of prayer is ever with us. Thus Vana R. Raye wrote:

> *Pray in the morning,*
> *Pray at the noontime,*
> *Pray in the evening,*
> *Pray all the time.*

Like a Vine

THOU hast brought a vine out of Egypt: thou hast cast out the heathen, and planted it. —80:8

The author used some poetic imagery in describing God's care of Israel. The vine which refers to God's people had been brought out of Egypt and planted in a new land. He had cast out the heathen to make room for the vine. The vine prospered, sending out its branches toward the Mediterranean Sea and the Euphrates River (ver. 11), the natural boundaries of the country promised to Abraham.

But the hedges which are usually around a vineyard were broken down, leaving no enclosure, exposing the grapes to be picked off by all that passed by. Wild men, compared to swine and beasts, came in and devoured it (vers. 12, 13).

In asking for Divine help, they acknowledged they were at fault: "So will not we go back from thee: quicken us, and we will call upon thy name" (ver. 18). *Will not go back from thee* — implies they had. *Will call upon Thy name* — suggests they had neglected this.

A practical lesson for us is: a vine should bear fruit; if it doesn't, it loses its right for special care and protection from the tiller. In a comparison of the disciples to branches, the Lord taught that they must bear fruit — or be severed:

EVERY branch in me that beareth not fruit he taketh away: and every branch that beareth fruit, he purgeth it, that it may bring forth more fruit. —John 15:2

Great Expectations

I AM the Lord thy God, which brought thee out of
the land of Egypt: open thy mouth wide, and I will
fill it. —81:10

The text is one of great expectations. Perhaps it
is based on a true scene of nature. The poet probably
had observed the little bird open wide its mouth to
receive food from the parent-bird.

The Psalm assured the people that they would not
be disappointed in their hope. "And I will fill it" is
the promise made to the anticipating mouth.

> *'Tis expectation makes a blessing dear*
> *—Sir John Suckling*

As you see from the text, faith in God makes you
an optimist. He that lives in hope gets ready to receive — just like a little bird.

One of the great rules of success can be stated in
one word — expectation. You don't ordinarily get what
you don't expect. So for a fuller life let us keep up
our song of anticipation:

> *Through the night of doubt and sorrow*
> *Onward goes the pilgrim band,*
> *Singing songs of expectation,*
> *Marching to the promised land.*
> *—Sabine Baring-Gould*

God Gave Them Up

So I gave them up unto their own hearts' lust. —81:12

This is one of the most tragic accounts in all the Bible. Some well-favored people had to be given up. God withdrew from them, leaving them to follow their own stubborn will in their own lust. This is frightful. A similar fate is recorded in Hosea 4:17: "Ephraim is joined to idols: let him alone." No need to offer leadership to apostates who don't want to follow.

In this case they had to be given up. Of course, God is God and man is man, which is to say that God could have forced them to obey; but this would have denied man his lofty nature and made him no more than a puppet on a string. This would not have been in humanity's interest; for if man obeys at all, he must do it through his own volition.

And it was a continual refusal to hearken that finally caused God to let them go their own way: "But my people would not hearken to my voice; and Israel would none of me (ver. 11). They would have none of God, which forced Him to have none of them. This is just the way the relationship works. He doesn't think it proper to walk with those who won't honor His company.

Even today in the church, as unpleasant as it is, we have to follow the same course of withdrawal (II Thessalonians 3:6). This is God's way.

Poor Counsel

AND they walked in their own counsels. —81:12

The first part of the verse, as seen in the previous essay, tells of a people so rebellious they had to be given up. They were allowed to do as they pleased. For in the end their own decisions rebuked them. This, however, is God's way of dealing with hardened people. Examples are numerous: (1) Israel clamored for a king and God gave them Saul (I Samuel 12). (2) The prodigal was not hindered from going into a far country (Luke 15). (3) Demas was not stopped from walking out on Paul (II Timothy 4:10).

Now we see from the text that Israel, having rejected the Divine counsel, was left with no counsel but their own. Poor counsel indeed! If their counsel had been smart, they wouldn't have given up God's instruction. Human advice — that's what they chose. You can get plenty of it free; but it won't be cheap if you follow most of it, for with every word a future will die.

They could have said a thousand times, "It's our life. We'll do as we please." Of course! But later when they had to suffer, it would have given no comfort to say, "This is our life." Yes, each has his life. And his misery. And his joy. So let's make it a life of joy and success by following God:

BECAUSE the foolishness of God is wiser than men.
—I Corinthians 1:25

It Might Have Been

Oн that my people had hearkened unto me, and Israel had walked in my ways! I should soon have subdued their enemies, and turned my hand against their adversaries . . . He should have fed them also with the finest of the wheat: and with honey out of the rock should I have satisfied thee. —81:13-16

The text gives a very human account — the story of what might have been — neglected duties, lost opportunities. Israel's enemies would have been subdued. God's people would have been fed. But they missed what they could have had because they would not hearken. Much was at stake, and they lost it because they wouldn't listen. Deaf ears have denied legions the call to opportunity, and later all they could hear was, "It might have been."

Of all the sad words
Of tongue and pen,
The saddest are these:
It might have been.

—John Greenleaf Whittier

Oh, the haunting echoes of what might have been! Countless numbers who once were so close to a better way are now following courses of failure and sorrow. Oh! had they only hearkened to a better voice! But every new day presents another chance. Thank God for it! Learn from your *might have beens*. Go out and meet the challenge of *what might be.*

Ruling in Ignorance

THEY know not, neither will they understand. —82:5

The men in the text were magistrates. They had three distinctions and all three were wrong: *didn't know;* topped by the second, *didn't know they didn't know;* and still worse, *didn't care to understand.* Their glory was in their superficiality where they unashamedly rested their honor in unwitting decisions.

> *Blind and naked Ignorance*
> *Delivers brawling judgments, unashamed,*
> *On all things all day long.*
>
> *—Alfred Tennyson*

Ignorance is a foe of justice. It's impossible to administer justice unless you have the complete facts. Judging with only a few facts is "like trying to tell what happens inside a house by watching what goes in by the door and what comes out by the chimney," declared Claude Bernard.

Though it's an official ignorance dressed in the ill-fitting clothes of an iller intelligence, it still hurts. The people want liberty, freedom and justice for all. They will swim the oceans to reach the land that offers it. And as they do, what a welcome sight is the inscription on the Statue of Liberty, New York Harbor:

> *Give me your tired, your poor,*
> *Your huddled masses yearning to breathe free,*
> *The wretched refuse of your teeming shore,*
> *Send these, the homeless, the tempest-tossed, to me:*
> *I lift my lamp beside the golden door.*

Destroying the Foundations

ALL the foundations of the earth are out of course [are shaken, A. S. V.]. —82:5

Civil injustice breaks the foundations of society: spreads bitterness; inflames disrespect for law and order; and festers anarchy in the land. History is replete with what occurs when rulers rule too fiercely.

It seems paradoxical, but injustice can occur in a democracy — especially among people not organized to be heard; for politicians have ears sensitive to the voices of organized voters. Self-serving politicians can pave their pathway to victory with special considerations for those who can turn out the votes. This can saddle some citizens with galling inequities while it gives the favored a flash-in-the-pan glee. Yes, flash-in-the-pan jubilation. For nothing can endure that is not based on honesty, fairness and justice for all.

A government red with blood will someday turn ghastly pale in death. Blood — that's life. And the sacrifice of wealth — that's also life. For it takes so much life to produce a dollar. Life can be taken on the field of labor as well as on the field of battle. One is a once- for- all sacrifice, the other a day-by-day bleeding. When government demands too much, it destroys the incentive to produce, undermines its foundations and topples its own prosperity.

Let us, therefore, hold dear the sacred view that government should exist for the benefit of the governed — not the governors.

Rulers Must Die Too

I HAVE said, Ye are gods: and all of you are children of the Most High. But ye shall die like men, and fall like one of the princes. —82:6, 7

Rulers were called "gods" because of their role in humanity's affairs. But beneath those royal robes is a mortality as fragile as the obscure peasant. The king is subject to heart failure, stroke, ruptured appendix, malignancy and all other ills, plus creeping old age, like the mass of mankind. Renown will not ease the pain of disease nor stop it from taking its toll. The pale horse with its rider called Death is galloping not far behind him as well as us.

> *Seeing that death a necessary end,*
> *Will come when it will come.*
> *—William Shakespeare*

I was more deeply impressed with man's frailty and superficial values when I visited the old home of Andrew Jackson. After going through the dwelling place of the heroic President, popularized for his stonewall courage, I went out to the family burial ground. There I stood and meditated at the grave of a man who held the highest office in the land. Then I walked over to the grave of his trusted slave. There I searched my soul as I pondered the state of man. And I thought — it doesn't make much difference when the end comes whether you are President or slave, for both must die and sleep in the same dust.

Hidden Under Thy Wings

THEY have taken crafty counsel against thy people, and consulted against thy hidden ones. —83:3

The *hidden ones* are identified in the verse as *thy people*. They were hiding "under the Shadow of the Almighty" (91:1).

There are times when we want to fly away: get away from the grind, the greed, the superficiality of a society that aches because of its self-caused pains. This craving of the soul for a place of concealment was expressed by the psalmist in beautiful language: "Oh that I had wings like a dove! for then I would fly away, and be at rest" (55:6). What we really want to get away from is not the *here* but the *strain* of what's here: however, we attain it not in geography but "in the secret place of the Most High" (91:1).

So, in the poetic wording of David, we pray: "Keep me as the apple of the eye; hide me under the shadow of thy wings" (17:8). And we sing —

> *Hide me, O my Savior, hide me*
> *In Thy holy place;*
> *Resting there beneath Thy glory,*
> *O let me see Thy face.*
> *Hide me, when the storm is raging*
> *O'er life's troubled sea;*
> *Like a dove on ocean's billows,*
> *O let me fly to Thee.*
>
> *—Fanny J. Crosby*

JEHOVAH

THAT men may know that thou, whose name alone is
JEHOVAH, art the Most High over all the earth.
—83:18

JEHOVAH — I AM, the eternal living one.

When Moses was given the command to deliver
Israel from Egyptian bondage, the Almighty made
plain to him the name that he should use in giving
the credentials of his mission: "And God said unto
Moses, I AM THAT I AM: and he said, Thus shalt
thou say unto the children of Israel, I AM hath sent
me unto you" (Exodus 3:14).

> *Tell them I AM, Jehovah said*
> *To Moses; while earth heard in dread,*
> *And smitten to the heart,*
> *At once above, beneath, around,*
> *All nature, without voice or sound,*
> *Replied, O Lord, Thou art.*
>
> *—Christopher Smart*
> *A Song to David* (1763)

Jehovah alone is the true, almighty, holy Being, a
spirit so personal that He is the father of our spirits
(Numbers 16:22).

Jehovah is the Most High. He is over all the earth.

Oh! that men knew this!

> *Ye sons of earth, in reverence bend;*
> *Ye nations, wait his nod;*
> *And bid the choral song ascend*
> *To celebrate our God.*
>
> *—H. Kirke White*

From Strength to Strength

THEY go from strength to strength, every one of them in Zion appeareth before God. —84:7

Their ardor and character were gaining strength. That's the way a child of God should develop: "Though the outward man perish, yet the inward man is renewed day by day" (II Corinthians 4:16).

Gaining strength is an inside job; each must do it within himself. For strength is largely mental. It's not the size of the dog in the fight but the size of the fight in the dog that makes the difference. So —

> *Be strong:*
> *Sing to your heart a little song.*
> *—Edwin Markham*

Victorious singing keeps the mind victoriously conditioned.

With mind made up, then give yourself to one-directional living. Go one way. For it weakens a person to be torn between this and that, chased back and forth. Be like Paul who said, "This one thing I do."

I like the way Isaiah put this matter of obtaining strength: "They that wait upon the Lord shall renew their strength" (Isaiah 40:31).

In conclusion, the way you live determines your moral and spiritual power. There's no getting around the law of cause and effect: "As thy days, so shall thy strength be" (Deuteronomy 33:25).

The Surest Superlative

For a day in thy courts is better than a thousand. I
had rather be a doorkeeper in the house of my God,
than to dwell in the tents of wickedness. —84:10

A day spent in the courts of God will do more to
bring peace and satisfaction to the soul than a thous-
and days spent in worldly indulgence, social-mixing,
honor-looking, self-seeking and money-chasing, com-
bined.

When we start reviewing the past, we find that
those days spent seeking pleasures were rather empty
and disappointing. The satisfactions we sought were
always over yonder, and when we got there they were
still over yonder. They were the fleeing mirages that
kept ahead of us.

'Tis greatly wise to talk with our past hours
And ask them what report they bore to heaven.
—Edward Young

We find peace in a relationship — not in seeking it.
The communion of our spirit with the Great Spirit,
believing in Him, hoping in Him, brings a special
delight not experienced in common pastimes.

Out of the hardness of heart and of will,
Out of the longings which nothing could fill,
Out of the bitterness, madness, and strife,
Out of myself and all I called life,
Into the having of all things with Him!
Into an ecstasy full to the brim!

Revive Us Again

WILT thou not revive us again: that thy people may rejoice in thee? —85:6

The petition, "revive us again," implies there was life, but it also suggests that their spiritual life had declined and was in need of revival. The causes of this cooling state were many; and as they were removed, the fervor of the soul would be restored.

Those people were like a countryside swept by the wintry blasts: cold, barren, in need of spring's revival. Their zeal had lost its glow. The once-burning fire within them was now just some dying embers. They had left their first love; it was no longer first.

In the plea for renewal, the poet gave this reason: "that thy people may rejoice in thee." Clearly, the joyous life is incompatible with a weak, inactive religion.

A soul-stirring awakening is needed throughout the land. Oh, the warmth, the zeal, the invigoration, if we would live in a constant revival with no changing seasons, no winter — perpetual summer. Then there would be the voice of a vibrant life, the jubilee of salvation, the song of holiness and the hallelujah of praise. Great results would follow. Needing a revival, Israel sang of it. So should we:

Revive us again: Fill each heart with Thy love;
May each soul be rekindled with fire from above.
Hallelujah! Thine the glory; Hallelujah! Amen;
Hallelujah! Thine the glory; revive us again.

—William P. Mackay

The Kiss of Reconciliation

MERCY and truth are met together; righteousness and peace have kissed each other. —85:10

The story of an unusual trial has been told. It occurred in a land that demanded unyielding penalties for the disobedience of laws. A young man who had destroyed both eyes of another was brought to trial. The law required an eye for an eye — two in this case. The trial judge was his own father, who was torn between the conflicting cries of mercy and truth. Mercy pleaded for acquittal. But truth had to be honored — his son was guilty. Finally the father-judge said, "As your judge I must uphold the law. The verdict is: two eyes must be given for the two destroyed. But, as your father, I offer one of mine to help meet the demands of justice."

Mercy and truth met together and found a way of reconciliation. They do not necessarily conflict with each other. Human governments, however, have ever had the issue of assessing the proper proportions of each.

The Divine government has no such problem; for mercy permits an escape from justice—because change occurs in the heart of the offender, and this is what God wants. So in what seems to be an estrangement and alienation between mercy and truth, God unites them and, like alienated friends kiss when reconciled, they, too, kiss for they have been brought together in the loveliness and beauty of unity.

Utterances of a Distressed Soul

Bow down thine ear, O Lord, hear me: for I am poor
and needy . . . . —86:1

Here are the earnest utterances of the trustful but
distressed poet, as expressed in the Psalm:

— "O Lord, hear me." And he believed God would.
"Thou wilt answer me," he confidently stated.

— "I am poor and needy." But the poorer the state
of man, the richer can be the mercy of God.

— "Preserve my soul." The Creator is also the
Preserver. "O thou preserver of men" (Job 7:20).

— "Save thy servant that trusteth in thee." For "none
of them that trust in him shall be desolate" (34:22).

— "Be merciful unto me." He asked that his unworthiness be disregarded. This was a common request for the psalmist; and rightly, for "the Lord is
very pitiful, and of tender mercy" (James 5:11).

— "I cry unto thee daily." The cry of the mouth
was merely the echo of the heart's need.

— "Rejoice the soul of thy servant." He pleaded
that sorrow and anxiety be replaced with joy and peace.

So trust, faint heart, thy Master!
He doeth all things well,
He loveth more than heart can guess
And more than tongue can tell.

The Incomparable God

AMONG the gods there is none like unto thee, O Lord; neither are there any works like unto thy works. —86:8

A comparison of the one God to false gods was only an accommodation to the superstitions of men — not that they exist, except in the misconceptions of men. In a land where many people were devoted to heathen gods, the poet paid tribute to the true God by stating, "there is none like unto thee":

— "For thou, Lord, art good" (ver. 5).

— "Ready to forgive" (ver. 5).

— "Thou wilt answer me" (ver. 7).

— "A God full of compassion" (ver. 15).

— "Plenteous in mercy and truth" (ver. 15).

— "Thou art great" (ver. 10).

— "Doest wondrous things" (ver. 10).

— "Thou art God alone" (ver. 10).

For there is "one God and Father of all, who is above all," uncaused, invisible, spiritual, described in one word — *love*. He is not limited to the do-nothing role of the so-called gods. What men call gods are not gods. They are not self-existent, all-knowing, all-powerful beings. They are only man-made, and to serve them is idolatry.

Gods fade, but God abides and in man's heart
Speaks with the clear unconquerable cry
Of energies and hopes that cannot die.

—John Addington Symonds

Unite My Heart

TEACH me thy way, O Lord; I will walk in thy truth: unite my heart to fear thy name. —86:11

A few years ago a man came to my office for consultation. He bore all the signs of a distraught, desperate creature. His skin was tormented with a nervous rash. His eyes showed loss of sleep. His voice was unsteady. His hands were shaky. After conversing for a while, I said, "Your trouble is a divided heart. You are trying to follow two ways of life that completely contradict each other. You have too much conscience to do wrong, but not enough consecration to do right. You can't have two masters in the same heart. *No man can serve two masters* is an incontrovertible principle of happiness and success. By making God the master-passion of your heart, you can pull your shattered life together. In fact, this is the only satisfactory remedy for the contradictions and rivalries that now rage within you.

"Your problem is as old as man — and as human. Many great men have suffered the pain that is yours, including David. You can learn from him. You should pray his prayer (we turned and read from Psalms): *unite my heart to fear thy name.* And you should live as you pray. You will never have peace and security until you unify your heart."

This is the remedy — single heart, single eye — for many of humanity's frustrations. Our Lord taught it:

IF therefore thine eye be single, thy whole body shall be full of light. —Matthew 6:22

The Divine Count

THE Lord shall count, when he writeth up the people,
that this man was born there. —87:6

God would honor those born in Zion (vers. 5, 6).
When a census of the people was taken or an enroll-
ment was made, those whose birthplace was Zion would
be given special distinction.

Some practical truths from the text are:

*First, there is great distinction for those born into
his church,* the spiritual Jerusalem. It is God's house
or family — "the house of God, which is the church
of the living God" (I Timothy 3:15) — and we are
born into it, born again, which is an absolute requirement of this preferential recognition (John 3:3). In
this we enjoy a nobility of birth — neither degener-
ates nor improves by ancestors — that is strictly personal. Truly, to nobly live and nobly die befits such
a noble birth.

Second, God is interested in counts. Luke recorded
that 3,000 were added to the church in one day (Acts
2:41), and that a few days later the number jumped
to 5,000 men (Acts 4:4). We should never depreciate
numbers when they apply to people, for every person
is an invaluable number.

*Third, God does have a personal and complete know-
ledge of His people.* God's "book of life" is the spiritual
biography of us all (Revelation 3:5).

So when the saints go marching in may we be
among that number.

The Most Mournful Psalm

O LORD God of my salvation, I have cried day and night before thee . . . for my soul is full of troubles: and my life draweth nigh unto the grave. I am counted with them that go down into the pit: I am as a man that hath no strength. Thou hast laid me in the lowest pit, in darkness, in the deeps. Thy wrath lieth hard upon me, and thou hast afflicted me . . . Thou hast put away mine acquaintance far from me; thou hast made me an abomination unto them . . . Mine eye mourneth by reason of affliction . . . while I suffer thy terrors I am distracted . . . They came round about me daily . . . they compassed me. —88

This Psalm has been called the most mournful of the Psalms, the saddest of all. The poet — we are not certain who he was — expected to die, but didn't anticipate it. His heart was filled with gloom, showing no consolation.

It is unlike the most of the Psalms which relate to sickness and sorrow, defeat and disappointment, in that they generally end with a ray of hope, a cheerful note and a triumphant rhetoric. But not this one. Yet the author held on. He prayed daily. In all his troubles he recognized the hand of God. His faith carried him onward as he kept his pace to the grave.

Art is long, and Time is fleeting,
And our hearts, though stout and brave,
Still, like muffled drums, are beating
Funeral marches to the grave.

—Henry Wadsworth Longfellow

Distracted

I Am afflicted and ready to die from my youth up:
while I suffer thy terrors I am distracted. —88:15

Some severe ailment had racked the poet's body for
years. His trouble and affliction had been of long
continuance — "ready to die from my youth up." His
strength was nearly gone. He didn't think he could
endure much longer. Moving toward death, he was
tormented with terrors. He was afraid.

Beset with fears, he said, "I am distracted." Exhausted. Bewildered. It was hard to pursue a normal,
settled course of straight thinking because he was possessed with fears. He was the victim of contending feelings. Composure was gone and so was clear thinking.

The death bed is not the best place to weigh the
claims of religion, or to write wills, or to reconcile
any of the differences of life. The better time is in
the vigor of health when the mind is sharp and the
thinking is clear. Then when sickness comes and
your thinking is impaired, you wll have nothing to
do but to enjoy the comfort of a long and faithful
life spent in God's service and the anticipation of a
better tomorrow—immortality. And as the end draws
nearer, you can confidently answer, "Must I go?" with
the hope, "Let me go."

> *O Captain! my Captain!*
> *My fearful trip is done!*
> *The ship has weather'd every rock,*
> *The prize we sought is won.*
>
> *—Walt Whitman*

God Is Faithful

WITH my mouth will I make known thy faithfulness to all generations. —89:1

As I awoke this morning, the sun was just peeping over the eastern hills. Enthralled in the quiet splendor of a new dawn, my soul exclaimed, "God is faithful."

The day wore on and clouds formed in the heavens. As I cast my eyes toward them, I surveyed in ecstasy the beautiful multi-colored rainbow, and I thought of what it symbolizes—the covenant God made with man that he would never send another flood—then my mouth whispered the praise of my heart, "God is faithful."

A bird flew by and I was reminded: "Your heavenly Father feedeth them. Are ye not much better than they" (Matthew 6:26)? And I said, "God is faithful."

Later in the day I wrote a letter and dated it with an A.D. date, in the year of our Lord, which marks the fulfillment of God's promise to send the world a Redeemer. And in the deepest gratitude my lips praised Him, "God is faithful."

Night came on and I looked into the heavens and was lifted by the beauty of a million stars twinkling in their glory. Then I recalled the power that keeps them in orbit — the word of God (II Peter 3:7) — and my whole being sought expression in the utterance: "God is faithful."

Then, as the closing thought for the day, I asked myself the question, "Am I?"

Fearing God the Right Way

GOD is greatly to be feared in the assembly of the saints, and to be had in reverence of all them that are about him. —89:7.

The fear that is enjoined upon man is not the ordinary fear — terror, horror, fright and dread. "God hath not given us the spirit of fear; but of power, and of love, and of a sound mind" (II Timothy 1:7). The fear we should have of God is a constructive fear — reverence, awe and respect. The Bible states that we should "serve God acceptably with reverence and godly fear" (Hebrews 12:28); however the words "godly fear" are rendered "awe" in the American Standard Version. Hence the fear we should have is:

— The awe of God's greatness.
— The reverence of His name.
— The veneration of His authority.
— The temper that prefers to please Him.
— The submission to His will.
— The adoration that bows in worship.

In the command to fear God it was not intended that man be terrorized at the thought of Him; for man is also commanded to love God, which is not compatible with fright. For "perfect love casteth out fear" (I John 4:18). The fear of God and the love of God complement each other, and as they enlarge in the heart they give power to religion by providing the motives for the closest walk with God.

How Short Is My Time

REMEMBER how short my time is: wherefore hast thou made all men in vain? —89:47

Life is brief. "Man that is born of a woman is of few days" (Job 14:1). And those few pass so quickly. Time moves on crutches only for youth; a little later it takes to the jets. So there's not but one reasonable conclusion —

MAKE HASTE TO LIVE

Make haste, O man! to live,
For thou so soon must die;
Time hurries past thee like the breeze;
How swift its moments fly.
Make haste, O man! to live.

Make haste, O man! to do
Whatever must be done;
Thou hast no time to lose in sloth,
Thy day will soon be gone.
Make haste, O man! to live.

The useful, not the great,
The thing that never dies;
The silent toil that is not lost,
Set these before thine eyes.
Make haste, O man! to live.

Make haste, O man! to live.
Thy time is almost o'er;
Oh! sleep not, dream not, but arise,
The Judge is at the door.
Make haste, O man! to live.

Blessed Thoughts of God

Lord, thou . . . . —90:1-4

We have in this Psalm some of the loftiest theological concepts — blessed thoughts of God:

His personal relation to man: "Thou hast been our dwelling place in all generations" (ver. 1). "For in him we live, and move, and have our being" (Acts 17:28). It would make no sense to have an impersonal God; the thesis that He exists requires a second — that we live in Him.

God's almighty power: "Thou ... formed the earth and the world" (ver. 2). There had to be a super power behind creation, for it couldn't have created itself.

His eternal existence: "Even from everlasting to everlasting, thou art God" (ver. 2). He is a self-existent Being, uncaused, unchangeable. He "was set up from everlasting, from the beginning, or ever the earth was" (Proverbs 8:23).

His rulership: "Thou turnest man . . ." (ver. 3). It's a natural role for God to rule man.

God's timelessness: "A thousand years in thy sight are but as yesterday when it is past" (ver. 4). To Him who always existed and always will, how could it be otherwise? Time for Him will not run out.

> *One thought I have — my ample creed,*
> *So deep it is and broad,*
> *And equal to my every need —*
> *It is the thought of God.*
>
> *—Frederick Lucian Hosmer*

Our Fleeting Years

THE days of our years are threescore years and ten;
and if by reason of strength they be fourscore years,
yet is their strength labor and sorrow; for it is soon
cut off, and we fly away. —90:10

This is a melancholic meditation on the fewness of man's years. Threescore. By reason of strength, fourscore. But whether the strength is little or much, "it is soon cut off, and we fly away." Our years are like a passing shadow; a fleeting breath; the folding of a shepherd's tent — time to move on.

> *God stands winding His lonely horn,*
> *And time and the world are ever in flight.*
> *—William B. Yeats*

Consequently, it was incumbent upon the psalmist to exhort: "So teach us to number our days, that we may apply our hearts unto wisdom" (ver. 12). Fill our days with the best and worthiest living. Therefore it is fitting that we ask ourselves —

> *Out of eternity*
> *This new day is born;*
> *Into eternity*
> *At night will return.*
>
> *Here hath been dawning*
> *Another blue day;*
> *Think; wilt thou let it*
> *Slip useless away?*
>
> *—Thomas Carlyle*

Pray for Your Work

ESTABLISH thou the work of our hands upon us; yea, the work of our hands establish thou it. —90:17

This portion of the Psalm invoked the favor of God upon their plans and purposes. It was a prayer of the heart that accompanied the work of the hands. The repetition of the request indicates how intense the feeling was.

In rebuilding the walls of Jerusalem, the builders prayed as well as worked. "The people had a mind to work" and a mind to pray: "we made our prayer unto our God" (Nehemiah 4:6, 9). The two powers that raise walls, tame wildernesses, erect cities, ascend heights and enlarge the kingdom of God are work and prayer.

When you work and pray, there is the combination of man's labor and God's help. This is enough.

"But is my work worthy of praying the blessings of God upon it?" you ask. Does it sustain your family? Does it help others? Does it aid the cause of God? If the answer is "Yes" to any of the questions, then you should work hard and pray much.

> *Sing, pray, and swerve not from your work;*
> *But do thine own part faithfully;*
> *Trust his rich promises of grace,*
> *So shall they be fulfilled in thee.*
>
> —*George Neumarck*

My God

My God; in him will I trust. —91:2

One of the high and blessed attainments is to be able to say in the language of the author, "My God." There is a special significance attached to what we call our own. There is always more preciousness in anything that is ours. Oh! the depth of meaning and the far-flung value in those two priceless words, "My God." The open profession. The closeness. The deep trust. The spirituality. The security.

Take note of the charm with which others used the expression: (1) Nehemiah — "Think upon me, my God, for good" (Nehemiah 5:19). (2) Isaiah — "My soul shall be joyful in my God" (Isaiah 61:10). (3) Jesus — "My God, my God, why hast thou forsaken me" (Matthew 27:46)? (4) Thomas — "My Lord and my God" (John 20:28).

The utterance, "My God," does not mean I have exclusive possession of Him. Yet He is mine, like this country is mine, though it belongs also to others. From the viewpoint of ownership, He owns me — not that I own Him. For "whatsoever is under the whole heaven is" His (Job 41:11). Knowing this, knowing He is mine and I am His, my soul declares —

All that I have or am
Is wholly Thine,
So is my soul at peace,
For Thou art mine.

Protected by the Angels

For he shall give his angels charge over thee, to keep thee in all thy ways. They shall bear thee up in their hands, lest thou dash thy foot against a stone. —91:11, 12

Satan quoted this passage when he tempted Christ, urging Him to fling Himself down from the pinnacle of the temple (Matthew 4:5, 6). Satan applied the Psalms text to that occasion, but Jesus didn't for He didn't jump. While the Bible teaches aid by the angels, it does not teach that man should allow Satan to interpret the occasion and the extent. Satan is hardly a correct interpreter of Scripture; rather his skill is in interpreting Scripture to his own purpose.

The devil can cite Scripture for his purpose.
—William Shakespeare

Since man is "a little lower than the angels" (Psalms 8:5), then the angels are in a higher position than man.

They are the "ministering spirits" of God (Hebrews 1:14).

As the servants of God, they feel a deep interest in man. Thus the Saviour says, "There is joy in the presence of the angels of God over one sinner that repenteth" (Luke 15:10).

God Blesses Those Who Love Him

BECAUSE he hath set his love upon me .... —91:14-16

Jehovah is the speaker. He states the blessings He will grant to the person who loves Him, namely:

— "Deliver him" from evil (ver. 10). Individually, each needs some kind of deliverance.

— "I will set him on high." Exalt him. Honor him. God smiles on those who love Him.

— "He shall call upon me, and I will answer him." Prayer is a privilege not everyone enjoys for spiritual reasons. Only the person who loves God has the Divine promise that God will answer — not always as he asks, but ever in the way that is best.

— "I will be with him in trouble." There will be trouble, but God will be with him when it comes.

— "With long life will I satisfy him." This is very understandable. The life prescribed by true religion — calmness, moderation, temperance, faithful industry and freedom from excesses — contributes to health and longer days.

— "Show him my salvation." The previously mentioned blessings are temporal, but this one is spiritual, reaching beyond the grave, for now and for ever.

Oh! the triumph of loving God!

If I truly love the One,
All the loves are mine;
Alien to my heart is none
And life grows Divine.

How Great Are Thy Works

O LORD, how great are thy works! and thy thoughts
are very deep. A brutish man knoweth not; neither
doth a fool understand this. —92:5, 6

Something great is going on. Are we observant
enough to see it? Do we have the faith to recognize
the power behind the greatness? And the gratitude
to praise God for it?

The grandeur and enormity of His works overwhelm
us, and though we meditate on them the longest and
the fullest we're still just primary students forced to
say, "Thy thoughts are very deep." Too deep for
complete comprehension. They have a vastness and
eternity that swallow up man's littleness and tem-
porality. Job's question is still only rhetorical: "Canst
thou find out the Almighty unto perfection?" (Job
11:7). But I don't have to fully understand Him to
appreciate Him, no more than a child has to know
all about cake to like it.

His works are beyond my perfect comprehension,
but I do understand their source and appreciate them.
This is something "a brutish man knoweth not."
"Neither doth a fool understand this." The stupid
man, like the brute, does not have the rationality to
relate creation to Divinity. Stupefied by sin, his concept
of the marvelousness of God's counsels and works is
very minimum. But whether a person sees it or not —

There lives and works a soul in all things,
And that soul is God.

—William Cowper

Fruit in Old Age

THEY shall bring forth fruit in old age. —92:14

This is encouraging. Beautiful. Years of industry, sobriety, temperance and sound thinking form a fruitful way of life that is not apt to be broken by just some birthdays. There is, of course, a lessening of physical strength, but it is offset by the enhancement of other powers (II Corinthians 4:16).

As a rule, the generals are older men; so are bank presidents and executives of other large businesses. Furthermore, age is a qualification of bishops or elders in the church. Age must have something going for it. God thinks so; and so does man. The people demand maturity, seasoning, experience and wisdom of the person who fills the most responsible job — they don't care if he is no longer able to triumph in football or to win the mile race in a track meet. They want something from his mind and heart; and they feel that the years enrich both. And they are right!

WITH aged men is wisdom, and in length of days understanding. —Job 12:12

He who gets wiser with time qualifies himself to bring forth a special fruit in old age.

For age is opportunity no less
Than youth itself, though in another dress,
And as the evening twilight fades away
The sky is filled with stars invisible by day.

God's Testimonies Are Sure

THY testimonies are very sure. —93:5

All of God's testimonies are true: every word He spoke, every command He gave, every promise He made and every prophecy He uttered. And in their surety they:

Make the simple wise: "The testimony of the Lord is sure, making wise the simple" (19:7).

> *The Bible is an invaluable and inexhaustible mine of knowledge and virtue.*
> —*John Quincy Adams*

Rejoice the heart: "The statutes of the Lord are right, rejoicing the heart" (19:8).

Enlighten the eyes: "The commandment of the Lord is pure, enlightening the eyes" (19:8).

Warn man: "Moreover by them is thy servant warned" (19:11).

Restrict man: " . . . nor walked in his law, nor in his statutes, nor in his testimonies" (Jeremiah 44:23).

Bless those that keep them: "Blessed are they that keep his testimonies" (119:2).

In a society of imperfect and changeable people, it is heartening to have something sure and certain — the testimonies of God, our heritage forever (119:111). And when we near the journey's end may we be able to repeat this blessed expression: "I have stuck unto thy testimonies" (119:31).

Holiness in God's House

HOLINESS becometh thine house, O Lord, for ever.
—93:5

Holiness is cleanness on the inside, without which no dimming of lights, or bowing in prayer, or retiring in solitude or keeping quiet will make a person that way.

Holiness should prevail in the house of God. There truth should be the cardinal distinction and righteousness the dominant influence. God's house should be free of corruption, worldliness, politics, pride, ostentation, respect of persons, hate and hypocrisy. Sincerity and purity should characterize those within it.

Let us bear in mind, we get the crowd we appeal to. Appeal to those who prefer vaudeville and that's what you get — but not for long, for you are not good enough actors to hold them. But contrariwise, appeal to the spiritual and you get them — and their continued support, for you are appealing to the heart.

Since people become like what they worship and how they worship, this is God's plan for man:

WORSHIP the Lord in the beauty of holiness.
—I Chronicles 16:29

So this is our prayer:

Take my life and let it be
Consecrated, Lord, to Thee.
Take my moments and my days;
Let them flow in ceaseless praise.

—Frances Ridley Havergal

Self-evident Logic

UNDERSTAND . . . when will ye be wise? —94:8-10

The religion of God is founded on reason. Here are some questions that prove it:

— "He that planteth the ear, shall he not hear" (ver. 9)? That makes sense.

— "He that formed the eye, shall he not see" (ver. 9)? A study of the structure of the eye impresses us with the skill and power of its Creator. It is not possible that the God who gave man vision is lacking in that quality.

— "He that chastiseth the heathen, shall not he correct" (ver. 10)? Surely He who rebukes and controls the nations corrects and reproves the individual for sin.

— "He that teacheth man knowledge, shall not he know" (ver. 10)? God had to possess intelligence, truth and wisdom, or it could not have come from Him. He knows what's going on — even in the hearts of men (ver. 11).

As these questions argue for a wise, powerful and personal God, our hearts resound in holy praise —

> *Among so many can He care?*
> *Can special love be everywhere?*
> *A myriad homes — a myriad ways —*
> *And God's eye over every place?*
> *I asked; my soul bethought of this:*
> *In just that very place of His*
> *Where He hath put and keepeth you,*
> *God hath no other thing to do.*
>
> *—Adeline Dutton Train Whitney*

Rest From Adversity

BLESSED is the man whom thou chastenest, O Lord,
and teachest him out of thy law; that thou mayest
give him rest from the days of adversity. —94:12, 13

Blessed or happy is the person who understands
God's plan of ups and downs; who knows that our
earthly stay requires some "bread of adversity and
water of affliction" (Isaiah 30:10); who understands
that —

Prosperity is not without many fears and dis-
tastes; and adversity is not without comforts and
hopes.

—Francis Bacon

When a person is strengthened with the positive
view, engendered by God's teachings on reverses, then
when trouble abounds he will have the hope to be
calm and the confidence to continue. Reverses are
easier to take when we realize they can be the means
to a higher end.

Sweet are the uses of adversity,
Which, like the toad, ugly and venomous,
Wears yet a precious jewel in his head.

—William Shakespeare

Thus every setback must be judged in the light of how
it affects us.

Whatever your trouble is, it will pass. And oh! the
rest from adversity, how sweet it will be! And just
as the winter beautifies the spring, so adversity will
sweeten your prosperity.

When I Was Slipping

UNLESS the Lord had been my help, my soul had almost dwelt in silence. When I said, My foot slippeth; thy mercy, O Lord, held me up. —94:17, 18

If it had not been for God: for God's guidance to direct, for God's promise to sustain, for God's comfort to cheer and for God's mercy to rescue, the poet would have fallen. He had been in a slippery place and had almost lost his balance. A little longer and he would not have been able to stand. If relief had not come, he would have gone down to the grave of silence. But, in that threatening hour, the mercy of God held him up.

In a similar statement the author said, "I had fainted, unless I had believed to see the goodness of the Lord in the land of the living" (27:13). His belief saved him from despair — they never fill the same heart.

How frail is man without the help of God. How invincible he is with it. So in traversing the slippery ground let us:

— Believe in God (I John 5:4).

— Watch and pray (Matthew 26:41).

— Draw nigh to God (James 4:8).

— Hide the Word in our heart (119:11).

And that gives security.

No Fellowship

SHALL the throne of iniquity have fellowship with thee, which frameth mischief by a law? —94:20

The question is an emphatic negative — No! God does not sit on thrones with the rulers of iniquity. The oppressors of mankind do not have His fellowship. They frame laws to further mischief. They condemn the innocent blood (ver. 21). Consequently, God shall make them to fall into the snare of "their own iniquity, and shall cast them off in their own wickedness" (ver. 23).

Here are some other pertinent questions (II Corinthians 6:14-17):

"What fellowship hath righteousness with unrighteousness?"

"What communion hath light with darkness?"

"What concord hath Christ with Belial?"

"What part hath he that believeth with an infidel?"

"What agreement hath the temple of God with idols?"

None! So "come ye out from among them, and be ye separate, saith the Lord."

As seen, fellowship requires more than association, more than contact; it requires unity, unity of beliefs, unity of aims. "Can two walk together, except they be agreed" (Amos 3:3)? This is the prerequisite of fellowship — agreement, like views, like goals. And this unity of spirits with God and with others is one of earth's sweetest joys.

O Come Let Us Worship

O COME, let us worship and bow down: let us kneel before the Lord our maker. For he is our God; and we are the people of his pasture, and the sheep of his hand. —95:6, 7

The text gives two reasons for worship: (1) God is man's maker — it is natural for a product to laud its maker. (2) Man is the tended being of God — "we are the people of his pasture, and the sheep of his hand." These are sufficient reasons to incite within him the feelings of praise.

It is as innate for man to worship as it is to breathe. For he has a spirit that craves communion with the Great Spirit. As a spirit being, *he will worship.* His nature leads him to bow before a superior being. The history of the races is the history of this feeling, however blindly it may have expressed itself. Man's thirst within his soul finds satisfaction only in the worship of God:

MY soul thirsteth for God, for the living God: when shall I come and appear before God? —42:2

Possessed with this urgency to worship, we further say:

When all Thy mercies, O my God,
My rising soul surveys,
Transported with the view, I'm lost
In wonder, love and praise.

—Joseph Addison

Harden Not Your Heart

TODAY if ye will hear his voice, harden not your heart,
as in the provocation, and as in the day of temptation
in the wilderness. —95:7, 8

Paul not only quoted this passage, he attributed its
source to the Holy Spirit: "Wherefore as the Holy
Ghost saith, To-day if ye will hear his voice, harden
not your hearts, as in the provocation . . ." (Hebrews 3:7, 8). "The Holy Ghost saith" — not man!
Thus the New Testament writer placed the stamp of
inspiration on Psalms. It's an inspired message — not
human folklore.

Today! The commands of God relate to the present.
They are too important to be postponed.

Harden not your heart. It's an act of man. And
there are many ways it is produced: (1) Refusing
the call of God hastens the petrifying process. (2)
Man's every effort to have his own way firms the mind
in false reasoning. (3) Every doubt sets up the harden-
ing action. (4) Resisting right dulls the sensitivity
and makes it easier the next time. (5) Trying to
justify wrong sears the conscience a little deeper.
(6) When deceived by sin the heart is stripped of
feeling. (7) A heart that beats only for self hardens
a little with every throb. And (8) a heart that is
filled with hate, how like iron it becomes.

> *Hate-hardened heart, O heart of iron.*
> *—Marianne Moore*

From Day to Day

SING unto the Lord, bless his name; show forth his salvation from day to day. —96:2

From day to day is God's plan for man. It is simple. All that is required of man is to do his duty daily. It's a plan for the *now*. One of constancy. One of practicality. One of appropriation.

Every day presents its opportunities — seize them.

Each day brings its responsibilities — shoulder them.

Every day showers its blessings — thank God for them.

Each day brings us closer to the end — don't look back.

Life is wrapped up in today. Now is the time to be good and happy.

"Sufficient unto the day," was the theme of the Master Teacher.

> *Tomorrow — oh, 'twill never be,*
> *If we should live a thousand years!*
> *Our time is all today, today.*
>
> *—James Montgomery*

So this is our prayer —

> *Only today is mine,*
> *And that I owe to Thee;*
> *Help me to make it Thine;*
> *As pure as it may be;*
> *Let it see something done,*
> *Let it see something won,*
> *Then at the setting sun*
> *I'll give it back to Thee.*
>
> *—Henry Burton*

The Righteous Judgment

HE shall judge the people righteously —96:10

Justice Gray of the Supreme Court once said in a lower court to a man who would have been sentenced, except for a technicality: "I know that you are guilty and you know it, and I wish you to remember that one day you will stand before a better and wiser Judge, and there you will be dealt with according to justice and not according to law."

How assuring to the people of God! How frightening to those who are not!

God the Creator, God the Provider, is also God the Righteous Judge, better and wiser than man. He is the all-pure, never-corruptible, all-knowing, all-merciful Judge of souls. "He shall judge the world with righteousness, and the people with his truth" (ver. 13).

Judgment Day will be a day of great rejoicing for the people of God, rewarding time, the crowning day—

HENCEFORTH there is laid up for me a crown of righteousness, which the Lord, the righteous judge, shall give me at that day: and not to me only, but unto all them also that love his appearing. —II Timothy 4:8

It will be the day for which we have lived to hear Him say, "Well done, good and faithful servant . . . enter thou into the joy of thy lord" (Matthew 25:23).

They That Serve Graven Images

CONFOUNDED be all they that serve graven images, that boast themselves of idols: worship him all ye gods. —97:7

Confounded be the idolaters. Let them be ashamed. Let them be disappointed. Let them learn that their idols are not real gods. May their boasting be in vain.

The heathen had their idols; but the people of God at times have also drifted into idolatry. The Israelites once made a golden calf and said, "These are thy gods, O Israel, which brought thee up out of the land of Egypt" (Exodus 32:8). Of course, they knew the golden calf which could not walk did not bring them out of Egypt, for it says in the fifth verse that they made "a feast to the Lord." So the calf was only a symbol of deity; nevertheless Paul called it idolatry (I Corinthians 10:7).

Then why did the people resort to image-making? Because they wanted a concrete manifestation of the prototype. Man thinks it is difficult to remain close to a being he cannot see with the naked eye; therefore he creates some symbol to represent the being. But this is not needed, for our relationship to God is one of faith, not of sight (II Corinthians 5:7).

The Ten Commandments forbid the making and worshiping of images:

THOU shalt not make unto thee any graven image, or any likeness of any thing that is in heaven above, or that is in the earth beneath, or that is in the water under the earth: Thou shalt not bow down thyself to them, nor serve them. —Exodus 20:4, 5

Gladness for the Upright

LIGHT is sown for the righteous, and gladness for the
upright in heart. —97:11

I have never heard of a School of Happiness; yet
we evidently can be taught some principles that help
us to develop gladness, for the Bible gives them — and
surely to some avail.

The righteous person sows for himself a harvest of
joy. It will spring up and thrive around him. "For
whatsoever a man soweth, that shall he also reap"
(Galatians 6:7). The happy people are reaping what
they have sown.

Sow the seed of thinking you are happy. "For as
he thinketh in his heart, so is he" (Proverbs 23:7).

> *No man can be happy who does not think him-*
> *self so; for it signifies not how exalted soever your*
> *station may be, if it appear to you bad.*
>
> *—Lucius Annaeus Seneca*
> 8 B.C.-A.D. 65

Sow the seed of righteousness. It gives an approving conscience. "And herein do I exercise myself, to
have always a conscience void of offense toward God,
and toward men" (Acts 24:16).

Sow the seed of trust. It produces optimism. "The
righteous shall be glad in the Lord, and shall trust
in him" (64:10).

Sow the seed of helpfulness. It brings satisfaction.
We find happiness by taking an interest in people. "It
is more blessed to give than to receive" (Acts 20:35).

Our Marvelous God

O SING unto the Lord a new song; for he hath done marvelous things. —98:1

The story goes that a king in the Orient once set before his three sons three sealed urns, one of gold, the second of amber and the third of clay. He asked them to pick the one that appeared to contain the greatest treasure. The eldest chose the golden vase whereon was written "Empire." When he opened it he beheld it full of blood. The second chose the vessel of amber on which was written "Glory." He opened it and found it full of the ashes of men who had only made names for themselves. The third son selected the vessel of clay which had the word "God" engraved on the bottom. Within it was a single Scripture: "Which doeth great things and unsearchable; marvelous things without number" (Job 5:9). The wise men in the king's court voted the third was the most valuable, basing their decision on the belief that it contained the whole of everything that is precious and priceless.

How right they were!

Everything about God is marvelous: His self-existence. His omnificence. His omnivision. His omnipotence. His love. His mercy. His forgiveness.

To think upon His marvelous works inspires within us a new song: a song of praise and thanksgiving.

In all eternity no tone can be so sweet
As where man's heart with God in unison doth beat.
                        —Johannes Scheffler

Let the Whole Creation Praise Him

MAKE a joyful noise unto the Lord, all the earth: make a loud noise, and rejoice, and sing praise . . . Let the sea roar, and the fulness thereof; the world, and they that dwell therein, let the floods clap their hands: let the hills be joyful together before the Lord.
—98:4-9

Let there be one grand and continuous chorus of praise to the glorious God. May the saints declare His glory from pole to pole and from shore to shore. May everything in nature — the heavens, the snow-capped mountains, the green valleys, the roaring seas, the sparkling dewdrops, the singing birds, the flashing lightning, the desert sands, the quiet dawn and the golden sunset — shout the praise of the Creator.

It was customary in a mountainous country, as the sun was going down, for a man on one of the peaks to loudly shout through his horn, "Praise ye the Lord." Higher up the mountains another and another would take up the sublime anthem until the mountains rang with the praises of God.

Hallelujah! Here. There. Everywhere. Today. Tomorrow. Forever. For it is one exercise that will continue in the next world.

As a little boy lay critically ill his older brother tried to teach him to say, "Hallelujah." But death came before he learned it. When the older one was told of his passing, he silently stared into nothingness for a few moments and then said, "Johnny can say 'Hallelujah' now, mother."

For He Is Holy

EXALT ye the Lord our God, and worship at his footstool; for he is holy. —99:5

In three different verses the Psalm exalts the holiness of God as a leading characteristic of the Just One.

Isaiah, in moving and beautiful eloquence, also emphasizes this Divine trait: "Holy, holy, holy, is the Lord of hosts: the whole earth is full of his glory" (Isaiah 6:3).

A modern poet was inspired by Isaiah's passage to write for today's worshipers this popular hymn:

Holy, holy, holy! Lord God Almighty!
Early in the morning our song shall rise to Thee;
Holy, holy, holy! merciful and mighty!
God over all, and blest eternally.

Holy, holy, holy! tho' the darkness hide Thee,
Tho' the eye of sinful man Thy glory may not see;
Only Thou art holy! there is none beside Thee,
Perfect in pow'r, in love, and purity.

—Reginald Heber

His holiness touches our hearts and moves us to praise Him. For He is "above all the people" (ver. 2); equitable, just and righteous (ver. 4); and forgiving (ver. 8), without which we would be doomed forever. Therefore it is incumbent upon us that we "exalt the Lord our God, and worship at his holy hill; for the Lord our God is holy" (ver. 9). Holy, holy, holy, is He!

Pray and Obey

THEY called upon the Lord, and he answered them...
they kept his testimonies, and the ordinance that he
gave them. —99:6, 7

In speaking of some outstanding men — Moses,
Aaron and Samuel — the composer stated that they
prayed to God and kept His testimonies. They prayed
and obeyed.

This is a worthy pattern for us to follow — pray
and obey — whereby we are given a ready hearing
before the throne of God:

AND whatsoever we ask, we receive of him, because
we keep his commandments, and do those things that
are pleasing in his sight. —I John 3:22

The believer cannot afford to dispense with the
privilege of prayer. It is effectual, first, because God
answers prayer. Of all the truths taught in the Scriptures perhaps there is none more verified by human
experience than this — that God answers prayer.
Second, it is fruitful because of the therapeutic value
afforded the praying person by expressing his deepest
and most locked up feelings.

God answers prayer, but only if we have the disposition to obey; otherwise our lisped words are vain.
Hence this question is ever fitting: "And why call ye
me, Lord, Lord, and do not the things which I say"
(Luke 6:46) ?

> *I may as well kneel down*
> *And worship gods of stone,*
> *As offer to the living God*
> *A prayer of words alone.*
>
> *—John Burton*

The Forgiving God

THOU wast a God that forgavest them, though thou tookest vengeance of their inventions. —99:8

Years ago a distressed woman came to our home on a Sunday afternoon. Caught up in sin, remorseful, ashamed, she felt her only escape was suicide.

"If you believe the way I do, you could get a new start in life," I suggested.

"What do you mean?" she inquired.

"I believe in the God of forgiveness."

It was this thought — the thought of forgiveness — that took the woman's mind from self-destruction and enabled her to find her better self in a new life.

It was heartening to the psalmist to recall that God forgave Moses, Aaron, Samuel and other greats (ver. 6). They were not perfect; they were sinners; yet God showed them mercy and forgave them. He manifested displeasure at their follies; nevertheless He pardoned their shortcomings and answered their prayers.

The God who cannot overlook sins can forgive them. This is our hope and our greatest attainment — forgiveness:

Forgiveness is man's deepest need and highest achievement.
—Horace Bushnell

It is more than the remission of sins — it is the restoration of a broken fellowship. Cleansed of guilt and reunited with our Maker, we have a new slate and a new opportunity — all because God is forgiving.

God and Man

MAKE a joyful noise unto the Lord, all ye lands. Serve the Lord with gladness: come before his presence with singing. Know ye that the Lord he is God: it is he that hath made us, and not we ourselves; we are his people, and the sheep of his pasture. Enter into his gates with thanksgiving, and into his courts with praise: be thankful unto him, and bless his name. For the Lord is good; his mercy is everlasting; and his truth endureth to all generations. —100

This Psalm pertains to God's greatness and man's duty:

God's greatness:

— "The Lord he is God."
— "It is he that hath made us, and not we ourselves."
— "The Lord is good."
— "His mercy is everlasting."
— "His truth endureth to all generations."

Man's duty to God:

— "Make a joyful noise unto the Lord."
— "Serve the Lord with gladness."
— "Come before his presence with singing."
— "We are his people, and the sheep of his pasture."
— "Enter into his gates with thanksgiving."
— "Enter . . . into his courts with praise."
— "Be thankful unto him."
— "Bless his name."

So it's God and man, man and God, the story of civilization.

Man Did Not Make Himself

KNOW ye that the Lord he is God: it is he that hath made us, and not we ourselves. —100:3

I look at my watch, knowing that every tick is more than a tick of time, that it is a tick to the genius of its maker — for it never made itself.

As the light from the incandescent lamp drives out the darkness, I know the bulb never made itself — it shines to the glory of its inventor.

I turn on the television, and I know it is the product of a manufacturer, that it never made itself.

Neither did my house evolve. It's the work of a builder. In recognition of this fundamental truth, the Bible says, "For every house is builded by some man; but he that built all things is God" (Hebrews 3:4).

In keeping with the same common sense, our text gives this explanation of the origin of man: God created him; he never made himself (Genesis 1:27; 2:7).

This is reasonable. And therefore as long as watches, light bulbs, televisions and houses are unable to make themselves — have to be made by a superior power — just that long I must hold to the idea that man is the creation of a Higher Power.

So this is my song —

Thou art the workman, I the frame;
Lord to the glory of Thy name
I raise my voice in lofty strain,
I praise, I sing this old refrain.

Fourteen Resolutions

I Will . . . . —101

The Psalm gives the fixed determinations of a king:

— "I will sing of mercy and judgment."

— "I will behave myself wisely in a perfect way."

— "I will walk . . . . with a perfect heart."

— "I will set no wicked thing before mine eyes."

— "The work of them that turn aside, it shall not cleave to me."

— "A froward heart shall depart from me."

— "I will not know a wicked person [evil things, A.S.V.]."

— "Whoso privily slandereth his neighbor, him will I cut off."

— "Him that hath a high look . . . will not I suffer."

— "Mine eyes shall be upon the faithful of the land . . . ."

— "He that walketh in a perfect way, he shall serve me."

— "He that worketh deceit shall not dwell within my house."

— "He that telleth lies shall not tarry in my sight."

— "I will early destroy all the wicked of the land; that I may cut off all wicked doers from the city of the Lord."

These were the resolutions of a great king. Don't you think they would be appropriate in our own Capitol?

The Days of Man

For my days are . . . . —102:3

The Bible contains some very descriptive and meaningful statements on the days of man:

1) "My days are consumed like smoke" (ver. 3).

2) "My days are like a shadow that declineth" (ver. 11).

3) "I am withered like grass" (ver. 11).

4) "Shall wax old like a garment" (ver. 26).

5) "They were but flesh; a wind that passeth away, and cometh not again" (78:39).

6) "We spend our years as a tale that is told" (90:9).

7) "As the days of a tree are the days of my people" (Isaiah 65:22).

8) "For we . . . are as water spilt on the ground, which cannot be gathered up again" (II Samuel 14:14).

9) "For what is your life? It is even a vapor . . . appeareth for a little time . . . vanisheth away" (James 4:14)

10) "He . . . like a flower . . . is cut down" (Job 14:2).

As the life of a flower, as a breath or a sigh,
So the years that we live, as a dream, hasten by;
True, today we are here, but tomorrow may see
Just a grave in the vale, and a memory of me.

—*Laura E. Newell*

11) "Are not his days also like the days of a hireling [looks for his reward]" (Job 7:1)? The award awaits us.

Depression Likened to Three Birds

I AM like . . . . —102:6, 7

At times life can get pretty rough. The blues can sink us low. We can feel awfully lonely. The poet, no less human than the rest of us, was caught up in this very human experience of melancholy when he wrote the Psalm. He stated, "I am in trouble"; "my heart is smitten, and withered like grass, so that I forget to eat my bread." Then he compared himself to three sorrowful birds:

1) "I am like a pelican in the wilderness" (ver. 6). This bird is a striking image of grimness and loneliness. Its solemnity and austerity are most visible. David referred to it to illustrate his own dismals.

2) "I am like an owl of the desert" (ver. 6). The owl is known as a bird that dwells in solitary places. Just to look at it is enough to give you the blues; and to hear its doleful cry in the night strikes a tune of desolation in your heart.

3) "I watch, and am as a sparrow alone upon the housetop" (ver. 7). David watched through the sleepless nights. Grief would not let him sleep. He likened his state to the sparrow. When it loses a mate it will sit on the housetop alone and mourn in sad bereavement.

All of this called for a conquering faith and a perservering patience, which he expressed in the last verse.

Now in a touch of relevancy, conquer your melancholy. The best is yet to come.

Let Me Live

I SAID, O my God, take me not away in the midst of
my days. —102:24

This prayer for more days gets down to where a
person lives — and dies. Hezekiah stated, "O Lord,
by these things men live" (Isaiah 38:16).

> *Even throughout life, 'tis death*
> *that makes life live.*
> —*Robert Browning*

We don't like the idea of getting old, but we prefer
it over the alternative. Life smiles at its problems
and pulls back from the grave. Because for every
ounce of gall there is a ton of honey, and for every
thorn there is a garden of roses. The urge to live is
especially compelling when so many of our plans have
not yet come to fruition.

The psalmist's supplication is a pitieous one. He
feared that he might not live to see the restoration
of Zion (ver. 13). He was concerned that his plight
might be like that of Moses whose life was cut short
of his entrance into the promised land.

A prayer for longevity is proper, but the specific
answer must wait on the will of God. Now as we
pray for more days, let us properly use the ones we
have, and trust Him who is the giver and taker of
life for whatever lies ahead.

Remember God's Benefits

BLESS the Lord, O my soul, and forget not all his benefits. —103:2

David was resolved not to forget the wonderful things God was doing for him. And in the Psalm he mentioned the following benefits from God: forgiveness (ver. 3); restoration of health (ver. 3); rescue from danger (ver. 4); kindness and mercy (ver. 4); things that satisfy the mouth (ver. 5); and renewal of youth (ver. 5).

One of David's outstanding virtues was his thankfulness. It is definitely one of the requisites of a lofty life, and one the psalmist constantly mentioned; for instance:

ENTER into his gates with thanksgiving, and into his courts with praise: be thankful unto him, and bless his name. —100:4

Gratitude signifies a greatness of heart. Definitely so! It has a good memory — does not forget.

An appreciativeness on the part of the recipient is commended and lauded the world over; however ingratitude is despised and rebuked as one of the blackest sins. Ingratitude reveals that one is lacking in goodness and nobility. It is a glaring flaw in character.

So in the language of David, we say to ourselves: "forget not all his benefits" — nor the blessings from man. For gratitude is one of the sweetest flowers that blossoms in the garden of virtue.

Like a Father

LIKE as a father pitieth his children, so the **Lord** pitieth them that fear him. —103:13

If a son should lead a revolution to unseat his father that he might occupy the throne; and if the son should lose his life in the struggle, that loving father will lament and mourn his passing in overwhelming grief. David is our example. When he learned the fate of his revolutionary son, he "was much moved, and went up to the chamber over the gate, and wept: and as he went, thus he said, O my son Absalom! my son, my son Absalom! would God I had died for thee, O Absalom, my son, my son!" (II Samuel 18:33) The heartbreak and depth of feeling has been described by Longfellow:

There is no far nor near,
There is neither there nor here,
There is neither soon nor late,
In that Chamber over the Gate.
Nor any long ago
To that cry of human woe,
"O Absalom, my son!"

That 'tis a common grief
Bringeth but slight relief;
Ours is the bitterest loss,
Ours is the heaviest cross;
And forever the cry will be,
"Would God I had died for thee,
"O Absalom, my son!"

Like a father, God pities His children.

God Knows We Are Weak

For he knoweth our frame; he remembereth that we are dust. —103:14

He knows how we are made. He fashioned us — of dust. He understands our feebleness and is sympathetic toward our weakness. He knows that we are frail and may break under pressure; that we are weak and may yield to temptation. This is special reason for his pity toward us (ver. 13). Would that men were as considerate of one another's frailty.

When the issues call for rugged strength and we seem so breakable, it is assuring to recall that He pities our humanity.

When our work is imperfect and our life is stained with sin, though our intentions are pure and our efforts stir from faith and spring from love, it is then that we are in dire need of the pity that comes from Him who knows our frame. It is a boon to drooping spirits to remember that all men are made of the same dust, and that to the apostles who evidently had some superior traits, Jesus said:

WATCH and pray, that ye enter not into temptation: the spirit indeed is willing, but the flesh is weak.
—Matthew 26:41

He who knows the weakness of His children has in every age owned them, directed them, blessed them and forgiven them — as they believed and obeyed. Hence imperfect people are able to maintain a blessed relationship with Him — provided they try.

Our Wonderful World

O Lᴏʀᴅ my God, thou art very great. —104:1

For Thou gave us this marvelous world.
Light is our benefaction (ver. 2).
The heavens stretch out like a canopy (ver. 2).
The foundations of the earth are solid forever (ver. 5).

We have seas of water and stretches of dry land with permanent boundaries, because the waters that once stood above the mountains fled at the rebuke of God (vers. 6-9).

The springs that run from the hills remind us of a hidden source of water ready for our tapping — for the good of man and beasts and fowls (vers. 10-12).

The growing grass for cattle and the thriving herbs for man are . . . provisions of God (ver. 14).

Drinking in God's rain, the trees flourish in beauty and usefulness. The cedars of Lebanon grow to God's glory and man's good (vers. 16, 17).

The high hills are a refuge for the goats, and among the rocks is the home of the conies (ver. 18).

The moon adds to the beauty and efficacy of our world; and the sun rises and sets with dependability (ver. 19).

So inviting and productive is the earth that man goes forth unto his work and labors in hope (ver. 23).

The seas are filled with innumerable things (vers. 25, 26).

"O Lord, how manifold are thy works! in wisdom hast thou made them all: the earth is full of thy riches" (ver. 24).

The Open Hand of God

THESE wait all upon thee; that thou mayest give them their meat in due season. That thou givest them [what] they gather: thou openest thine hand, they are filled with good. —104:27, 28

We wait on God the Great Provider for our blessings. Having no means of our own, we are wholly dependent on Him. We are needy creatures, but His hand is open to us. From it we are "filled with good."

In rapturous wonder we praise His name, saying, "Thou openest thine hand, and satisfiest the desire of every living thing" (145:16). And we pray:

MY times are in thy hand; deliver me from the hand of mine enemies, and from them that persecute me. —31:15

LET thine hand help me. —119:173

And now with all our fears allayed we put our little hand over in His big open hand. For He has said, "I the Lord have called thee in righteousness, and will hold thine hand, and will keep thee" (Isaiah 42:6).

A little girl, walking home one dark night with her father, suggested, "Take my hand, papa! I can take only a little piece of yours, but you can hold all of mine." In his strong grasp she seemed comforted, but suddenly asked, "Papa, are you afraid?" When he assured her he wasn't, she confidently stated: "All wight! If you isn't, I isn't."

Sweet Meditations

MY meditation of him shall be sweet: I will be glad
in the Lord. —104:34

I shall find a sweet joy in meditating on the character and works of God. This is the purpose of these
365 devotionals on the Psalms. The ageless Psalms
are such unique and rich sources for contemplation.

The very first Psalm says this of the blessed man:
"His delight is in the law of the Lord; and in his law
doth he meditate day and night." That there could
be delight in such musing tells us of a heart that
beats in tune with the heart of God.

In the world's great art galleries the lovers of art
will spend hours before a single masterpiece. They
go away and return the next day. In spellbound
ecstasy with charmed eyes they survey the wondrous
beauty. Through prolonged meditation it seems to
them the world stops and they get off, and standing
there in rapturous thought they discover new beauties
and new joys.

This is what you do in meditation. You close your
eyes to the beckoning scenes to see one sight. You
deafen your ears to a thousand calls to hear one voice.

Close up his eyes and draw the curtain close;
And let us all to meditation.

—William Shakespeare

Responding to God's Providence

ALL his wondrous works. —105:2

What should our response be to the providential wonders of God? The answer is given in the Psalm:

Gratitude: "O give thanks unto the Lord" (ver. 1). Thank the tree that bears your fruit; and the bridge that carries you safely over; and the sun you take for granted; and the God man often forgets.

Publication: "Make known his deeds among the people" (ver. 1). As much as you have in you, tell it (Romans 1:15); because you have something to say that compels you to say it (Jeremiah 20:9).

Praise: "Sing unto him, sing psalms unto him: talk ye of all his wondrous works" (ver. 2). Men, worthy or unworthy, are praised because they die; but God never dies — praise Him because He lives and for ten thousand other reasons.

Joy: "Let the heart of them rejoice that seek the Lord" (ver. 3). God's motto for us is:

Enjoy living.

Endeavor: "Seek the Lord, and his strength: seek his face evermore" (ver. 4). "Seek, and ye shall find" (Matthew 7:7). The non-seekers are the non-finders in every field.

Remembrance: "Remember his marvelous works that he hath done; his wonders, and the judgments of his mouth" (ver. 5). Remember and your soul shall be renewed.

The Purpose of Life and Prosperity

AND he . . . gave them the lands of the heathen: and they inherited the labor of the people; that they might observe his statutes, and keep his laws. Praise ye the Lord. —105:44, 45

The design and purpose of all the guiding, protecting, feeding and sustaining of those so few and weak (leading them into the promised land) was "that they might observe his statutes and keep his laws." The end of all God's providential care was to establish a God-fearing nation, a nation with character, moral, spiritual and holy. By keeping His laws, they could partake of His own holiness and thereby achieve the ideal that God had set for them.

Today the principle is the same. We are given life, breath and all things that we might glorify Him (Matthew 5:16). Life has a greater end than counting birthdays.

Hence when prosperity smiles upon us, may it correct us — not corrupt us; and may we use it — not abuse it. For its purpose is lofty and its effect is revealing. It won't take long for it to show what a person is.

> *Prosperity doth best discover vice.*
> *—Francis Bacon*

As the manna keeps dropping, let us remember: *we are prospered to serve.* Every blessing is a mercy-drop from heaven. Receive it graciously. Use it advantageously.

Extenuating Circumstances

> THEY angered him also at the waters of strife, so that
> it went ill with Moses for their sakes: Because they
> provoked his spirit, so that he spake unadvisedly with
> his lips. —106:32, 33

Moses was guilty. No question about it. This is why "it went ill" with him. But there were mitigative circumstances.

This is what occurred: The people complained and blamed Moses when things got rough with them; one of their trials was no water to drink. In supplying this need, God ordered Moses to gather the congregation together and to speak unto the rock, promising that water would gush forth. But under the strain of all their murmurs and reproaches, Moses went beyond the command of God and said, "Hear now, ye rebels; must we fetch water out of this rock?" (Numbers 22:10). Then he "smote the rock twice."

This was God's reaction: "Because ye believed me not, to sanctify me in the eyes of the children of Israel, therefore ye shall not bring this congregation into the land which I have given them" (Numbers 20:12). But Moses had been provoked, which justly needed to be considered; so God permitted him to glimpse the land, though he could not enter (Deuteronomy 34:1-5).

Here are two morals from the story:

First, one man's sin may cause another to sin.

Second, when one's mistake is the result of another's incitement, we should soften our censure of it. Provocation begs consideration.

Nevertheless He Regarded Them

NEVERTHELESS he regarded their affliction, when he heard their cry. —106:44

The "nevertheless" of God's mercy is the theme of the whole Psalm. They were in dire and constant need of mercy because their sins were so grievous and numerous.

They "were brought low for their iniquity" (ver. 43). Sin is very degrading. There is nothing elevating about it.

What had thy done? Here is a list of their transgressions: 1. Fear at the Red Sea (ver. 7). 2. Lust (ver. 14). 3. Putting God to the test (ver. 14). 4. Envy (ver. 16). 5. Idolatry (ver. 19). 6. Contempt for the pleasant land (ver. 24). 7. Disbelief (ver. 24). 8. Murmur (ver. 25). 9. License (ver. 25). 10. Eating sacrifices to false gods (ver. 28). 11. Provoking of Moses (ver. 33). 12. Self-will (ver. 34). 13. Acquiring sinful works from heathen people (vers. 35-39).

The worst thing God could have done to them was to do nothing — leave them alone — but He did not ignore them. They were on His heart, the object of His attention; and consequently He chastened them, giving "them into the hand of the heathen" (ver. 41), for their good. Inspite of all their sins He regarded their affliction and remembered His covenant (vers. 44, 45). They were His children. And He forgave them when they came back to Him. Oh! what mercy spared Israel! A mercy equalled only by the mercy that spares us.

Let the Redeemed Say So

LET the redeemed of the Lord say so, whom he hath redeemed from the hand of the enemy. —107:2

The redeemed — they are especially qualified to say so. Having been rescued by the loving mercy and the outstretched hand of God, they are prepared to say so.

The redeemed — in this particular usage it refers to a deliverance from danger, probably to the deliverance from Babylonian captivity (Isaiah 43:3, 4). But more, there was a blotting out of their sins: "I have blotted out as a thick cloud, thy transgressions, and, as a cloud, thy sins: return unto me; for I have redeemed thee" (Isaiah 44:22).

The redeemed — we belong to this number if we have been washed in the blood of the Lamb (Hebrews 9:12-14). And now in the language of Job, we say, "For I know that my Redeemer liveth" (Job 19:25). This is our assurance; so let us sing it:

REDEEMED

Redeemed — how I love to proclaim it.
Redeemed by the blood of the Lamb;
Redeemed thro' His infinite mercy,
His child, and forever, I am.

I know I shall see in His beauty
The King in whose law I delight;
Who lovingly guardeth my footsteps,
And giveth me songs in the night.

Redeemed by the blood of the Lamb;
His child, and forever, I am.

—Fanny J. Crosby

Praise the Lord

OH that men would praise the Lord for his goodness,
and for his wonderful works to the children of men!
—107:8

This verse is given verbatim three more times in
the Psalm (vers. 15, 21, 31). Four times in one Psalm
should impress the mind of the reader with the urgency
of the message. Those who have been blessed by the
wonderful works of God should praise Him for His
goodness — not just in words but in life.

Neither should the praise of God be just a little
temporary expression of emotion, but rather a life-
feeling. David viewed it as a lifetime attitude, avow-
ing: "As long as I live: I will sing praise to my God"
(104:33).

Nor should it be lip service. David's whole being
was committed to the praise of God: "I will praise
thee, O Lord, with my whole heart" (9:1). When
man's whole being pulsates with thanksgiving and
praise, he approaches an ideal that each should have.
Aware of this, we pray for a fuller life of praise:

> *Fill thou my life, O Lord my God,*
> *In every part with praise,*
> *That my whole being may proclaim*
> *Thy Being and Thy ways.*
>
> *Not for the lip of praise alone,*
> *Nor e'en the praising heart,*
> *I ask, but for a life made up*
> *Of praise in every part.*
>
> —*Horatius Bonar*

Tongue-praising is a good thing, but living the praise
is better.

At Their Wit's End

AND are at their wit's end. —107:27

The context presents a maritime scene. A ship is struck by a storm which stirs up high and hammering waves (ver. 26). The soul of the mariners is "melted because of trouble." Fearful, seasick, reeling "too and fro like a drunken man," they "are at their wit's end." All their wisdom is swallowed up. No human power avails. Helpless, feeling that God is their only rescue, they pray; and He speaks peace to the storm and the waves are settled (vers. 28, 29).

Sometimes we, too, are at our wit's end. Our little sea turns angry and we become fearful, sick and dismayed. Everything fails. Our heart bleeds over a problem that seems to have no solution. Helpless, we do what men should be doing all along — earnestly pray. For prayer is needed in smooth waters as well as in stormy seas. And the God who calmed the briny deep for the Israelites and stilled the waters for the disciples (Mark 4:38) can quiet those raging waves that threaten us.

> *Master, the tempest is raging!*
> *The billows are tossing high!*
> *The sky is o'er shadowed with blackness;*
> *No shelter or help is nigh,*
> *"Carest Thou not that we perish?"*
>
> —*Mary A. Baker*

Yes, He cares. Remember — when man is at his wit's end, it could be God's beginning of help.

The Fixed Heart

O GOD, my heart is fixed; I will sing and give praise, even with my glory. —108:1

His mind is made up. No vacillation. His slogan is: *All steps ahead.* No turning back. When success smiles and when failure frowns; when friends stand by and when they betray; when you are praised and when you are condemned. Hence the fixed heart does not depend on outward circumstances . . . but on an inward state.

The fixed heart brings the whole man into the effort, uniting and coordinating his labors; and this awakens the slumbering giant:

> *Every human mind is a great slumbering power until awakened by keen desire and by definite resolution to do.*
> —*Edgar Roberts*

The fixed heart holds you to a purpose.

> *When my resolution is taken, all is forgotten except what will make it succeed.*
> —*Napoleon I*

The fixed heart makes for favorable winds. Otherwise —

> *When a man does not know what harbor he is making for, no wind is right.*
> —*Latin Proverb*

The fixed heart, summed up, is the way of success.

> *The secret of success is constancy of purpose.*
> —*Benjamin Disraeli*

Early to Rise

I MYSELF will awake early. —108:2

The psalmist awoke early to better look after his spiritual duties and privileges. By rising early he started the day aright. He shortened his sleep for the sake of praise and prayer.

We also have Jesus as an example of early morning religion. He got "up a great while before day, and departed into a solitary place, and there prayed" (Mark 1:35). This was refreshing to His crowded life.

Later, after His death, Mary Magdalene went at an early hour to the tomb of Jesus (John 20:1). It is easier to find the break of pressure in the break of dawn.

I know a minister who habitually arises at 4:30 that he may have some time for reading, meditation and prayer before he gets caught up in the daily whirl of things.

Another friend of mine, a business man, arises at 5:30, two hours before going to work, that he may have time to read and think before his world starts turning so fast.

One mistake most people make is getting up too late. Then when they arise, life becomes a wild, frantic, nerve-wracking comedy (or should we say tragedy?) on how to get to work, or even to church, on time. One way a hurrying, out-of-breath, restless people could find peace and tranquility is just to get up thirty minutes earlier. By shortening their sleep they could lengthen their day.

The Valiant

THROUGH God we shall do valiantly: for he it is that shall tread down our enemies. —108:13

Bravery — how humanity loves it. The world salutes the brave man, regardless of his weaknesses. For bravery alone we're willing to pin a medal on him. But the coward, though he has a thousand virtues, is held in contempt. And justly so. For his fainthearted-ness nullifies his excellencies.

> *A great deal of talent is lost to the world for the want of a little courage.*
> *—Sydney Smith*

O spirit of courage! what you can do for me! In every hour of danger you can favor me in the struggle.

> *Fortune favors the brave.*
> *—Virgil*
> 70-19 B. C.

In a world crowded with fears and dreads, anybody with a plan to generate a little more courage is welcome.

In giving the answer, David declared that valiance is found in God. Through Him we gather strength to go forth with spirit and courage. With God at our side, we say, "I will fear no evil" (23:4). Not that we always win according to our wishes, but we always try.

It's better to suffer a few defeats than to live in that dismal cowardice that knows neither victory nor defeat.

The courage to try and try, again and again, en-rolls our names among the valiant.

Enemies Without Cause

THEY compassed me about also with words of hatred; and fought against me without a cause. —109:3

David spoke of enemies he had not caused. They hurt him severely. His heart was wounded (ver. 22). Furthermore, he had become a reproach unto men who looked upon him and shook their heads (ver. 25).

Yet he had not caused the enmity. Instead, he had treated them kindly, but his love was recompensed with hate and his goodness was rewarded with evil (ver. 5).

This is not an uncommon reaction — enemies for no cause. Here are the despicable reasons for it:

— Having what another likes may drive him to fight you.

— Holding to truth may alienate those who don't want it.

— Knowing something bad on a person makes him despise you.

— Being harmed by another tends to make him hate you.

— The feeling that you are a threat to one's job, honor or success may prompt him to detest you.

— An inferior person's trying to feel bigger or cleaner can cause him to disparage you.

— Seeking an outlet for frustration may move the frustrated to pick on you.

— The feeling that one is dependent on you may cause him to loathe you.

The New King

THE Lord said unto my Lord, Sit thou at my right hand,
until I make thine enemies thy footstool.... —110:1-7

If you believe in prophecy here is a Psalm for you
to proclaim, one in which you can exult. It is Davidic
in authorship and prophetically Messianic in subject.
We say this because Jesus attributed its authorship
to David and its fulfillment to Himself:

WHILE the Pharisees were gathered together, Jesus
asked them, saying, What think ye of Christ? whose
son is he? They say unto him, The son of David. He
saith unto them, How then doth David in spirit call
him Lord, saying, *The Lord said unto my Lord, Sit
thou on my right hand, till I make thine enemies thy
footstool?* If David then call him Lord, how is he
his son? And no man was able to answer him.
—Matthew 22:41-46

Peter also applied this Psalm to the Messiah (Acts
2:33-35); and so did the writer of Hebrews (5:6;
7:17, 21).

The Psalm touches on the Messiah's kingdom, His
priesthood and His final victory over the power of
evil. It sets forth His glory and the conquest that
some day shall be His. It states that His strength
or ruling power would go forth from Jerusalem and
be exercised in the midst of His enemies (ver. 2). His
people shall be willing, for (recognizing human volition) the Messiah can rule over only willing subjects
(ver. 3). His role would be greater than either king
or priest — the combination of the two, like that of
Melchizedek (ver. 4). He shall exercise judgment
over all the nations and shall rule until all enemies
are put down (ver. 1; I Corinthians 15:23-26).

Something Sure

ALL his commandments are sure. They stand fast for
ever and ever, and are done in truth and uprightness.
—111:7, 8

In a world of crumbling standards, "the commandments of God are sure," and "stand fast for ever
and ever." They are true, for He is truth. They are
the criterion, for He is the standard. They shall endure, for He shall be around to see that they do.

His commandments (except in some rites and ceremonies) have not changed. His moral injunctions
have withstood the testing of time. The frustrations
and defects of humanity have not relegated them to
a place of irrelevancy. The more defeats men suffer
the more convinced they become that they need to
get back to a *Thus saith the Lord*. Laid low by imperfect, human views, they see the need of society's
adhering to a sure and workable standard, lest we
turn mad and destroy ourselves.

His regulations have been the bread of life, the pil-
grim's staff, the mariner's compass and the soldier's
sword. They have fed us. They have steadied us.
They have directed us. They have defended us.

Say what you will, it is easy to see the practicality
of: "Thou shalt not kill"; "Thou shalt not steal";
"Thou shalt not bear false witness"; "honor thy father
and thy mother"; and all other moral directives. They
are as relevant today as yesterday, and shall be as
urgent tomorrow.

Reverence His Name

HOLY and reverend is his name. —111:9

This is no light matter.

Man *can* and *must* hold the name of God in awe and exaltation. As we touch and taste the works of God, let us lisp the praise His holy name requires.

When we look at nature, stirred by its grandeur, we exclaim, "Holy and reverend is his name."

As we read the Scriptures, blessed by their practicality, we declare, "Holy and reverend is his name."

Having been laundered in the fountain of mercy and cleansed in the waters of forgiveness, we exuberantly say, "Holy and reverend is his name."

Convinced that victory belongs to those who walk with God, we proclaim, "Holy and reverend is his name."

So awake my soul in joyful exclamation and pay the tribute His name so richly deserves. I know that I can no more do His name justice than I can count the stars. But I *can* reverence it! I *can* venerate it! I *can* refrain from degrading it in vain and ugly speech!

> *It chills my blood to hear the blest Supreme*
> *Rudely appealed to on each trifling theme;*
> *Maintain your rank, vulgarity despise;*
> *To swear is neither brave, polite, nor wise.*
> *You would not swear upon the bed of death;*
> *Reflect! Your Maker yet may stop your breath.*
>
> —*William Cowper*

Blessings Follow

BLESSED is the man that feareth the Lord, that de-
lighteth greatly in his commandments . . . . —112

As seen in the beginning verse, blessings are promised to those who fear God and delight in His commandments. No question about it—blessings are found
in virtue, and this plus the care and providence of
God shower them on the God-fearing man:

— His descendants shall be mighty and blessed (ver.
2). Influence perpetuates goodness from generation to
generation.

— Wealth shall be his (ver. 3). Obedience to God's
laws tends to gather riches.

— He has a lamp to guide him in the darkness
(119:105). It gives direction and drives out gloom.

— He is endued with kindness (ver. 4). Since like
begets like, he receives kindness.

— His discretion holds his affairs in order (ver. 5).
The indiscreet are sure to have what they call *hard luck*.

— His memory shall be held in perpetual pleasantness (ver. 6). When we bury the dead we never bury
their good.

— He is not fearful of bad news (vers. 7, 8). Mis-
fortune comes to all, but he does not anticipate it.

— His generosity exalts him in honor (ver. 9). It
speaks well for him.

— His goodness robs the wicked of power to do him
lasting harm (ver. 10). There is not much to attack.

The godly man has always been blessed, then and now.

Prosperity

WEALTH and riches shall be in his house. —112:3

God's directives tend to accumulate the good things of life. Note these necessary conditions of prosperity:

Work: "If any would not work, neither should he eat" (II Thessalonians 3:10).

Self-reliance: A lack of this defeated the one-talent man (Matthew 25:14-30).

Vision: "Where there is no vision, the people perish" (Proverbs 29:18).

Enthusiasm: "Whatsoever thy hand findeth to do, do it with thy might" (Ecclesiastes 9:10).

Analysis: "For which of you, intending to build a tower, sitteth not down first and counteth the cost..." (Luke 14:28-30).

Multiplied strength through numbers: "Two are better than one; because they have a good reward for their labor" (Ecclesiastes 4:9).

Time element: "Go to the ant . . . Consider her ways, and be wise . . . provideth her meat in the summer, and gathereth her food in the harvest" (Proverbs 6:6-8).

Thrift: "Gather up the fragments that remain, that nothing be lost" (John 6:12).

Investments: The parable of talents or coins establishes the need of investments (Matthew 25:14-30).

Prosperity has a price. But poverty costs more.

Stability

A GOOD man . . . surely he shall not be moved for ever.
—112:5, 6

He is not forever on the move. He is not driven by restlessness, frustration and defeat from pillar to post. He is stable, solid and firm. He shall have:

— *A permanent home.*
— *A solid reputation.*
— *A continuous influence.*
— *A firm prosperity.*

An old proverb is, "Two moves are as bad as a fire." Instability is very expensive: loss of thought, time, energy and money. Productivity requires stickability. Oh! that some people had glue that would hold them to their opportunity. Before the sown seed can ripen in harvest, they abandon the field. The pasture is not always greener on the other side of the fence — just looks that way. The saddest day in a person's life is when he decides to be a rolling stone.

For success and happiness, each needs to be —

> *Steady of heart, and stout of hand.*
> *—Sir Walter Scott*

This is no disparagement of a move that betters a person; for you can be stable without standing still. In the fable of *The Hare and the Tortoise,* Aesop said: "Slow and steady wins the race."

Praise God for He Is Able

PRAISE ye the Lord. Praise, O ye servants of the Lord, praise the name of the Lord. Blessed be the name of the Lord from this time forth and for evermore. From the rising of the sun unto the going down of the same the Lord's name is to be praised. The Lord is high above all nations, and his glory above the heavens. Who is like unto the Lord our God, who dwelleth on high, who humbleth himself to behold the things that are in heaven, and in the earth! He raiseth up the poor out of the dust, and lifteth the needy out of the dunghill; that he may set him with princes, even with the princes of his people. He maketh the barren woman to keep house, and to be a joyful mother of children. Praise ye the Lord. —113

We have given in full this Psalm which has proven to be very popular in church services.

Praise to God is "from this time forth and for ever more." "From the rising of the sun unto the [its] going down" — from the farthest east to the farthest west.

Why such timeless and universal acclamation for God? Because God is able! Though He "dwelleth on high," God is never too far away or too busy or too preoccupied to "humble himself," as the text states, and come to our help. No distance can ever hide man's needs from God's eyes.

In contrast to the problems of rulers and nations, the barrenness of one woman may have seemed insignificant. But the God who could lift up a ruler and bless a nation could also bless a barren woman. Sarah knew it; Hannah knew it; and so did Elizabeth.

God is able! To handle your problem! Big or Small!

Poetic Beauty

WHEN Israel went out of Egypt... —114:1-8

This is one of the most poetic of all the Psalms, more like the poetry of the modern poet. In it, nature's wonders are personified, pictured alive and responsive to the presence and power of the Omnipotent one, and in such eloquent and lofty rhetoric. The psalmist portrays the sea as having eyes that saw Israel approaching and then fled for their passage; and Jordan, accommodating as it were, pulled back for them to cross over into the promised land. Referring to the agitations of Sinai's peaks when God gave the Law (Exodus 19:16-20:18), the poet pictures the mountains skipping "like rams, and the little hills like lambs" leaping for joy. The whole earth trembled, because God was there. And in this graphic style it states that the rock Moses struck was turned into a standing water and the flint was made a fountain.

This impressive language was employed to celebrate the praises of God in delivering Israel from Egyptian bondage. It is the expression of triumph, delighting in the merciful interpositions of God in this never-to-be-forgotten deliverance.

As they sang the Psalm, it generated cheer and optimism to face the unknown future. It emphasized that *the all-powerful God cares*. This was enough to keep their spirits up. And this is enough for us.

Not for Our Glory

NOT unto us, O Lord, not unto us, but unto thy name give glory, for thy mercy, and for thy truth's sake.
—115:1

When man properly relates himself to God, he puts self in the background.

He wears the Lord's name to glorify Him — not self (I Peter 4:16).

He shines to His glory — not to be applauded (Matthew 5:16).

He gives of his means because he has given self — not to be seen of men (Matthew 6:1-4).

He prays to be heard of God — not to be acclaimed (Matthew 6:5).

Now these personal questions:

Why attend church? To worship God or to hold up our reputation?

Why construct a new church building? To glorify God or to exalt ourselves?

Why do we give? To please God or man?

Why do we seek a church office or position? To serve God or to dignify ourselves?

If we follow a make-believe religion to impress people, our only reward will come from people — none from God (Matthew 6:5).

He that does good for good's sake seeks neither praise nor reward, though sure of both at last.
—*William Penn*

Idle Idols

THEIR idols are silver and gold, the work of men's hands . . . —115:4-8

The denunciation of idols is a common characteristic of Psalms. This was urgent. For these people lived in the midst of idolatry where the scorning of idol-deities was constantly needed.

In the Psalm there is a contrast in the powerful God and the powerless idols. It says of God, "he hath done whatsoever he pleased." But all that could be said of the idols is:

"They have mouths, but they speak not.
"They have ears, but they hear not.
"Noses have they, but they smell not.
"They have hands, but they handle not.
"Feet have they, but they walk not."

Idle idols — they have the organs, but not the sensibilities.

They are the deified representations of a people's own frailties and passions. And a study of a nation's gods will give you a nation's history.

Idols are only "the work of men's hands." Having been made by man, they are inferior to him; and if there should be any worshiping of either, they ought to worship man. So to make idolatry all the worse, it is practiced in reverse.

WE know that an idol is nothing in the world, and that there is none other God but one. —I Corinthians 8:4

The Small and the Great

Hᴇ will bless them that fear the Lord, both small and
great. —115:13

"Nobody big. Nobody little. Everybody same." These
are the leveling words some young boys painted inside their little, unpretentious club house.

Quite appropriate. At least they represent the feelings of God. To Him all look alike. Money doesn't
impress Him — He has all there is. Neither does education — He knows everything. So the *small* and the
great stand the same height in His sight. Accordingly,
He blesses all who fear Him, both *small* and *great*.
Surely, God loves the *small*, for there are so many
of them; and the mighty should, for if there were
no little ones there would be no big ones. God also
loves the *great*, for He made them, too.

Many *greats* in the Bible stand out in faith. But
as a whole, the little people have been more inclined
to honor God. Since human nature is the same, therefore there must be exterior causes which affect the
hearts of one group more than another: money, power,
popularity, intellectual pride and the cares of the
world.

Gʀᴇᴀᴛ men are not always wise. —Job 32:9

So if you permit the things of the world to blind
you, don't blame God if you can't see Him.

But the Earth Belongs to Man

THE heaven, even the heavens, are the Lord's: but the
earth hath he given to the children of men. —115:16

God formed and reserved the heavens as His dis-
tinctive abode. But the earth He gave to man as a
home. And in man's down-to-earth living he is to
employ his skills, earn his bread and live out his days
in hope of a home better than earth.

However, man's poor job as keeper of the earth
has defiled it. Unquestionably — "The earth also is
defiled under the inhabitants thereof; because they
have transgressed . . . " (Isaiah 24:5). Believing that
the last best hope of earth is in man's conformity to
the Landlord's wishes and to nature's restrictions,
we say —

> *There is no sense, as I can see,*
> *In mortals such as you and me*
> *A-faulting nature's wise intents*
> *And locking horns with Providence.*

For if we would justify our brief moment here, we
must feel and live —

> *. . . my God, Thou hast*
> *So brave a place built, O dwell in it*
> *That it may dwell with thee at last.*
> *Till then, afford us so much wit*
> *That, as the world serves us, we may serve Thee,*
> *And both thy servants be.*
>
> *—George Herbert*

The Energetic Faith

I Believed, therefore have I spoken. —116:10

Paul used this passage to emphasize the faith that proclaimed the gospel, despite all opposition. He said, "For we which live are alway delivered unto death . . . We having the same spirit of faith, according as it is written, *I believed, and therefore have I spoken;* we also believe, and therefore speak" (II Corinthians 4:13).

The faith of the psalmist found a tongue. He could not be silent. His faith spoke.

Furthermore, his faith found legs. He declared, "I will walk before the Lord in the land of the living" (ver. 9).

Talk and walk — the effects of faith.

Faith *moves:* "By faith Noah . . . moved . . . prepared an ark" (Hebrews 11:7). Faith is the great vigorous force that will move your mountain — at least, tunnel through it. For faith doesn't stop at the mountain — it grabs a shovel.

> *Faith is the force of life.*
> *—Tolstoy*

Over the entrance to the Temple of Life are these words:

> *Ye must have faith.*

Hasty Words

I SAID in my haste, All men are liars. —116:11

His fault is a common one — hasty words, hasty charges. Many things precipitate fast speech:

Illness. "I was greatly afflicted" (ver. 10). Tormented by suffering, one may say things he would not normally say. Feeling neglected, he may be tempted to impugn the character of others.

Disappointment. Occasionally we shall be disappointed in others. We may reach the hasty conclusion that all persons are liars and cheats. But no one instance should indict the whole race.

Projection. A charge against another may be only the expression of one's own guilt.

Anger. Rash words come fast from hot tempers.

Ignorance. It's faster and easier to assassinate character than to investigate.

Hate. Give the hater the slightest chance and he will jam the air waves with his calumny; and if the chance doesn't come, he will make it.

Protection. One may accuse another of lying to protect himself in his own lies.

In conclusion, "be slow to speak" (James 1:19). And if it's something bad about somebody else, be a thousand times slower.

BE not rash with thy mouth, and let not thine heart be hasty to utter any thing before God. —Ecclesiastes 5:2

Open Religion

I WILL pay my vows unto the Lord now in the presence of all his people. —116:14

Before them all.

Not ashamed.

Not afraid.

There are two kinds of hypocrisy: (1) The showing of religion to gain praise. (2) The hiding of religion to escape censure. The latter is more popular in this age. In either case, one is failing to be his true self; and this is hypocritical.

God went public with His religion. In its very nature it relates to others which negates secrecy.

Serving God is visible. "Let your light so shine before men, that they may see your good works, and glorify your father" (Matthew 5:16). As a devotee of God you are light, and the purpose of a light is to shine. Don't conceal it. Don't hide your light (Matthew 5:14).

Let us beware of two extremes: proud ostentation and false humility. We are opposed to pretentious parade, and just as opposed to feigned modesty. But there is a true and sincere ground between the two in which one practices open religion to the glory of God. No affectation. Just the real thing.

Be yourself, and be the person you hope to be.
—Robert Louis Stevenson

Precious Death

PRECIOUS in the sight of the Lord is the death of his saints. —116:15

To the Heavenly Father the death of His children is precious. It is essential to the accomplishment of His merciful and eternal purpose.

After Adam and Eve sinned, the compassionate God put them out of the Garden of Eden, separating them from the tree of life, lest they should live forever in a state of sin and rebellion (Genesis 3:22-24). Death became a little extra grace for man, giving him the way to reach a new and deathless life that he can live in perfection.

In death there is the separation of the two beings: fleshly and spiritual. "For as the body without the spirit is dead" (James 2:26). "Then shall the dust return to the earth as it was: and the spirit shall return unto God who gave it" (Ecclesiastes 12:7). This is what death is — separation! not extinction! And over there the Lord shall clothe man's spirit with a new body, like His own glorious body (Philippians 3:21).

There is no real death; what looks like it is transition. So when a loved one is called away, we ought not to count our grief more than his relief. He has gone home. It is precious.

> *I cannot say, and I will not say*
> *That he is dead! He is just away.*
>
> *—James Whitcomb Riley*

The Shortest Psalm

O PRAISE the Lord, all ye nations: praise him all ye people. For his merciful kindness is great toward us: and the truth of the Lord endureth forever. Praise ye the Lord. —117

This is the shortest Psalm, but not too short to reveal some foundation truths.

It recognizes God in national life. However, in this age some think He doesn't belong there. They say, "God, there's no place for you in the halls of Congress or in the assemblies of the United Nations. Run along to the little chapel — that's your field. Stick to your business and we'll stick to ours." What blasphemy! What shame! You can't assign God to only a little role in a chapel. He is the God of the universe.

The Psalm gives special reasons for praising Jehovah. For His merciful kindness and His truth that endures forever. Man's salvation requires both mercy and truth — praise his name — one without the other will not suffice. Nations rise, touch a little glory and fall. But God lives. So does His mercy. So does His truth.

Blessed Assurance!

> *Watching and waiting, looking above,*
> *Filled with His goodness, lost in His love.*
> *This is my story, this is my song,*
> *Praising my Savior all the day long.*
>
> *—Fanny J. Crosby*

The Lord on My Side

THE Lord is on my side; I will not fear: what can man do unto me? —118:6

There never has been a more assuring statement uttered by mortal man than this: *The Lord is on my side.* And He was. For God is no passive spectator of struggles between a child of His and Satan. He does not sit on the sidelines of neutrality, watching to see who wins before He does anything. He is involved with us in our fighting.

The psalmist declared, "The Lord taketh my part with them that help me" (ver. 7). Indeed, he had friends that aided him; but God was working with them, making their gestures and labors productive in the poet's behalf.

With God on his side, he fearlessly asked, "What can man do unto me?" For if God is for us, who can be against us?

> *No care can come where God doth guard;*
> *No ill befall whom He doth keep;*
> *In safety hid, of trouble rid,*
> *I lay me down in peace and sleep.*

Now concerning sides, two cannot be on the side of the third without all three being on the same side. So if we were all on the side of God, all would be on the same side; and God would be on the side of all. Hence it is appropriate that we ask, "Who is on the Lord's side?" (Exodus 32:26).

The Rejected Stone

THE stone which the builders refused is become the
head stone of the corner. —118:22

This is a poetic figure that alludes to the construction of a building. The masons cast aside the stones
they consider unfit to go into the walls. It compares
to any individual who is rejected by others.

It describes David who was despised among the
sons of Jessie, but raised to be the ruler of Israel.
And along with others, it applies to Zerubabel. He
and his work were loathed; nevertheless he began and
finished the building, and "brought forth the head-
stone with shoutings, crying, Grace, grace unto it"
(Zechariah 4:7-10).

But the analogy was fulfilled in the largest sense
by the Messiah. Though "his own received him not,"
He was destined to become the King of Kings and the
Prince of Peace. Peter applied the Psalm to Jesus
(Acts 4:11), and Jesus applied the Psalm to Himself:

AND he beheld them, and said, What is this then that
is written, The stone which the builders rejected, the
same is become the head of the corner? —Luke 20:17

Oftentimes the very person that others see no attainment in climbs the highest. The child that is considered dense may later turn the light on for millions—
Thomas A. Edison, the example.

Though all men should turn you down, there is still
the opportunity for the grandest honor and service: you
can be a living stone in the church of God (I Peter 2:5).

Look Well to This Day

THIS is the day which the Lord hath made; we will rejoice and be glad in it. —118:24

There is no day like today.

The Lord made it. For you and me.

It is the day to rejoice and be glad.

The day to work and pray.

And serve and grow; dream and hope.

Today I shall grow taller!

For I shall walk with God.

AN EXHORTATION TO DAWN

Listen to the Exhortation of the Dawn.
Look well to this Day! For it is Life,
  The very Life of Life.
In its brief course lie all the Verities
  And Realities of your Existence.
    The Bliss of Growth;
    The Glory of Action;
    The Splendor of Beauty.
    For Yesterday is but a Dream;
    And Tomorrow is only a Vision.
But Today well lived makes every Yesterday
  A Dream of Happiness.
    And Every Tomorrow A Vision of Hope.
    Look well, therefore, to this Day.
    Such is the Salutation of the Dawn.

Power of the Word

BLESSED are they that keep his testimonies, and that seek him with the whole heart. —119:2

In this masterpiece on the word of God — Psalm 119 — the poet said, "My tongue shall speak of thy word" (ver. 172). Concerning its efficacy, here are eleven distinct functions:

1) Cleanses: "Wherewithal shall a young man cleanse his way? by taking heed ... to thy word" (ver. 9).

2) Guards against sin: "Thy word have I hid in mine heart, that I might not sin against thee" (ver. 11).

3) Counsels: "Thy testimonies also are my delight, and my counselors" (ver. 24).

4) Gives hope: "Remember the word ... upon which thou hast caused me to hope" (ver. 49).

5) Quickens: "Thy word hath quickened me" (ver. 50).

6) Puts a song in the heart: "Thy statutes have been my songs in the house of my pilgrimage" (ver. 54).

7) Makes wise: "Thou through thy commandments hast made me wiser than mine enemies ... my teachers ... the ancients" (vers. 98-100).

8) Feeds the soul: "How sweet are thy words unto my taste! yea, sweeter than honey to my mouth" (ver. 103).

9) Gives light: "Thy word is a lamp unto my feet, and a light unto my path" (ver. 105).

10) Gives joy: "Thy testimonies ... a heritage for ever ... they are the rejoicing of my heart" (ver. 111).

11) Provides the only infallible way: "I esteem all thy precepts concerning all things to be right" (ver. 128).

Resolutions Related to the Word

I WILL keep thy statutes. —119:8

In his determination to keep the Word, the psalmist said, "I have sworn, and I will perform it, that I will keep thy righteous judgments" (ver. 106). Knowing that the blessings of the commandments are derived from keeping them, his mind was made up to abide by them to the very end: "I have inclined mine heart to perform thy statutes always, even unto the end" (ver. 112). Resolved, he said:

— "I will *meditate* in thy precepts" (ver. 15). "My meditation all the day" (ver. 97).

— "I will *delight* myself in thy statutes (ver. 16). For "I love thy commandments" (ver. 129).

— "Thy law: yea, I shall *observe* it with my whole heart" (ver. 34). For "Thy word is very pure" (ver. 140).

— "I will *speak* of thy testimonies" (ver. 46). For "Thy testimonies are wonderful (ver. 129).

— "I will *never forget* thy precepts" (ver. 93). For "my soul is continually in my hand" (ver. 109).

— "I will *keep* the commandments of my God" (ver. 115). "Continually for ever and ever" (ver. 44).

— "I will have *respect* unto thy statutes continually" (ver. 117). For "I esteem all thy precepts concerning all things to be right" (ver. 128).

We have to resolve to improve. So for the better life, let us clothe ourselves with higher intents.

Security for Youth

WHEREWITHAL shall a young man cleanse his way?
by taking heed thereto according to thy word. —119:9

How shall the young secure themselves? The same
way the aged do. By taking heed to God's word.

Youth is so susceptible to temptation and exploitation. In the lad and lassie days, passions clamor for
indulgence. The young mind, not satisfied with old
truths, seeks something new, something different from
what the fathers followed; and this makes him an
easy victim of doubt and unbelief. Impatient with
control, youth has a tendency to cast off all restraint.
Untaught and inexperienced, it is easy for him to
be ensnared.

In answer to the question of youth's security, Isaac
Watts gave the world this popular hymn:

HOW SHALL THE YOUNG SECURE THEIR HEARTS

> *How shall the young secure their hearts,*
> *And guard their lives from sin?*
> *Thy word the choicest rules imparts*
> *To keep the conscience clean.*
>
> *'Tis, like the sun, a heav'nly light,*
> *That guides us all the day;*
> *And, thro' the dangers of the night,*
> *A lamp to lead our way.*
>
> *Thy word is everlasting truth;*
> *How pure is ev'ry page!*
> *That holy book shall guide our youth*
> *And well support our age.*

The Enlarged Heart

I WILL run the way of thy commandments, when thou
shalt enlarge my heart. —119:32

The composer believed God would grant him the
necessary grace to expand his heart. The heart must
have something to stimulate its growth, and one of
the powerful stimulants is the word of His grace.
With God's word working in the human heart — de-
veloping faith, hope, love, humility and unselfishness
— that heart is sure to expand.

The Word produces faith, and faith enlarges the
heart. Walking by faith, you see a bigger world that
urges a bigger heart. A big faith can make a mighty
big heart.

Hope is another heart expander. However, when
hope is lacking, the heart starts shrinking. Indeed,
every shrunken heart lost hope. So don't take from
me great expectations.

Also, love is a vigorous influence in the heart that
urges its growth. Where love is, there's no lack. Stand
back, therefore, all you things that would deny me
of love.

Humility is likewise a factor in heart development.
We must guard against haughtiness, for it constricts
the heart. It was pride that lessened the stature of
the fallen angels.

Additionally, unselfishness swells the heart.

In conclusion, what humanity needs is bigger hearts.
For a good heart is better than all the heads in the
world.

I Thought on My Ways

I THOUGHT on my ways, and turned my feet unto thy testimonies. —119:59

The poet gives us the first step in turning to God — reflection. He thought on his ways and surceased in his course of folly. He examined himself, and what he saw he didn't like.

He had gone too far without thinking, which describes a lot of traffic on the highway of life. He had lived with presence of mind but absence of thought. Not thinking denies one the fuller life. For there can be no harvest-time of character without a seed-time of thought.

Thinking on one's conduct has the power to stop the evil and right the wrong. When the thief thinks on his ways the peasant gets his cow back.

> *There is always hope for an individual who stops to do some serious thinking about life.*
> *—Katherine Logan*

Thus, as we would expect, the first step in the Prodigal Son's long journey home was his coming to himself (Luke 15:17). Only after getting a person to think upon his condition — his guilt and its consequences — can you hope to change him.

Therefore, we need to stop to think, and think to stop. If there are things bad in our lives, a little thinking will help us see it's so.

Companions

I AM a companion of all them that fear thee, and of them that keep thy precepts. —119:63

Like views and goals make companions. "Birds of a feather flock together." Where there are similar ideals there is an affinity. The psalmist brought this out in the text, stating that he is a companion of all who fear the Lord and keep His testimonies. They share in a common interest and toil in a common cause. This generates a magnetic power that pulls them together. For this reason they are always glad to see each other.

THEY that fear the Lord will be glad when they see me. —119:74

You tell on yourself by the company you keep. When a church member has all his friends outside the church, it reflects on where his heart is. The seekers of God prefer each other. The association gives them strength in their calling.

Two are better than one. —Ecclesiastes 4:9

Also, association is one of man's sweetest joys.

'Tis the Almighty's gracious plan,
That man shall be the joy of man.

Sweet Are the Promptings
of Affliction

BEFORE I was afflicted I went astray: but now have
I kept thy word. —119:67

The psalmist appraised his sufferings as blessings
in disguise. His affliction let him see life from a different vantage, and it reclaimed him from straying.
He admitted that it had been good for him:

IT is good for me that I have been afflicted; that I
might learn thy statutes. —119:71

In time of health and prosperity, he had held false
values, forgotten his duty, neglected the right and em-
braced the wrong.

This is the experience of millions.

Hence affliction is often necessary to call us back
to our finer self. Adversity is a better keeper of the
Word than prosperity.

There are lessons to learn in illness that we can't
learn in health. We become cognizant of blessings we
had just taken for granted. Prayer becomes sweeter.
The Bible more meaningful. Going to church is no
longer a formality. Friends are dearer. Just a walk
in the yard is a delight. And a ride in the car is a
thrill. The whole world is more beautiful. And the
desire to do right is multiplied many fold. When this
occurs, then surely we, too, can say, "It is good for
me that I have been afflicted."

The Good Do Good

THOU art good, and doest good: teach me thy statutes.
—119:68

God does good because He is good. It is not mere policy! Not bare wish! Not simple sentiment! It is the natural outpouring from a natural, inexhaustible reserve of goodness. Just as the fountain gives what it is, so does God (James 3:11).

The same principle of bringing forth fruit in keeping with the tree you are is true of man (Matthew 7:17).

A GOOD man out of the good treasure of the heart bringeth forth good things. —Matthew 12:35

So the secret of doing good is being good; then it comes naturally. One might better try to fly than try to be good when he is bad.

True goodness springs from a man's own heart.
—Chinese Proverb

Though there is much wrong in the world, there is still an excellent chance for a good person. Where you were born and of whom matters little.

A good man's pedigree is little hunted up.
—Spanish Proverb

No need. The world is more interested in a person's works.

What Makes Men Smart

THOU through thy commandments hast made me wiser
than mine enemies . . . I have more understanding than
all my teachers: for thy testimonies are my meditation. I understand more than the ancients, because I
keep thy precepts. —119:98-100

The writer wasn't boasting, just stating a fact. He
wasn't exalting himself. He was lauding the Word
of God.

The commandments had made him wiser than his
enemies. The Word gives a wisdom far above the
cleverness of the worldly wise. It is as Moses stated:

BEHOLD, I have taught you statutes and judgments . . .
Keep therefore and do them; for this is your wisdom
and your understanding in the sight of the nations,
which shall hear all these statutes, and say, Surely
this nation is a wise and understanding people.
—Deuteronomy 4:5, 6

He had more understanding than all his teachers;
that is, the teachers of secular knowledge. They were
wise in their fields of worldly training, but unwise in
unworldly matters. Instructors can be well versed in
their specialty, but very lacking in wisdom and spiritual knowledge.

He had a deeper understanding than the ancients
or the aged. It was due to keeping the Divine precepts. "Years should teach wisdom," but sometimes
the aged don't learn (Job 32:7-9). Gray hair does
not necessarily indicate gray matter.

Antiquity is no help against stupidity.
—Martin Luther

May Iniquity Not Rule Over Me

ORDER my steps in thy word: and let not any iniquity have dominion over me. —119:133

The poet prays that no sin rule over him; that no passion enslave him. Even a little sin is so subtle it won't stay little long.

Sin multiplies. He that will serve one sin will have to serve many.

No person is prepared in heart to keep himself pure, if he has granted himself the privilege to indulge in a few or even one sin. It is no religion at all just to refrain from the sins that have no appeal to you. Everybody is against the sins that give him no pleasure. Obeying only what suits one is hardly obedience at all.

No man is master of himself who is slave to sin.

It is man's task to master the sin — not allow the sin to master him. The great issue of life is which is to be master — that's all.

And now may we be able to say —

*The wages of sin is death —
thank God I quit before pay day.*
—*Reamer Loomis*

Little Big People

I AM small and despised: yet do not I forget thy precepts. —119:141

I am small. The word *small* could mean small in number, or small in years, or small in rank.

And despised. Treated with contempt; passed by; loathed. It may have come as the result of rank, age, poverty or religion. Regardless of the cause, the pain of being despised surely hurt. It is hard to take reproach and ridicule.

Little — but he remembered the precepts of God. This made him big. Little in the eyes of men. Big in the eyes of God. The perfect God and the imperfect man have completely different standards of littleness and bigness, which make it possible for the same person to be so little and so big.

Life is made up of *littles* that are valuable. The day is filled with little beams of the sun, and the night is magnificent with the little twinklings of the stars. When nature chose to give the world something rare and beautiful she made it little: little diamonds, little pearls and little gold nuggets. The Sermon on the Mount is little, but the man who obeys it becomes a giant.

Let us not despise the little people. They may be the keepers of the precepts . . . and in that case, they are giants the world is too blind to recognize.

So here's to the *little* people — did I say little? — the mighty, mighty, big people!

Deliver Me From Lying Lips

DELIVER my soul, O Lord, from lying lips, and from a deceitful tongue. —120:2

Every person who has been misrepresented and maligned has cried out with anguish, "Deliver my soul, O Lord, from lying lips." There are few hurts more painful and widespread than slander.

And when it occurs, what do you do? The origin cannot always be traced; and if it could, the perpetrator often becomes all the more bitter and, behind your back, villifies you for approaching him. This only makes a bigger tale which adds a tinge of credibility to that which is false. Even if the slanderer should repent and try to right the wrong, the calumny has gone on the wind like feathers on a windy day.

Poor person! Retaliation will not help. Even if you wished, how could you black that which is already jet black? The calumniator fights in ways you cannot engage. Like the skunk, he gives off an odor that righteous people find hard to encounter. Like the wolf, he has fangs not to be matched with soft hands.

Maybe, about all that can be done is to pray. Your friends won't believe the rumor. And your enemies won't have it any other way.

Here's our prayer: From fabricators, gossipers, talebearers, anonymous writers, senders of newspaper clippings and all liars, dear Lord, deliver us.

Takes Two to Make Peace

MY soul hath long dwelt with him that hateth peace.
I am for peace: but when I speak, they are for war.
—120:6, 7

The poet had been exposed to the strife of people known for their war-like disposition. When he spoke to them of peace, they were for war. No proposal would satisfy them. They were averse to peace, set on hostility. There was nothing the psalmist could do to prevent it.

To be exposed constantly to a quarrel — in marriage, in the home, in business, or in world affairs — is extremely bitter. It is trying to live with maladjusted people, ever ready to pick a fuss.

Takes two to make peace. But what about the maxim, "Takes two to make war?" Takes two to make attack and counterattack. However one can attack; and, though the attacked refrains from hostility, it is still war — just one-sided strife. One person can cause trouble. But it takes two to make peace.

I saw this happen: One brother in the church fell out with another for no reason. There was nothing the second brother could do to change the feelings of the first one. Though he refused to retaliate, the perpetrator continued to fight and smear him behind his back. Only one could make war. But only one could not make peace. That required two.

How sorry a thing is war.

But peace can never rule the day, unless peace rules the hearts of both.

From Whence Comes My Help

I WILL lift up mine eyes unto the hills, from whence cometh my help. My help cometh from the Lord, which made heaven and earth. He will not suffer thy foot to be moved: he that keepeth thee will not slumber. Behold, he that keepeth Israel shall neither slumber nor sleep. The Lord is my keeper: the Lord is thy shade upon thy right hand. The sun shall not smite thee by day, nor the moon by night. The Lord shall preserve thee from all evil: he shall preserve thy soul. The Lord shall preserve thy going out and thy coming in from this time forth, and even for evermore. —121

We have given the Psalm in its completeness. It is one of blessed comfort and striking consolation. The author lifts up his eyes to the hills in anticipation of help. He finds confidence in the singular truth that God never sleeps; that He always watches over, cares for and protects His children "from this time forth, and even for evermore."

It has been called a New Year's Psalm. For whatever occasion the Psalm may have been written, it is well suited to New Year's thoughts, for daily meditation or for any circumstance.

The future is too uncertain not to have the assurance of which the Psalm so beautifully speaks; for one thing we struggling creatures need is help.

> *The very dimness of my sight*
> *Makes me secure;*
> *For groping in my misty way,*
> *I feel His hand; I hear Him say,*
> *"My help is sure."*
>
> —*John Parker*

The Thought of Worship Made Me Glad

I WAS glad when they said unto me, Let us go into the house of the Lord. —122:1

Going up to Jerusalem to worship wás a season of great joy for the writer. It produced a delight and satisfaction that transcended all other joys.

Here are seven benefits of worship, which produce gladness:

1) It is helpful for humanity to reach toward Divinity.

2) The feeling that we are in the presence of the Lord is sobering; brings us to our senses.

3) Worship is more inducive to soul-searching (I Corinthians 11:28), which is a prerequisite to improvement.

4) Obedience to the command to worship gives an approving conscience, while disobedience sears it. Man needs to keep his conscience sensitive.

5) Worship encourages the renewal of resolves, to once again say, "I will."

6) A pause from the world's slavish grind of materialism, a silence, a meditation on the spiritual, is invigorating.

7) Mixing and mingling with those of like ideals inspires good works (Hebrews 10:24).

Therefore —

It is only when men begin to worship
that they begin to grow.

—Calvin Coolidge

For the Sake of Others

PEACE be within thy walls, and prosperity within thy palaces. For my brethren and companions' sakes, I will now say, Peace be within thee. —122:7, 8

It was his prayer that there be peace within the defenses around Jerusalem; that tranquillity prevail within the rulers' palaces.

The particular reason was: *For my brethren and companions' sake.* Because some dwell there; others go there to worship; and all derive hope from the city. Thus he earnestly prayed, "Peace be within thee." For there their dreams and hopes were entwined.

The religion of God requires that we be concerned with others: "Look not every man on his own things, but every man also on the things of others" (Philippians 2:4). Jesus "came not to be ministered unto, but to minister" (Mark 10:45).

It is reputed that on the bells of a New England university are inscribed these words:

For him who in art beautifies life, I ring;
For him who in letters interprets life, I ring;
For the man of science who widens knowledge, I ring;
For the philosopher who ennobles life, I ring;
For the scholar who preserves learning, I ring;
For the preacher of the fear of the Lord, I ring;

But the one statement that strikes the major chord of humanity's heart is that on the first bell:

For him who in any station seeks not to
be ministered unto, but to minister, I ring.

The Lifted Eyes

UNTO thee lift I up mine eyes, O thou that dwellest in the heavens. —123:1

This is one of the compliments of man — the ability to lift up his eyes. The animals have no longing that prompts their eyes to look heavenward. But man is different. With eyes of faith, he penetrates the veil of space and lifts his vision in search of the unseen.

Lifted eyes indicate a heart that is very expressive:

Signifies reflection. The individual ponders the issues of life; helpless, he looks up to Him who rules and blesses man.

Testifies to faith. The infidel's vision is never above the earth.

Bespeaks obedience. The lifted eyes manifest obedient service: "Speak, Lord, I will hear, command, I will obey."

Suggests humility. The proud have eyes that see only themselves and their own glory.

Indicates need. Going around with our heads down is a good way to shrink our perspective. Bitter trials and vexing problems leave us in need of a longer and broader view, achieved only by lifting our eyes to God.

Denotes hope. The person desires and expects something this earth cannot supply.

The visionary eyes will give us a view of God and man; and this is what religion is all about — seeing God and serving man.

As the Eyes of a Servant

BEHOLD, as the eyes of servants look unto the hand of their masters, and as the eyes of a maiden unto the hand of her mistress; so our eyes wait upon the Lord our God, until that he hath mercy upon us. —123:2

The illustration is an apt portrayal of the believer's relationship to his God — that of a servant. The eyes of the servant and maiden are constantly set on the master and mistress to catch their every expression, ready to obey their wishes on the slightest signal.

We, too, need eyes focused on our Master, and a disposition that prays: "Not my will, but thine, be done" (Luke 22:42).

There are, however, differences in the relationship and servitude, which should prompt our services to come more gladly and freely: (1) Our Master, being perfect, never issues an unreasonable order. (2) Our Master has superior rewards to offer; greater protection; even eternal life. (3) Our Master is more understanding. (4) Good servants are made by good masters — this makes us the greatest. (5) Our servitude bestows greater honors — a nobility that outranks kings who are not His servants. (6) To serve our Master is not slavery; it is the highest form of liberty. (7) Our service can continue in the next world. And when everything else has passed away, what a joy it will be to hear Him say:

WELL done, thou good and faithful servant . . . enter thou into the joy of thy lord. —Matthew 25:21

God for Us

IF it had not been the Lord who was on our side,
when men rose up against us: Then they had swallowed
us up quick . . . . —124:2,3

There was unmistakable evidence that God had interposed and delivered them when they were assailed by their enemies.

The determining factor in their success was God. He was on their side. If it had not been for Jehovah, they would have been pulled down by opposing forces. God tilted the balance of strength in their favor.

The one all-important lesson to learn from Israel's successes and failures is that when God was on their side, they were strong and invincible; but when God was not with them, they were weak and vulnerable.

With God on our side, we have the Almighty to bear our burdens; stand by us in distress; dry our tears in time of sorrow; and give us strength in time of temptation. He will fight for us, and that means victory.

With God on our side, we cannot lose; without it, we do not deserve to win.

> *I have no answer, for myself or thee,*
> *Save that I learned beside my mother's knee;*
> *"All is of God that is, and is to be;*
> *And God is good." Let this suffice us still,*
> *Resting in childlike trust upon His will*
> *Who moves to His great ends unthwarted by the ill.*
>
> *—John Greenleaf Whittier*

Escape

OUR soul is escaped as a bird out of the snare of the
fowlers: the snare is broken, and we are escaped.
—124:7

Like a bird caught in the snare of the fowler, they
escaped. The net was broken and they were free.
This happens when the snare is not as strong as the
struggling bird; and, in the application of the illustration, it occurs when the snare is too weak to hold
a robust people made strong by the power of God.
For their help is "in the name of the Lord" (ver. 8).

It may be that we have been caught by a number
of ensnarements that restrict our freedom, snares
from which we desperately need to escape: *Doubt* —
confines us to only what we experience with our
senses, to what we see, hear, touch, taste and smell;
for we are devoid of faith. *Superstition* — locks us
within walls of unsupported fears. *Hate* — binds us
to a slavish and miserable life. *Unforgiveness* — tight-
ens the hold on the soul and squeezes the life out of
it. *Worry* — paces us in a narrow cage. *No vision* —
clips our wings and holds us to where we are.

All kinds of fowlers with every kind of a snare is
out there; but with God's help we can break loose.

May our yearning to escape cause us to cry out in
the language of Lot:

O LET me escape thither, and my soul shall live.
—Genesis 19:20

Unmovable Like a Mountain

THEY that trust in the Lord shall be as mount Zion, which cannot be removed, but abideth for ever. —125:1

The devout Jew beheld mount Zion with all its stability as a symbol of the dependability of God; and as a promise of what he could become, if he trusted Jehovah. This everyday scene, always there, always unchanged, conveyed a message to them — one that all humanity needs to hear.

Trust in God provides a firm foundation that saves us from slipping and tottering. It is only when trust is broken that the child of God becomes movable, as seen in the Scripture: "Take heed, brethren, lest there be in any of you an evil heart of unbelief [doubt, distrust] in departing from the living God" (Hebrews 3:12). Distrust is the earthquake that sends the rumblings through the soul and shifts it. However, when our trust in Him is full and undivided, we stand unmovable like a mountain. "Trust ye in the Lord for ever; for in the Lord Jehovah is everlasting strength" (Isaiah 26:4).

I SHALL NOT BE MOVED

Though the tempest rage round me,
Through the storm, my Lord, I see;
Standing like a mountain holy,
I shall not be moved from Thee.
I shall not be moved,
Anchored to the Rock of Ages,
I shall not be moved.

Reward the Good

Do good, O Lord, unto those that be good, and to them
that are upright in their hearts. —125:4

Because they are good, repay them with good, give
them the reaping of their sowing. This was the prayer
of the psalmist. It is in keeping with the scriptural
principle that *like deserves like*. "For whatsoever a
man soweth, that shall he also reap" (Galatians 6:7).

I cannot hold to the pessimism that good people do
not profit from their goodness. Good for the evil and
evil for the good is contrary to all the workings of
nature.

Things are drawn together by a natural affinity. The
good man draws good. And he should. For he is fit
to receive. "Righteousness tendeth unto life" is a
law of God (Proverbs 11:19).

> *Good, better, best;*
> *Never let it rest*
> *Till your good is better,*
> *And your better best.*
>
> —*Old Maxim*

Good is sure to come back to you for being your best.
The most good that comes, however, is comfort in the
hour of death. When Sir Walter Scott lay dying, he
called for his son-in-law and biographer, and said,
"Lockhart, be a good man. Be virtuous, be religious,
be a good man. Nothing else will give you any comfort when you come to lie here."

A Dream Come True

WHEN the Lord turned again the captivity of Zion,
we were like them that dream . . . . —126:1-3

The ecstasy was caused by the Lord's returning them
from captivity. The poet stated, "We were like them
that dream." It seemed too good to be true. But it
was. Their redemption from captivity was real; it
was marvelous . . . full of joy.

This is how it affected their personality:

"Then was our mouth filled with laughter." They
had something to cause them to laugh, and they did.

"And our tongue with singing." Their happiness
was expressed in songs, which is a natural way to
show a rapturous feeling. In an assembly of people
whose dreams have come true, there is always joyful
singing.

"The Lord had done great things for them." They
knew it. They felt it. They expressed it.

Dream! Be sure to dream! Then turn it over to
the Fulfiller of Dreams. Back of the dreamer there is
the God who makes the dream come true; for —

IF God be for us, who can be against us? —Romans 8:31

With His help, you can see what men have only
dreamed of seeing. But you must do your part —
wake up!

Bringing in the Sheaves

THEY that sow in tears shall reap in joy. He that goeth forth and weepeth, bearing precious seed, shall doubtless come again with rejoicing, bringing his sheaves with him. —126:5, 6

The passage particularly alludes to the long, weary march of the Jewish exiles to their native land. Comparing the ordeal to a harvest, it was a work of toil and tears; but there was joy when the journey was over, like bringing in the sheaves.

The sower's work is sometimes so burdensome that he sows in tears, yet reaps in joy. Many endeavors are beset with difficulties and require long laborious hours; but the joy of success more than compensates for the care and toil. This is true of the farmer's perspiration, the businessman's caution, the worker's loyalty, the teacher's patience, the student's application, the parent's training, the minister's proclamation and the missionary's concern — sometimes sowing in tears, always reaping in joy, bringing in the sheaves. This is stated so beautifully in the song:

BRINGING IN THE SHEAVES

Sowing in the morning, sowing seeds of kindness,
Sowing in the noontide and the dewy eves;
Waiting for the harvest and the time of reaping,
We shall come rejoicing, bringing in the sheaves.

Go then even weeping, sowing for the Master,
Though the loss sustained, our spirit often grieves;
When our weeping's over, He will bid us welcome,
We shall come rejoicing, bringing in the sheaves.

—Knowles Shaw

Except the Lord Build the House

ExCEPT the Lord build the house, they labor in vain that build it. Except the Lord keep the city, the watchman waketh but in vain. —127:1

God has a blueprint for construction and security that cannot be ignored without failure finally coming, no matter what the skill, or strength or industry of the worker may be.

As people build a home, a business, a school, a nation or a local church, a dependence on God as the builder should be uppermost in their minds.

Except the Lord build the house, they labor in vain that build it should be our motto. Churchmen should not be tempted to ignore God, to substitute the human for the Divine. We are too prone to discard the old scriptural plan for something less demanding. The material for the church is living stones, redeemed and sanctified; but the get-a-crowd-at-any-price builders throw caution to the wind, and use crumbling stones of impenitence, irreverence and worldliness. They swell church rolls and shrink sanctuaries.

As William Cowper stated, too often men have —

Built God a church, and laugh'd His word to scorn.

The inconsistency of such a builder was voiced by James Russell Lowell —

For though he builds glorious temples, 'tis odd
He leaves never a doorway to get in a god.

Children a Heritage

Lo, children are a heritage of the Lord: and the fruit of the womb is his reward. As arrows are in the hand of a mighty man; so are the children of the youth. Happy is the man that hath his quiver full of them: they shall not be ashamed, but they shall speak with the enemies in the gate. —127:3-5

The prosperity of a family and a nation depends on children. They are the reward of God. The lesson is enforced by an illustration: As arrows in the hand of a mighty man, children protect their aged parents; and when the father's cause is contested, they stand in the gate to take his part.

They protect the couple from selfishness. The parents are absorbed with the welfare of their offspring.

Children protect the home from boredom. With their hurts and ills, curiosity and learning, joys and smiles, sorrows and tears, each day bursts anew with challenges that bring a special interest.

Flesh of their flesh protects the home from separation. Surely there should be other reasons for togetherness, but children do tend to unify the parents. Drawn together by an object of mutual love and held by two tiny hands, one in the hand of the mother and the other in the hand of the father, they renew their commitment to each other.

Children protect the parents in old age. Nature has a way of balancing things. The little ones are cared for in their helpless state; and when years have passed and parents become helpless, they have their children to stand by and assist them.

A Lovely Home

BLESSED is every one that feareth the Lord; that walketh in his ways. For thou shalt eat the labor of thine hands: happy shalt thou be, and it shalt be well with thee. Thy wife shall be as a fruitful vine by the sides of thine house: thy children like olive plants round about thy table. —128:1-3

A family possessed with the fear of the Lord (ver. 1). This is a basic for the ideal home. The temperance, prudence, industry and thrift that go with keeping the commandments of God definitely bless the family.

A family that enjoys the labors of their own hands (ver. 2). Work brings a unique happiness, a satisfying contentment. It gives a feeling of accomplishment and independence, a sense of worthwhileness, which holds up their heads and allows them to look the world in the face.

A family with a fruitful wife (ver. 3). She is willing to do more than her part. A pleasant, industrious, thrifty, cooperative, helpful wife who loves her husband and her children is a precious blessing. He who finds her finds a good thing (Proverbs 18:22).

A family blessed with the patter of little feet (ver. 3). The "children are like olive plants" round about, growing up to take the place of the older ones when time takes its toll. They are stimulating blessings. They scatter sunshine and give strength.

*Be it ever so humble, there's no
place like home.*
—John Howard Payne

A Grandfather's Delight

BEHOLD, that thus shall the man be blessed that feareth the Lord . . . Yea, thou shalt see thy children's children, and peace upon Israel. —128:4-6

The promise to the God-fearing man to see "thy children's children" is literal, and one of the happiest experiences of life — to hold and love flesh of his flesh. "Children's children are the crown of old men" (Proverbs 17:6).

The very word (grandfather) speaks volumes. He is old enough to realize that the newly-arrived child from the hand of God is a link between two worlds. Grandfather can especially enjoy the childish sweetness, warm companionship and wide-eyed adoration of the grandchild. The years have seasoned him for it.

The godly man finds a distinct gladness in the thought he is leaving behind a pious lineage he hopes will continue. He rejoices in the expectation that his unfeigned faith will be handed down to succeeding generations, as was true of Lois, Eunice and Timothy (II Timothy 1:5). It is a sign of man's spiritual nature that it gives him joy to extend his life in the lives of his posterity.

Give us grandchildren!
Strong, healthy, talented ones:
Grandsons whom high hope inspires,
Granddaughters whom virtue fires,
Grandsons who honor their fathers,
Granddaughters who love mothers,
True, pure, faithful, useful ones;
Give us grandchildren, I say,
Give us grandchildren.

They Survived the Hardships

MANY a time have they afflicted me from my youth,
may Israel now say: Many a time have they afflicted
me from my youth: yet they have not prevailed against
me. The plowers plowed upon my back: they made long
their furrows. The Lord is righteous: he hath cut
asunder the cords of the wicked. —129:1-4

Israel's memory was one of constant affliction. Her
oppressions began in early youth, as soon as she became a nation.

The enemy was unmercifully cruel. "They plowed
upon my back," making long furrows, states the composer. Their oppressors had attempted to hold them
in bondage with strong cords.

However, the violence directed against Israel failed.
They withstood the afflictions in a commendable and
heroic way. It is amazing how much punishment
human beings can take when their will is forged by
an unbreakable faith. They could say, "Yet they have
not prevailed against me."

Other individuals and nations have passed through
similar trials, and have borne them courageously; and
perhaps were the bigger and purer because they suffered. On this point, Job said:

BUT he knoweth the way that I take: when he hath
tried me, I shall come forth as gold. —Job 23:10

Endurance was their crowning quality. It showed
a Divine grandeur.

*Not in the achievement, but in the endurance
of the human soul, does it show its divine grandeur,
and its alliance with the infinite God.*

—*E. H. Chapin*

As Grass on the Housetop

LET them all be confounded and turned back that hate Zion. Let them be as the grass upon the housetops, which withereth afore it groweth up: wherewith the mower filleth not his hand; nor he that bindeth sheaves his bosom. Neither do they which go by say, The blessing of the Lord be upon you: we bless you in the name of the Lord. —129:5-8

This is a prayer that God interpose and confound the enemies of Israel; turn them back; "let them be as the grass upon the housetops." The housetops were covered with earth where seeds would germinate and begin to grow, but later would wither because of the soil's shallowness — an apt illustration of feebleness.

In this case, those who passed by would not say, "The blessing of the Lord be upon you." It was customary when persons passed the harvest field to say to the reapers, "The blessing of the Lord be upon you." It was a token of goodwill, an expression of achievement and a hope of prosperity. But such a greeting would never be given the owners of grass on housetops. It would be ridiculous to apply the salutation to the gatherers of useless grass.

This is the psalmist's prayer in regard to the haters of Zion (ver. 5), that they not be given a prosperity that would evoke the congratulations and appreciation of their neighbors. Since it takes a harvest to keep an army going, then if it should be denied them, their aggressiveness would have to cease.

When a man projects himself into a future of no bread, the plowshare is more inviting than the sword.

If God Marked Iniquities

IF thou, Lord, shouldest mark iniquities, O Lord, who shall stand? But there is forgiveness with thee, that thou mayest be feared. —130:3, 4

But if He doesn't mark them, how can He forgive them? How can He erase what He hasn't marked? Obviously, it means God does not permanently and irrevocably mark iniquity. Though it is tallied, He is willing to blot it out and remember it no more (Hebrews 8:12). But if they were marked against us forever, "O Lord, who shall stand?" Nobody! "For all have sinned, and come short of the glory of God" (Romans 3:23).

What confident hope are these statements in the Psalm:

BUT there is forgiveness with thee. —ver. 4
WITH him is plenteous redemption. —ver. 7

With the Lord there is forgiveness. For those who care for it, it is available. It gives them another chance, and another, and another and another; for the Lord who taught us to forgive each other seventy times seven would not ask of man that which He is not willing to give. Knowing that Jehovah's forgiveness is inexhaustible, we pray:

Dear Lord and Father of mankind,
Forgive our foolish ways!
Reclothe us in our rightful mind,
In purer lives Thy service find,
In deeper reverence, praise.

—John Greenleaf Whittier

Therein I Hope

I WAIT for the Lord, my soul doth wait, and in his word do I hope. —130:5

It wasn't wishful thinking. It was a solid hope based on the bedrock of God's word. God had spoken; the poet believed it; therein was his hope. From God's word hope springs eternal in the human heart. On this point, Paul says, ". . . that we through patience and comfort of the Scriptures might have hope" (Romans 15:4). So the beacons of hope are the beacons of God's word.

"The Lord is not slack concerning his promises" (II Peter 3:9).

In all his distress, the psalmist was in a *waiting* posture, hoping, looking to the Lord to take his part. It gave patience and vitality to his endurance.

> *Let us, then, be up and doing,*
> *With a heart for any fate;*
> *Still achieving, still pursuing,*
> *Learn to labor and to wait.*
>
> *—Henry Wadsworth Longfellow*

Hope lets you dream —

> *Hope is a waking dream.*
> *—Aristotle*

You are awake — it's no sleeping dream. The hope is real. And in realistic anticipation you wait for it to come to pass.

Not Haughty

LORD, my heart is not haughty, nor mine eyes lofty:
neither do I exercise myself in great matters, or in
things too high for me. —131:1

It wasn't a counterfeit humility — a pride that apes
humility — but a humility so real that it would not
feign a standard so false that would keep it from
acknowledging itself.

His heart was not haughty. This gave him a special standing before God. Haughtiness — God will not
tolerate (Proverbs 6:17). As we observe in our ma-
turing years the vanity and vexation of the haughty,
this trait becomes more and more distasteful.

The composer's eyes were not lofty. Pride in the
heart especially manifests itself in the eyes. His eyes
were not fixed on the showy, ostentatious things that
easily impress those who fall for superficial signs of
greatness.

Neither did he exercise himself in things too high
for his capacity. Putting a realistic limit on our endeavors is an act of wisdom that saves us from un-
necessary frustrations. If we are not driven by pride,
nature permits us to gradually drift into the realm
where inclination, adaptation and capacity best fit us.
The ideal sphere for every person is the place where
affinity and ability naturally draw him.

So to all seeking a purer and happier life, we say:
May God save us from pride and hypocrisy. For —

> *He that is proud eats up himself.*
> *—William Shakespeare*

A House for God

> LORD, remember David, and all his afflictions: How he sware unto the Lord, and vowed unto the mighty God of Jacob; surely I will not come into the tabernacle of my house, nor go up into my bed; I will not give sleep to mine eyes, or slumber to mine eyelids, until I find out a place for the Lord, a habitation for the mighty God of Jacob. —132:1-5

David made an oath to secure for the Lord a special house of worship. He vowed to make the project his first business; not to go to his own house, nor sleep until he had found a place for the Lord — a place for the ark of God to safely and constantly remain. The ark had been moved from place to place, but David vowed to put it in a stationary location: first, a tent or tabernacle on Mount Zion, and then a magnificent structure, the temple. The latter was not realized by him but by his son Solomon. This was his reasoning:

> SEE now, I dwell in a house of cedar, but the ark of God dwelleth within curtains. —II Samuel 7:2

The contrast was very inconsistent with true dedication to God. It doesn't add up to true commitment for us to have the finest at home and the cheapest at church. Whatever concerns we have for our own houses are appropriate feelings for God's house — adequacy, beauty, carpets, cushions, new roof and fresh paint. And if our own grounds are well kept while the church grounds grow up in ugliness — how does God see it? and our neighbors?

The "If" in God's Promise

IF thy children will keep my covenant and my testimony
that I shall teach them, their children shall also sit
upon thy throne for evermore. —132:12

In the first part of the Psalm, David makes a vow
to God. In the last part, God makes one to David.
However, God's is conditional; "if" is attached: "if
thy children will keep my covenant and my testimony"
(ver. 12). When God issues a conditional promise to
bless man, all man has to do to get the blessing is to
meet the condition; but to expect the blessing without
complying is absurd.

It would be improper for the Just One to uncon-
ditionally promise to bless man, who might later turn
and misuse the benefaction to harm himself and his
Benefactor. God's doing His best for us may dictate
that He withhold the blessing and discipline us instead. This is what the Lord stated at the time He
made the promise to David (II Samuel 7:14, 15).

That God affixes conditions to His promises is very
wise:

— It tests faith and obedience.

— Preserves man's sense of dependence on God's
favor.

— Shows our worthiness or unworthiness to receive.

The Divinely stated "if" stands before all of us. If
we fail to meet the conditions, we lose all claim to
the promises — and it's our fault.

How Good and Pleasant Is Unity

BEHOLD, how good and how pleasant it is for brethren to dwell together in unity! It is like the precious ointment upon the head, that ran down upon the beard, even Aaron's beard: that went down to the skirts of his garments; as the dew of Hermon, and as the dew that descended upon the mountains of Zion: for there the Lord commanded the blessing, even life for evermore. —133:1-3

The unity of *brethren*—people with a common Father, a common faith and a common calling — is a state the composer extols as something good and pleasant.

The odor of this oneness is fragrant, he states, like the sacred ointment used in priestly consecration. The anointing oil was composed of several precious ingredients (Exodus 20:23, 24). The psalmist had a vision of its abundance running down from the head of Aaron to his beard and garments. The thought is: unity grants bountiful portions to man.

And it shines in beauty, like the dew on Mount Hermon.

However, to achieve it, we must adhere to a common standard: "walk by the same rule" (Philippians 3:16).

Concerning the necessity of oneness, it is something Paul commanded (Ephesians 4:3); and something for which Jesus prayed (John 17:20, 21).

When a group has to face the whole world, they had better stand together.

United we stand, divided we fall.
—G. P. Morris

Alternate Songs of Praise

BEHOLD, bless ye the Lord, all ye servants of the Lord, which by night stand in the house of the Lord. Lift up your hands in the sanctuary, and bless the Lord. The Lord that made heaven and earth bless thee out of Zion. —134:1-3

In this short Psalm there is a summons to praise and adoration.

Perhaps it was written to be sung by alternate singers: by the people who approached the temple, calling on the ministers of religion in the sanctuary to lift up their hands and praise God (vers. 1, 2); and then by the ministers who gave the response, pronouncing a blessing on the approaching worshipers who requested it, a blessing emanating from Zion (ver. 3).

In an adaptation of practicality we note:

1) Those who come to the new Zion, the church, seeking a blessing, shall not go away empty.

2) It is striking that the Psalm speaks of devotion in the night. When the world sleeps and we are alone with God; when noise has ceased and silence refuses to whisper; when nothing stirs except our thoughts of God; it gives us a deeper solemnity and better fits us for holy devotion. Significantly, it was during the night that Nicodemus went to Jesus (John 3:2). Also, even Jesus Himself chose the night to go "out into a mountain to pray" where he continued the whole "night in prayer to God" (Luke 6:12). Sometimes we can see in the night what the day never reveals.

Pleasant Worship

PRAISE the Lord; for the Lord is good: sing praises
unto his name; for it is pleasant. —135:3

Our hearts should be so tuned to the heart of God
that worship strikes a happy note. The house of God
should be a joyous place where worship is pleasant.
There is nothing to gain in being a church corpse,
sitting on coffin-colored pews, surrounded by depressing decoration, wondering if you can endure it until
you can get a little fresh air. God is alive. We are
alive. And worship to Him should be alive, moving
and pleasant — not something dead, rendered by the
dead, who dread it.

But for worship to be pleasant, *we* must be pleasant.
Resentful, disgruntled, seething-with-anger people are
not going to enjoy the worship.

Another thing — it must come from the spirit or
inner nature of man (John 4:24). Praise from the
mouth out could hardly expect to satisfy. To the true
worshiper, worship is not a hall of politics, not a
nest of trifles, not a fair of vanity, not an assembly
of babbling voices, nor a circus for misguided people
who use it for play acting.

Furthermore, worship must be in truth, according
to the truth God has commanded (John 4:24). After
all, the God that is being worshiped is the one to be
pleased — not the worshiper; and the only way we
know to please Him is to offer Him what He has commanded. And this gives peace.

God Does as He Pleases

WHATSOEVER the Lord pleased, that did he in heaven, and in earth, in the seas, and all deep places. —135:6

And why shouldn't He do as He pleases?

— Everything He wishes is perfect.
— Everything He does is infallible.
— His every act is merciful.
— Nothing is beyond His power.
— He cannot do wrong.

As the absolute sovereign, He has formed a perfect plan and carries it out infallibly.

But with man it is not so — the weak and vulnerable creature errs. It is not in him to direct his own steps. He needs guidance. His will needs to be bent to the will of the Perfect One. So our aim should be to do as God pleases.

WHAT PLEASETH GOD

What pleaseth God with joy receive;
Though storm-winds rage and billows heave
And earth's foundations all be rent,
Be comforted; to thee is sent
   What pleaseth God.

God's will is best; to this resigned,
How sweetly rests the weary mind!
Seek, then, this blessed conformity,
Desiring but to do and be
   What pleaseth God.

                              —Paul Gerhardt

Give Thanks Unto the Lord

O GIVE thanks unto the Lord; for he is good: for his mercy endureth for ever. —136:1

The Psalm gives these reasons for giving thanks unto Jehovah:

— "To him who alone doeth great wonders" (ver. 4).

— "To him that by wisdom made the heavens" (ver. 5).

— "To him that stretcheth out the earth above the waters" (ver. 6).

— "To him that made great lights . . . the sun to rule by day . . . the moon and stars to rule by night" (vers. 7-9).

— "To him that smote Egypt in their firstborn . . . and brought out Israel from among them . . . with a strong hand, and with a stretched out arm" (ver. 10-12).

— "To him which divided the Red Sea into parts . . . and made Israel to pass through the midst of it . . . but overthrew Pharoah and his host in the Red Sea" (vers. 13-15).

— "To him which led his people through the wilderness" (ver. 17).

— "To him which smote great kings . . . and slew famous kings . . . who remembered us in our low estate . . . and hath redeemed us from our enemies . . . who giveth food to all flesh" (vers. 17-25).

The God who did much for Israel also does much for us; and our thanks should be every bit as deep and expressive as the ancients.

Enduring Mercy

O GIVE thanks to the Lord of Lords: for his mercy endureth for ever. —136:3

There are twenty-six verses in the Psalm and all of them end exactly alike, with this note of praise: "for his mercy endureth for ever." Twenty-six times. Repetition. Repetition. But it cannot be said too often. It is one thing everybody needs — mercy — and something God has plenty of.

When temptation beckons and our weakness succumbs; when our foot stumbles and we fall; when the tide of fortune rolls out and leaves us stranded; when disease strikes and shatters the old body like a house torn to shambles; when sorrow pierces our heart and our eyes are turned to tears; when we are shrouded with loneliness because friends forsake; when the job we had counted on folds; when persecution inflicts without cause; when we are bewildered over a problem that seems to have no solution; when the burdens appear too heavy for our frailty — it is then that we can better appreciate the repetitious praise in the Psalm, "his mercy endureth for ever."

We must have help, or we shall lose the struggle. The mercy is granted. Help comes and we become victors. Now in the deepest gratitude, we express our thanks to Him whose "mercy endureth for ever."

Ye fearful saints, fresh courage take:
The clouds ye so much dread
Are big with mercy, and shall break
In blessings on your head.
—William Cowper

Memory's Tears

BY the rivers of Babylon, there we sat down, yea, we wept, when we remembered Zion. —137:1

Sitting on the banks of the rivers of Babylon (Euphrates and linking canals) the captives wept. Not because their character was weak (no crybaby tears), but because their memory was strong. They remembered who they were and what had happened to them — exiles in a strange land, inflicted with severe suffering.

It was the vivid recollection of the wrongs perpetrated against Jerusalem that sorrowed their hearts and opened wide the valves on their tear ducts. There by the river, they sat; they meditated; they remembered; they wept. Their harps hung on the willow trees, and no song graced their lips; instead, memory touched their heart strings and played the mournful melody of tears. A memory of their land — its former glory; its lost strength; the cruelties inflicted upon it; the devastations; the delightful days spent there in contrast with their Babylonian misery and humiliation; and, no doubt, their shortcomings which had brought them to their low estate. Former privileges versus present privations — this was their changed fortune; and it grieved them. The richer our treasure, the poorer our loss. The fuller our joy, the emptier we are when it is gone.

One priceless power they had left was memory.

> *Memory, the warder of the brain.*
> *—William Shakespeare*

When No Song Is in the Heart

FOR there they that carried us away captive required
of us a song; and they that wasted us required of us
mirth, saying, Sing us one of the songs of Zion. How
shall we sing the Lord's song in a strange land?
—137:3, 4

They didn't feel like singing. They felt like crying,
as mentioned in the previous essay. For they were
captives in Babylon, foot-sore, hand-calloused and
heart-wounded. Why the request came, we cannot be
sure. It may have been a taunt, hateful ridicule, mad
derision. However, it could have been no more than
curiosity, seeking to hear the songs of foreigners.

Their answer for not complying was, "How shall
we sing the Lord's song in a strange land?" It wasn't
the place. Nor the time. It was not proper to force
from their lips what the heart did not feel.

They were so opposed to the request and so outraged by it that they said, "If I forget thee, O Jerusalem, let my right hand forget her cunning . . . let
my tongue cleave to the roof of my mouth" (vers.
5, 6). They refused to forget Jerusalem's calamities.
It pressed them with anxiety and pain. One doesn't
sing and make merry when a loved one is dying, nor
when the flag of the oppressor is hoisted above him.
Under the circumstances, they felt that if they should
ever be tempted to act out of keeping with the sad
facts, it would be better for their right hand to be
stilled and their tongue to be silenced.

Their example inspires us.

Religion Before Pleasure

IF I forget thee, O Jerusalem, let my right hand forget
her cunning. If I do not remember thee, let my tongue
cleave to the roof of my mouth; if I prefer not Jerusalem above my chief joy. —137:5, 6

*If I prefer not Jerusalem (religion) above my chief
joy (pleasure)* — Here we have the thought of preferring religion before pleasure. Like the man in
the parable who searched for the pearl of great price
(Matthew 13:45, 46), he thought it wise to give up
the appeals of the world for the one great value —
his commitment to God.

Unfortunately, too many people have the secondary
view of religion. With them, the god of pleasure comes
first. They are "lovers of pleasures more than lovers
of God" (II Timothy 3:4).

However, the religion of God is one of rightly placed
affections: "Thou shalt love the Lord thy God with
all thy heart, and with all thy soul, and with all thy
mind. This is . . . first . . ." (Matthew 22:37, 38).
There is one thing sure — it is first in death; and
what is first in death ought to be first in life.

Actually, the sweetest joys spring from higher living: joy of faith, joy of conscience, joy of worship,
joy of soul-winning, joy of domestic life and joy of
honorable pursuits.

> *While I sought Happiness she fled*
> *Before me constantly.*
> *Weary, I turned to Duty's path,*
> *And Happiness sought me,*
> *Saying, "I walk this road today,*
> *I'll bear thee company."*

The Strongest Strength

IN the day when I cried thou answeredst me, and strengthenedst me with strength in my soul. —138:3

The passage speaks of the strongest strength — soul strength. Indeed, no person is strong unless he is strong on the inside. This is the stamina that comes from God. "Thou didst encourage me with strength in my soul" (A.S.V.). God's best blessings come to the inward being, the real *me*. Sometimes He does not change the outward circumstances for us, but does strengthen us inwardly to meet them. He did for Paul. He granted him the grace to bear the thorn in his flesh. He said to him: "My grace is sufficient for thee: for my strength is made perfect in weakness" (II Corinthians 12:9). This made Paul master of his ills and circumstances. Tested by beatings, stonings, shipwrecks, robbers, false brethren, weariness, painfulness, hunger, thirst, cold and nakedness, he was conqueror (II Corinthians 11:24-28).

No person is defeated unless he has lost heart. If God gives fortitude, then a man should ever be triumphant over the opposing circumstances. Truly — "they that wait upon the Lord shall renew their strength . . . I will strengthen thee . . . they that war against thee shall be as nothing, and as a thing of nought" (Isaiah 40:31—41:12).

Be strong!
It matters not how deep entrenched the wrong,
How hard the battle goes, the day how long;
Faint not — fight on! Tomorrow comes the song.
                    —*Maltbie Davenport Babcock*

Revived to Handle Trouble

THOUGH I walk in the midst of trouble, thou wilt revive me: thou shalt stretch forth thine hand against the wrath of mine enemies, and thy right hand shall save me. —138:7

The poet was experiencing some hard blows from trouble's cruel fist. However, he confidently stated that God would revive him with one hand and rebuff his enemies with the other. It's this hope that keeps us going.

Most of our troubles come from people, but their solution comes from God.

The price of living in the world is troubles; but when we think of the alternative, we are glad to have them. However, we do need God's reviving hand to bear them.

No one escapes trouble. Sometimes it closes in from every side. And if it's not handled correctly, anxiety haunts us by day and worry torments us by night. The stomach churns. Our hands tremble. Optimism dies. Pessimism makes a new convert. Now we have the worst troubles — growing, multiplying, self-made troubles, all because we didn't handle the initial problem. But we could have handled it, for "God is . . . a very present help in trouble" (46:1). His giving man power to persevere makes the person a genius.

> *Genius (which means transcendent capacity of taking trouble, first of all.)*
>
> *—Thomas Carlyle*

The Omniscience of God

O LORD, thou hast searched me, and known me. Thou knowest my downsitting and mine uprising; thou understandest my thought afar off. Thou compassest my path and my lying down, and art acquainted with all my ways. For there is not a word in my tongue, but, lo, O Lord, thou knowest it altogether. Thou hast beset me behind and before, and laid thine hand upon me. Such knowledge is too wonderful for me; it is high, I cannot attain unto it. —139:1-6

God has "searched me, and known me" — all my thoughts and feelings.

He "knowest my downsitting and mine uprising" — my every condition, posture, all the day long, even "my thought afar off" when it is just forming.

Jehovah "compassest [searchest, A.S.V.] my path and my lying down" — when I'm active and when I'm resting, all the time.

"There is not a word in my tongue" He doesn't know — my words, my deeds, even my thoughts, what is said and what is meant.

He is ever close to me, behind me and before me — thus His knowledge of me is complete.

This is wonderful knowledge — too wonderful for David, more than he could comprehend. It is too much for us poor mortals to fully understand God, but we do know enough to follow Him.

Therefore I come, thy gentle call obeying,
And lay my sins and sorrows at thy feet;
On everlasting strength my weakness staying,
Clothed in thy robe of righteousness complete.

The Omnipresence of God

> WHITHER shall I go from thy Spirit? or whither shall I flee from thy presence? If I ascend up into heaven, thou art there: if I make my bed in hell, behold, thou art there. If I take the wings of the morning, and dwell in the uttermost parts of the sea; even there shall thy hand lead me, and thy right hand shall hold me. —139:7-10.

"Tell me," said a philosopher, "where is God?" "First tell me," said the other, "where He is not."

God's presence cannot be escaped, for He is Spirit. This is understandable. For instance: You can be on the road to a cherished gathering. A tire blows. When others are meeting, you are beside the road. But you are at the meeting in spirit. You see them. You shake their hands. You hear their voices. If infinite man can be at a place in spirit when his body is absent, think how easy it is for the Eternal Spirit to be everywhere at the same time.

"If I ascend up into heaven," God is there.

"If I make my bed in hell" (*sheol*, the place of departed spirits), God is there."

"If I take the wings of the morning" and fly to the farthest parts of the sea, behold, God is there to lead me and to hold me.

On land or sea, above the earth, below the earth, day or night, God is with me. Anywhere, everywhere, God is there.

> *I know not where His islands lift*
> *Their fronded palms in air;*
> *I only know I cannot drift*
> *Beyond His love and care.*

The Omnivision of God

If I say, Surely the darkness shall cover me; even the night shall be light about me. Yea, the darkness hideth not from thee; but the night shineth as the day: the darkness and the light are both alike to thee.
—139:11, 12

If I should think that I might escape God's sight by departing into darkness, "even the night shall be light about me." The darkness hides nothing from God. To Him who has the all-seeing eye, "the darkness and the light are both alike."

"For the eyes of the Lord run to and fro throughout the whole earth" (II Chronicles 16:9).

"A land which the Lord thy God careth for: the eyes of the Lord thy God are always upon it, from the beginning of the year even unto the end of the year" (Deuteronomy 11:12).

"The eyes of the Lord are in every place, beholding the evil and the good" (Proverbs 15:3).

The thought that God sees is a terror to the unsaved, but a comfort to the redeemed. It is heartening to them to know that "the eyes of the Lord are upon the righteous" (I Peter 3:12).

> *My soul thou keepest,*
> *Who never sleepest;*
> *'Mid gloom the deepest*
> *There's light above;*
> *Thine eyes behold me,*
> *Thine arms enfold me;*
> *Thy word has told me*
> *That God is love.*

The Omnificence of God

For thou hast possessed my reins: thou hast covered me in my mother's womb. I will praise thee; for I am fearfully and wonderfully made: marvelous are thy works; and that my soul knoweth right well. My substance was not hid from thee when I was made in secret, and curiously wrought in the lowest parts of the earth. —139:13-15

King Canute, a Danish conqueror of Britain, was praised by his courtiers because of his power. Then the king requested that his throne be placed by the seaside, which he occupied. As the tide rolled in, he commanded the waves to stop. They didn't obey; whereupon he said to his flatterers, "Behold, how small is the might of kings."

But with God it is different. His power is unlimited.

Because of God's omnificence, I can praise Him for my nature; "for I am fearfully and wonderfully made." I say, "Marvelous are thy works."

My substance or frame was not hidden from God when I was secretly made or conceived. Indeed, I was "curiously wrought" in a place beyond human observation.

One thing the Psalms especially emphasizes is that God made man: "Thy hands have made me and fashioned me" (119:73). No matter how much we philosophize and conjecture, we finally have to get back to a First Cause, to the first verse in the Bible: "In the beginning God created the heaven and the earth." Herein is the mystery of creation explained.

Let Them Reap Their Own Mischief

As for the head of those that compass me about, let the mischief of their own lips cover them. —140:9

David was threatened by mischievous enemies: "The evil man." "The violent man." Those who "imagine mischief in their heart." Those "gathered together for war." Those who had "sharpened their tongues like a serpent." "The proud" who had hidden a snare for him.

Obviously, the threat was severe; at least, David prayed about it. In the prayer, he requested that God "let the mischief of their own lips cover them." This is in keeping with what God does. He allows man to reap what he sows (Galatians 6:7). He permits a person to fall into the pit he digs for another: "They have digged a pit before me, into the midst whereof they are fallen themselves" (57:6). And the Just One allows the mischief of lips to cover its perpetrator with disarray and defeat. The danger he designs against others becomes his own downfall.

We have seen this happen again and again. It makes us wonder why the mischievous can't see it.

It is the principle of reaping what is sown, a principle ordained of God and confirmed by nature.

> *Sow truth if thou the true wouldst reap;*
> *Who sows the false shall reap the vain;*
> *Erect and sound thy conscience keep;*
> *From wicked words and deeds refrain.*
>
> —*Horatius Bonar*

Reject the Self-seeking Politician

LET not an evil speaker be established in the earth.
—140:11

David was king. As mentioned in the previous essay, his enemies threatened the structure and stability of the kingdom. Hence the text has a political significance. The king admonishes: do not establish an evil speaker (a man of tongue) in the land. His words are ulterior. He has a self-seeking aim.

In our age in which many politicians appeal to the voters with the rhetoric of promise, offering various groups everything from earth to heaven, we must say that the passage is unusually relevant. It is possible to use the taxpayers' money and the country's welfare to get elected. But when the game of fantasy finally plays out, what happens then?

We need a voice in America that will address itself more to the cause of our woes than to its effects. Remedy the cause and the effects will take care of themselves.

Instead of listening to the self-seekers, don't you think we ought to heed the text? If we do, we shall have statesmen rather than politicians.

But many people are saying to the candidate what was said to Isaiah: Speak "not unto us right things, speak unto us smooth things, [speak] deceits" (Isaiah 30:10). So, in the last analysis, the fault is in the people.

A Kind Lick

LET the righteous smite me; it shall be a kindness: and let him reprove me; it shall be an excellent oil, which shall not break my head: for yet my prayer also shall be in their calamities. —141:5

The smiting or lick spoken of is reproof. The psalmist welcomed it from the righteous. They would give it in keeping with facts. And in the right spirit.

A person can hardly reject whatever is for his good. David gladly received personal rebuke as an act of kindness. To do this, he had to be humble and eager to improve. With these attitudes, reprimand was to him like oil poured on the head of a sufferer — a welcome cure.

The intended kindness of the righteous reprover should be accepted profitably by the reproved. It should never provoke sullenness, anger and vengeance, but rather an appreciation that manifests itself in prayer for the rebuker. It tells that one is wise.

REPROVE not a scorner, lest he hate thee: rebuke a wise man, and he will love thee. —Proverbs 9:8

But the foolish harden themselves against censure, and thereby destroy themselves:

HE, that being often reproved hardeneth his neck, shall suddenly be destroyed, and that without remedy.
—Proverbs 29:1

Therefore let us welcome each reproof.

Then They Shall Hear

WHEN their judges are overthrown in stony places, they shall hear my words; for they are sweet. —141:6

David believed that when his enemies were overthrown, the people would hear his words. For his words would be pleasant, equitable and just, in contrast with the deceit and bitterness of evil men. It was his conviction that when the ringleaders who had been cruel persecutors of the people (ver. 7) were hurled down "in stony places," the rest would listen to godly instruction.

Calamity often opens hearts to receive teaching. In the midst of health and prosperity, there are those who have no disposition to listen. But when the storm strikes and they are left beaten and bruised amidst the wreckage, they are more inclined to take heed. Standing there on the rubbish of disappointment and insecurity, stripped of haughtiness, arrogance and self-sufficiency, the aching heart is more receptive.

Joseph's brethren had to be brought low before they were ready to look up (Genesis 44:16).

Jonah had to be swallowed by the big fish before he would listen (Jonah 2, 3).

Paul had to be struck blind before he could see (Acts 9:1-6).

Indeed, some people can never sail to a fairer land except on the vessel called *hardship;* for when they board the luxury liner they head for the opposite port.

In the Cave He Prayed

I CRIED unto the Lord with my voice; with my voice
unto the Lord did I make my supplication .... —142:1-7

The title of the Psalm states this of David: "A
prayer when he was in the cave." The cave may have
been that of Adullam (I Samuel 22:1), or that of
Engedi (I Samuel 23:29). David had fled to escape
from Saul. And there he prayed. Feeling that he
was forsaken by friends and pursued by enemies, he
was left entirely to the mercy of God. It is interesting
to note the points in the prayer:

— "I poured out my complaint before him."
— "Thou knewest my path."
— "They privily laid a snare for me."
— "There was no man that would know me."
— "Refuge failed me."
— "No man cared for my soul."
— "Thou art my refuge and my portion in the land
of the living."
— "Attend unto my cry; for I am brought very low."
— "Deliver me from my persecutors; for they are
stronger than I."
— "Bring my soul out of prison, that I may praise
thy name."
— "The righteous shall compass me about."
— "Thou shalt deal bountifully with me."

The prayer ends with an optimistic note. He believed the time would come when the righteous would
gather around him and rejoice with him.

No One Cares

I LOOKED on my right hand, and beheld, but there
was no man that would know me: refuge failed me;
no man cared for my soul. —142:4

When David looked about for human assistance,
there was no one to help. No person would even
acknowledge knowing him. He was deserted in his
trouble. The cave where he had fled was miserable
quarters, but there was no other refuge. His sad comment was, "No man cared for my soul."

The word *soul*, used in the text, means *life*. No one
sought to save his life. Nobody thought it was worth
saving. If David could feel this way then, surely
there are legions who feel this way now. No helping
hand comes their way. No effort is made to ease their
burdens . . . to enrich their lives.

In all fairness, not every person who thinks no
man cares has sized up the matter correctly. Really,
there are many who care, though they have not been
brought face to face with the person who feels otherwise. But each time the church meets it prays for
him. And many workers do go out seeking the lost
and the helpless. There are public school teachers,
Sunday School teachers, social workers, physicians,
dentists, ministers, missionaries — many who care,
each anxious to help in his own field.

Many care for you. But if no one should, you can
still make it, provided (1) you are aware that God
cares, and (2) you care for yourself.

No Man Living Is Justified

AND enter not into judgment with thy servant: for in thy sight shall no man living be justified. —143:2

David prays that God will not deal with him on the basis of strict justice. He stated in another prayer that no one could stand, if God marked — never forgave — sin against man:

IF thou, Lord, shouldest mark iniquities, O Lord, who shall stand? —130:3

Simply, the psalmist understood that he was a sinner; and, as such, he would have to rely on the mercy and forgiveness of God. "For in thy sight shall no man living be justified" on his own merit. He is not so sinless as to be totally innocent and fully free of all blame. For one to plead that he is, only marks him as being more perverse:

IF I justify myself, mine own mouth shall condemn me: if I say, I am perfect, it shall also prove me perverse. —Job 9:20

However, in David's prayer he does not plead for God's favor on the basis of human perfection, but rather on the grounds of Divine mercy.

David's hope is our hope — the mercy of God. For if we get justice, we shall be forever doomed; but as the objects of Divine grace, we can be forgiven.

Golden Age of Peace and Prosperity

> RID me, and deliver me from the hand of strange children, whose mouth speaketh vanity, and their right hand is a right hand of falsehood: That our sons may be as plants grown up in their youth; that our daughters may be as corner stones, polished after the similitude of a palace: That our garners may be full, affording all manner of store; that our sheep may bring forth thousands and ten thousands in our streets: That our oxen may be strong to labor; that there be no breaking in, nor going out; that there be no complaining in our streets. —144:11-14

Man dreams of a golden age of peace and prosperity. David prayed for it:

— That they be delivered from fierce enemies whose word is false and whose covenants are worthless.

— That their sons be permitted to grow up as plants. With nothing between the plant and heaven, it is free to reach toward the sun. Not restricted to the tents of war and the fields of battle, their sons could follow a life of personal freedom and development.

— That their daughters be as polished corner stones. That they be fair and beautiful, like the ornaments on a palace.

— That their garners be full. That their fields yield an abundance of every sort of produce and grain.

— That their sheep and oxen multiply, which were essential to their national prosperity.

— That their property be safe and secure. No breaking in of the animals, and no escape of them.

— That there be no complaining in the streets. No outcry, no clamor, no strife.

This is what the world seeks. Why can't we have it?

Happy Is That People

HAPPY is that people, that is in such a case: yea, happy
is that people, whose God is the Lord. —144:15

Happy or blessed is the people whose God is JE-
HOVAH, a people who worship and serve Him. The
religion of God is constituted and adapted to make
a happy people. It gives peace and quietude. God
provides a hope that keeps one perservering. He
teaches the principles of prosperity and happiness:
work, diligence, thrift, love and goodwill. His way
guards one from bitterness and strife, freeing his
energies to go into a productive life.

The good life is no accident. It is produced by a
cause — God's directives.

The best security for any nation is adherence to
God's plan. A remembrance of God has always prospered nations. It's the nations that forget Him that
regress and destroy themselves. "The wicked shall be
turned into hell, and all the nations that forget God"
(9:17).

A friend of mine had a car with a transmission defect: it would run; it would move; but it always went
in reverse. It burned up energy to go the wrong way.

The illustration aptly describes a people that forgets
God. They are moving backwards to destruction. Their
own forgetfulness of God withholds from them the
happy life, as the prophet Jeremiah stated:

YOUR iniquities have turned away these things, and
your sins have withholden good things from you.
—Jeremiah 5:25

From Generation to Generation

ONE generation shall praise thy works to another, and shall declare thy mighty acts. —145:4

Here we have a sacred charge.

This is a Divinely enforced duty: "The father to the children shall make known thy truth" (Isaiah 38:19). "And these words, which I command thee this day, shall be in thine heart: And thou shalt teach them diligently unto thy children" (Deuteronomy 6:6, 7).

Handing down the praise of God from generation to generation is an inviolable trust. Like a relay race, the torch of truth is given to another. One generation passes to the next one the store of accumulated knowledge and wisdom gathered by succeeding generations. We are the heirs of all the ages. And this makes us debtors to the past, and especially to those who walked with God and transferred to us the knowledge of His ways.

As the oldsters declared to us a blessed knowledge of God, so we must do the same for the youngsters who reach out to us as our steps begin to tire.

This service is to be carried out individually by each family. What the home *is* usually determines what the children *become*.

> *What the parents spin the children must reel.*
> —*German Proverb*

Parents have been given much, and of them much is required. They must not break the trust.

God Our Help

Happy is he that hath the God of Jacob for his help, whose hope is in the Lord his God. —146:5

In this Psalm God is praised as our only sure and adequate help.

Our trust is not to be put in man, not even in princes, for they are mortal (vers. 3, 4). They soon return to the earth and their thoughts perish. In them is little aid.

Oh, how disappointed
Is that poor man that hangs on princes' favors!

God is the only qualified Being, equipped with longevity, power, love and mercy to help us. The Psalm gives ten reasons for man to rely on Him for assistance:

1) He is the creator of all the universe (ver. 6).

2) Keeps truth forever (ver. 6).

3) Executes judgment for the oppressed (ver. 7).

4) Looses the prisoners (ver. 7).

5) Opens the eyes of the blind (ver. 8).

6) Lifts up the bowed down (ver. 8).

7) Loves the righteous (ver. 8).

8) Preserves the strangers (ver. 9).

9) Relieves the fatherless and widow (ver. 9).

10) He shall reign forever (ver. 10).

While measures of trust in men are pleasant and essential, we find in God alone our soul's refuge and our heart's satisfaction.

God Heals the Broken Heart

HE healeth the broken in heart, and bindeth up their wounds. —147:3

In another of the Hallelujah Psalms that begin and end the same way — "Praise ye the Lord" — the poet mentions a number of reasons for praising God; one of which is, "He healeth the broken in heart." Only those who have languished with broken hearts, eased by God's healing balm, can fully appreciate this as one of the most praiseworthy blessings.

> *Only the soul that knows the mighty grief can know the mighty rapture.*
>
> *—Edwin Markham*

The text refers primarily to the healing God administered to those whose hearts were crushed and broken in their long captivity. He fortified their courage and dried their tears during their stay, and gave them complete comfort by returning them to their native soil. However, the language is general in describing a characteristic of God — it is His nature to heal the broken-hearted among His people.

THE Lord is nigh unto them that are of a broken heart. —34:17

When sorrow invades the mind, when trouble vexes the spirit, when the heart is saddened, we may turn to God for the remedy. Read His remedial, therapeutic Scriptures, filled with direction and promise. Trust Him. For there has never been a tear He couldn't dry, nor an aching heart He couldn't heal.

Let All Creation Praise Him

PRAISE ye the Lord. Praise ye the Lord from the heavens: praise him in the heights. Praise ye him, all his angels . . . Praise the Lord from the earth . . . .
—148:1-14

In this Hallelujah Psalm the poet is in a jubilant, exultant mood. The clouds have vanished. Sunshine beams on his path. Joy fills his heart and praise graces his lips.

He calls for the whole universe to praise God: angels; inanimate objects; beasts, cattle, creeping things and flying fowls; all people: kings, princes, judges, "young men, and maidens; old men and children" — all are to praise the Ever-existent First Cause that brought them into creation.

All the hills and mountains, rivers and valleys, trees and plants, beasts and fowls speak His praise. For He made them. Their very existence declares the glory of God. All creation shouts: "Praise ye the Lord."

But man, a creature of intelligence, must do more than breathe to laud God; he must praise his Maker from his heart, out of his own volition. And with a little reflection this should come easily. So we in our own time and in our own way sing:

> *Praise the Lord, ye heav'ns adore Him!*
> *Praise Him angels in the height;*
> *Sun and moon rejoice before Him;*
> *Praise Him, all ye stars of light.*
>
> *—J. Kempthorne*

Beautified With Salvation

FOR the Lord taketh pleasure in his people: he will
beautify the meek with salvation. —149:4

In another Hallelujah Psalm the writer praised the
Lord, among other things, for the beauty of salvation.

This is the beauty that cannot be matched by any
outward appearance. It's the heart that makes the
person attractive. True beauty is the best of all we
know — not the physique or profile we see. And if
"pretty is as pretty does," then the lovely-spirited
person is prepared to win all beauty contests.

The inward beauty is the real person — not the
earthly house in which he or she lives a few fleeting
years. It's the beauty that never ages, but renews
with vigor and attraction with the passing of every
hour (II Corinthians 4:16).

This is why outward "beauty is vain" (Proverbs
31:30) ; and why wise men through the centuries have
placed the greatest value on internal appearance.

And if we could wave a wand and make all people
beautiful, we would wave it on the inside of man.
This is where God's word works; and for each who
receives it, God begins the beauty treatment. That
person has no need to fear his or her appearance.

Who walks with Beauty has no need of fear;
The sun and moon and stars keep pace with him;
Invisible hands restore the ruined year,
And time, itself, grows beautifully dim.

—David Morton

Praise the Lord

PRAISE ye the Lord . . . Let every thing that hath
breath praise the Lord. Praise ye the Lord. —150:1-6

The last five Psalms all begin and end the same
way — with praise! Hallelujah! This is a fitting ending to the wondrous, superb, popular book it concludes. With four grand words this book of inspiration and comfort closes: *Praise ye the Lord.*

In view of all the sacred volume discloses about
God and man — God's power, man's frailty; God's
eagerness to help, man's need of assistance — it is
highly appropriate that it ends with an expressive
laudation of the majesty of God. After all it says
about man's trials, conflicts, persecutions, bondages,
temptations, sicknesses, disappointments, sorrows, sufferings, troubles, tears, defeats, steps of faith, glorious
victories, overflowing joys and beckoning hopes — all
that accompanied their chequered and eventful lives
— it is proper that the Book of Psalms concludes
with exuberant praise, rejoicings and Hallelujahs.

The closing Psalm grandly rises from verse to verse
to end in a grander climax: *Let everything that hath
breath praise the Lord.*

> *Through every period of my life*
> *Thy goodness I'll pursue;*
> *And after death, in distant worlds,*
> *The glorious theme renew.*
> *Through all eternity to Thee*
> *A joyful song I'll raise;*
> *But, oh! eternity's too short*
> *To utter all thy praise.*
>
> *—Joseph Addison*

We have walked on sacred ground.
Divinity has stirred within us.